EU Security Policy

EU Security Policy

What It Is,

How It Works,

Why It Matters

Michael Merlingen

LYNNE
RIENNER
PUBLISHERS

BOULDER
LONDON

Published in the United States of America in 2012 by
Lynne Rienner Publishers, Inc.
1800 30th Street, Boulder, Colorado 80301
www.rienner.com

and in the United Kingdom by
Lynne Rienner Publishers, Inc.
3 Henrietta Street, Covent Garden, London WC2E 8LU

Library of Congress Cataloging-in-Publication Data
Merlingen, Michael, 1964–
EU security policy : what it is, how it works, why it matters / Michael Merlingen.
    p. cm. — Includes bibliographical references and index.
  ISBN 978-1-58826-774-0 (hardcover : alk. paper)
  ISBN 978-1-58826-799-3 (pbk. : alk. paper)
  1. Common Security and Defence Policy. 2. European Union countries—
Military policy. 3. European Union countries—Defenses. I. Title.
  UA646.3.M373 2011
  355'.03354—dc23

                                                              2011020128

British Cataloguing in Publication Data
A Cataloguing in Publication record for this book
is available from the British Library.

Printed and bound in the United States of America

  The paper used in this publication meets the requirements
∞ of the American National Standard for Permanence of
  Paper for Printed Library Materials Z39.48-1992.

  5 4 3 2 1

To my wife,
for all her love and support throughout the years

Contents

EU Security Policy

CHAPTER 1

Introduction

THE GOAL OF THIS BOOK IS TO INTRODUCE READERS TO THE security and defense policy of the European Union (EU). The thesis that animates the book is that in EU jargon what is known as the Common Security and Defence Policy (CSDP) is important to international security affairs and to the management of global order. Moreover, through whatever theoretical lens one looks at the CSDP, structural dynamics both internal and external to the EU push it toward becoming a powerful global security actor—which is not to deny its many shortcomings.

The fact that the EU is a security actor that matters and is bound to matter more in the future is not widely known. Undoubtedly, this has to do with the fact that the CSDP is a relatively young venture, launched in 1999. Moreover, the CSDP has specialized in stabilization and reconstruction operations, rather than fighting wars. As it is war fighting that captures most of the public's attention rather than the dull business of nation-building, the CSDP has gotten less publicity than it deserves. Yet the EU is not blameless when it comes to the lack of public awareness of and knowledge about the CSDP. The CSDP is unduly complex and complicated. Those inside the beltway of the EU headquarters in Brussels use unfamiliar acronyms when they write and speak about it. They refer to the RRF, CPCC, CONOPS, and lessons learned as if it were self-evident what these terms mean. They invent awkward and difficult-to-understand phrases such as *external action service* to replace perfectly good and understandable ones such

1

as *diplomatic service*. While the EU sports a nice-looking Web portal, anyone who has ever tried to use it to get beyond generalities and official statements knows that the portal yields little information about the ins and outs of the CSDP. The seemingly transparent EU is actually quite opaque. Even well-informed observers of the CSDP often find it hard to understand what goes on behind closed doors in Brussels and on the ground in theaters of operation. In short, the CSDP is not user-friendly. The book addresses this problem.

The book offers a descriptive analysis of the CSDP and covers what happens at EU headquarters and among Brussels and the capitals of the EU states in the making of the CSDP. Moreover, it discusses what happens in CSDP theaters of operation and how the CSDP has affected transatlantic relations, including the North Atlantic Treaty Organization (NATO) and relations with Russia. In addition to this descriptive analysis, the book provides an in-depth overview of what the main international relations and EU studies theories have to say about the CSDP. The empirical chapters that make up the bulk of the book draw on the concepts and insights laid out in Chapter 2. Finally, the book makes predictions, based on theoretically informed scenarios, about the future of the CSDP and its impact on European security and world order. Based on existing evidence, it evaluates the plausibility of these contrasting predictions.

Why the CSDP Matters

There are at least four reasons why students and interested observers of international relations ought to familiarize themselves with the CSDP. First, with the CSDP the EU has graduated from security receiver to security provider, quickly evolving into a "recognised and sought-after security actor."[1] While this may sound like self-congratulatory hype, it is not. As this book will show, the conclusion of a RAND Corporation team investigating six European-led military nation-building missions can be generalized to the more than twenty civilian and military peacekeeping, stabilization, and reconstruction operations fielded so far by the CSDP, which have established "a short but respectably positive record in the field" (Dobbins et al. 2008: xxxiv).

The second reason why it is important to study the CSDP is that the EU's role in international security management is bound to grow as global security interdependence rises, which has sharply increased since the end of the Cold War and will continue to do so. Global security interdependence is driven by a number of factors, notably technological progress, the growing importance of transnationally operating nonstate actors such as organized crime and terrorist networks, and the proliferation of nontraditional security threats such as those associated with failed states and energy dependency. To deal effectively with the proliferation of sources of insecurity and the intensification of security threats brought about by deepening security interdependence, the EU will have to upgrade its foreign policy toolbox, including the CSDP.

The third reason why the CSDP matters is that the growth of the EU's military power will hasten the end of the US unipolar period in international security affairs. Even as national defense outlays have stagnated, EU governments have built up their collective military capabilities through reinforcing their cooperation on military research and development, procurement, and the pooling of capabilities. The global financial crisis of the late 2000s, whose ramifications have badly affected some of the weaker EU economies, even threatening the survival of the EU's Economic and Monetary Union, has put further pressure on EU nations to join forces. Military cooperation saves money and enhances the collective punch that the EU countries can pack on the international stage. Extrapolating from its current development trajectory, the CSDP will be one of the elements shaping the posthegemonic international security order that is likely to arise in coming decades. It is important to know how the CSDP has emerged, what it is, how it works, and its current contribution to global security in order to get a sense of where it is headed and how it will impact the world.

Finally, students of world politics cannot afford to ignore the CSDP as a real-world laboratory in which academic theories can be tested. The main theories in the study of international relations and the EU have very different explanations of the causes and workings of the CSDP and very different predictions of where it is headed. It is only recently that scholars have become aware of the theoretical significance of the CSDP. Much remains to be done to develop and systematically apply contrasting theories to the CSDP and to evaluate their relative explanatory power.

While there are powerful reasons to study the CSDP, so far only a charmed circle of mostly European scholars, analysts, and journalists have explored the CSDP in any depth. The inevitable result is confusion about the policy. Take the following two widely differing assessments by two well-known US observers of international affairs. Robert Kagan likened the foreign and security policy of the EU to the chorus in a classical Greek tragedy: "It comments on the action. It reacts with horror and praise. It interacts in various ways with the protagonists. But the singers themselves play no part in the plot" (cited in *The Economist* 2005). Conversely, Andrew Moravcsik referred to the EU as the quiet superpower, attributing to it nearly as much global influence as to the United States. The EU, Moravcsik argued, was "the world's pre-eminent civilian power, and its second military power" (2009: 403; 2010). This book will debunk such exaggerated views and enable readers to get a more accurate understanding of EU security and defense policy.

What the CSDP Is (and What It Is Not)

What the CSDP is seems simple enough. But a closer look reveals that the answer is far from straightforward. The CSDP is an integral part of the EU's Common Foreign and Security Policy (CFSP), which is one component of the multilayered European foreign policy system. The other components of this multilayered system are the separate national foreign policies of the EU states and the supranational foreign policy managed by the European Commission, which includes trade and development policy. The CFSP is not (yet) the main component of European foreign policy. Furthermore, for the time being, the CSDP is not (yet) about the territorial defense of the EU, the "D" in its name notwithstanding. As it stands, the CSDP gives the EU an operational capacity to carry out military and civilian stabilization and reconstruction operations abroad. Planning and preparations are under way in the EU to enable the CSDP to do more robust interventions such as peace enforcement.

The CSDP is shaped by what the EU is not. Because the EU is not a nation-state, the CSDP cannot draw on a European army. Nor does it have an EU peace corps whose members go out into the world to be a force for good and conduits of European soft power. Moreover, the community of military action created by the CSDP is less integrated than that created by NATO. Unlike the alliance, the CSDP does not have a supreme commander responsible in peacetime for planning the battles of the future and in war for the overall command of military operations. The CSDP is a sophisticated framework for cooperation on security and defense policy among EU nations.

The CSDP relies on the voluntary pooling of national manpower and capabilities and the convergence of national political will. It works well in cases in which EU governments share similar views of the security threats and challenges they face and when they agree that the CSDP is the best tool to tackle them. In cases when such cross-national convergence of views is absent, the CSDP becomes a paper tiger. In short, the CSDP is an intergovernmental capability pool run by EU governments on the basis of consensus decisionmaking. Yet this is not the whole story. The day-to-day operation of the pool generates supranational dynamics. EU rules, norms, and ways of doing things influence—often only at the margins but sometimes in more fundamental ways—how EU governments interpret security problems and how they define their national interests.

Plan of the Book

The book is organized into four parts. Part 1 defines the CSDP, Part 2 looks at the CSDP operations, Part 3 analyzes how the CSDP has affected transatlantic relations and EU relations with Russia, and Part 4 offers scenario-based predictions about the likely future of military power in Europe. To keep the text reader friendly, the book consistently refers to the EU and the CSDP even when it refers to the pre-Maastricht European Community (EC) and the pre-Lisbon European Security and Defence Policy (ESDP). Only Chapter 3, which puts the CSDP in historical context, uses chronologically correct labeling.

Chapter 2 provides an overview of the main theories of the creation, development, and functioning of the CSDP. The chapters that follow make use of the arguments and concepts discussed in Chapter 2. Chapter 3 traces the post-1945 precursors of the CSDP as well as its proper development. In the 1950s and 1960s, innovative and ambitious Western European efforts to develop common foreign, security, and defense policies failed. In the 1970s, a more modest project to coordinate foreign policy succeeded, which allowed EU states to fashion a common European identity on the international stage. Since the end of the Cold War, the EU has transformed itself into a military actor. In the new millennium, considerable progress has been made. Chapters 4 and 5 draw on the notion of principal-agent relations to explore the CSDP policymaking process. Chapter 4 focuses on the key political actors—the principals—and discusses their competencies and functions in the CSDP policy process. It shows that the CSDP is at core an intergovernmental policy system shaped by EU governments and the high representative of the EU for foreign affairs and security policy. Yet there is more to the CSDP than intergovernmentalism. This is highlighted in Chapter 5, which brings into focus the supranational processes that loosen the grip of the member states on the CSDP. Brussels-based national delegates and EU officials—the agents—enjoy some leeway in shaping the CSDP.

Chapter 6 looks at the civilian and military capabilities available to the CSDP and considers what the EU has achieved so far and where it has fallen short of expectations. Chapter 7 draws on the concept of Europeanization to examine to what extent national threat perceptions, security policies, and institutions have converged across the EU. It analyzes the European Security Strategy (ESS), including the security philosophy that underpins it, and the EU-level pressures on member states to adapt their security policies and structures. The impact of Europeanization has been patchy. Important cross-national cleavages remain in relation to the CSDP and are the topic of the second part of the chapter.

Chapter 8 discusses the process by which military and civilian operations are planned, launched, and run. Chapters 9 and 10 map and analyze all CSDP operations that have been launched so far. Each mission is contextualized, in terms of both the security problems faced by the host country and the EU motives for the deployment. This sets the stage for the investigation of mission objectives, the internal and external challenges faced by the mission, and its impact on the ground. Drawing conclusions from the discussion of the operations, Chapter 11 looks at their performances, employing different criteria to offer a nuanced judgment of the CSDP record so far. Moreover, it identifies the main reasons for performance shortcomings.

Chapter 12 focuses on transatlantic relations. In the wake of the end of the Cold War, the EU and the United States started to build a new European security architecture. The construction has been a conflictual process of trial and error that has pitted supporters of NATO and the CSDP against each other. At first, Washington was concerned about the impact of the CSDP on transatlantic relations. The diplomatic fallout from the 2003 US-led invasion of Iraq nearly killed the CSDP. However, the challenges of global security management prompted the United States and the EU to focus on pragmatic cooperation. In the absence of an overall grand strategy, a new transatlantic division of labor in security affairs has emerged. The EU has acquired the capabilities to deputize for the United States in lower-intensity peacekeeping, stabilization, and reconstruction missions. Yet shortcomings in EU-NATO cooperation remain, and US support for the CSDP remains qualified.

Chapter 13 looks at EU-Russia security relations since the end of the Cold War. It shows that the CSDP has been one, albeit not the most important, element in the relationship. Initially, the EU had high hopes for integrating an enfeebled Russia into a European security order centered on the EU. Yet the EU's Eastern policy did not bear fruit. After the Kremlin took measures to reverse the country's decline, its foreign policy became once again more assertive. By the middle of the 2000s, frictions had markedly increased in relations between Brussels and Moscow, especially in relation to regional and energy security. Though internally divided over the right policy toward Russia, the EU has hardened its Eastern policy in response to Moscow's new assertiveness. It has mustered the political will to act more resolutely in post-Soviet space, including through the CSDP. EU-Russia cooperation on the CSDP, about which Moscow initially was optimistic, has suffered from the accumulation of disagreements and conflicts. Unlike in the transatlantic case, there is little prospect for transforming the CSDP into an opportunity for improving EU-Russia relations.

The final chapter draws on the theories laid out in Chapter 2 to extrapolate two contrasting futures of military power in Europe. The chapter asks where the CSDP is headed and what its impact on international order will be. The available empirical evidence is used to assess the plausibility of the two scenarios.

Note

1. This is how the foreign ministers of Germany, France, and Poland characterized the CSDP in a joint letter to EU foreign policy chief Catherine Ashton (Rettman 2010).

CHAPTER 2

Exploring Theories and Concepts

IN RECENT YEARS A NUMBER OF THEORETICAL APPROACHES have been used to study different aspects of the CSDP (for overviews, see Bickerton et al. 2011; Kurowska and Breuer forthcoming). This chapter discusses the main theories, focusing especially on two big questions: What are the causes driving the development of the CSDP, and who runs it? Later chapters refer back to arguments and concepts laid out here.[1]

Constructivist Approaches: Identity, Institutions, and Socialization

In the study of international relations, constructivist approaches came of age in the wake of the Cold War. Their rise was associated with the failure of realist and liberal international relations theories to predict the collapse of the bipolar world. Furthermore, neither of the two main theories at the time seemed to offer convincing explanations concerning the timing and unfolding of the dramatic events that ended decades of Cold War confrontation. To many critics, the problem with the principal international relations theories was their lack of attention to ideas, beliefs, norms, values, and social identities. Constructivist approaches argue that the "identities, interests and behavior of political agents are socially constructed by collective meanings, interpretations and assumptions about the world" (Adler

1997: 324). A corollary of this argument is that political actors often act in accordance with what they and their social environment consider appropriate conduct (March and Olsen 2009). This differs from the type of social action at the heart of realism and liberalism. Actors do what they do because they want to maximize their utility calculus. In brief, constructivist approaches argue that ideational factors are an important determinant of international relations.

In studies of EU foreign and security policy, constructivist approaches have long been neglected. In recent years, however, this has changed (a milestone in this development was Tonra and Christiansen 2004). By now, constructivism is arguably the most prominent approach in this field of study. Numerous scholars use sociological and historical institutionalism, the Europeanization framework, and more generic constructivist perspectives centered on the role of social identities to explore the development and the policy process of the CFSP.

Sociological and historical institutionalist perspectives argue that EU-level structures for making and implementing foreign and security policy matter because they shape the identities, interests, and interpretations of actors and how they organize themselves (for a general discussion, see Hall and Taylor 1996; March and Olsen 1989).[2] Hence, a key focus of constructivist institutionalist research is to explore to what extent European foreign and security policy has been institutionalized and to analyze the effects of any such institutionalization. A number of scholars have examined the sociological and organizational processes set in motion by the launch of European Political Cooperation (EPC) in 1970 and its impact on foreign policy cooperation. While the EPC was launched for mainly instrumental reasons, one of its unintended effects was that it created a social environment that fostered cognitive and behavioral role changes. The successor of the EPC, the CFSP, consolidated this social environment and reinforced its effects. Brussels-based actors participating in the EPC, and the CFSP in the 1990s, came to share common expectations about appropriate EU foreign and security policy, were increasingly bound by rules and norms, and developed considerable autonomy from national capitals (Glarbo 1999; Nuttall 2000; Smith 2004a; Tonra 1997, 2003). These changes led to the creation of a "Diplomatic Republic of Europe" (Jørgensen 1997), which has been characterized by a transformation in how EU states make foreign policy. Instrumental rationality has been constrained and on occasion even replaced by a collective rationality that emphasizes general principles, legitimate procedures, and joint problem-solving as opposed to conflictual bargaining. Also, the diplomatic republic has generated pressure on national diplomacies to reorganize themselves in line with the EU's methods. Finally, the new EU-level governance system has created path dependencies. Initial policy decisions have conditioned subsequent policy as common norms have thickened and expectations among participating national representatives have converged. In this view, the CSDP is an outgrowth of, and its functioning is shaped by, the sociological and organizational processes associated with institutionalization (Breuer forthcoming; Juncos 2011; Menon 2011; Petrov 2011; Watanabe 2010).

Some scholars have taken a broader view of the institutionalist dynamics that they say have shaped the CSDP. Adding to the previous arguments, they claim that the interpenetration of most EU armed forces under the umbrella of NATO has created a common set of social representations that predisposes EU soldiers to look at military security policy no longer from the perspective of just their nation-states. Their attitudes have become internationalized (Mérand 2008, 2010). The upshot of the NATO-induced institutionalization of European defense policy is that traditional sovereignty concerns, which normally make cooperation and integration in the field of high politics difficult, have been dissolved. This change, in turn, has been a key condition of possibility of the CSDP.[3] In this view, NATO has been the midwife of the CSDP.

Institutionalist research of the CSDP policy process qualifies the claim of realist and liberal theories that national interests and intergovernmental negotiations are the key ingredients in the making of EU security policy. Institutionalists highlight the "Brusselization" of policymaking. The term refers to the growing role of Brussels-based national representatives and EU civil servants in the CSDP policy process (Allen 1998). In particular, researchers employing institutionalism have explored the cognitive and policy consequences of the extended exposure of CSDP diplomats to the Brussels scene (Duke and Vanhoonacker 2006; Howorth 2010; Juncos and Pomorska 2006; Juncos and Reynolds 2007; Meyer 2006). They have documented the development of a shared corporate identity among the members of CSDP structures, the induction of new members into existing bodies, social learning, and the gradual emergence in CSDP institutions of a European strategic culture.

Another constructivist perspective that has proven fruitful in analyzing the development of European foreign and security policy centers on the notion of Europeanization. The term denotes the construction and institutionalization of EU-level rules and practices and their subsequent integration into the logic of national policymaking (Ladrech 2010; Major 2005; Radaelli 2000). Scholars employing the Europeanization framework have looked at different aspects of the Europeanization of EU security and defense policy (Giegerich 2006; Gross 2009a; Irondelle 2003; Larsen 2005; Miskimmon 2007; Rieker 2006; Tonra 2001). Some have analyzed the pressures (normative and functional) faced by EU states to adapt their own national rules and practices governing foreign and security policy to those prevailing at the EU level so as to minimize any misfit. This is the downloading aspect of Europeanization. Other scholars have explored how EU states strive to shape EU-level security and defense policy and policymaking in accordance with their national preferences. This is the uploading aspect of Europeanization. Finally, some scholars have looked at how the EU provides the context for and facilitates the transfer of best practice in the security and defense field across member state borders. This is the cross-loading aspect of Europeanization.

Generic constructivist perspectives look at EU foreign and security policy through the lens of the policy roles and identities of the EU and member states. For instance, some analysts argue that EU states "are using foreign, security and defense policy to nation-build; that is, to create pride and popular support for the European project" (Anderson 2008: 176; for a less radical discussion, see Keukeleire and MacNaughtan 2008: 333). In this view, the CSDP is little more than an exercise in military bodybuilding. It is aimed not at improving the EU's punching power but at strengthening its self-confidence and prestige both at home and in the world (Sommer 2004). EU governments employ the symbolism of the high politics of defense to create a European identity and strengthen support for the EU at a time when popular discontent with and apathy toward the EU are high.

Generic constructivist arguments also figure prominently in many accounts of the EU's self-conception as an international security actor. In particular, numerous studies analyze the emergence of the EU as a normative or ethical power and the challenges it faces. As a normative power, the EU is said to pursue foreign and security policies that are shaped more by values than by egoistical material interests (Aggestam 2008; Khaliq 2008; Lucarelli and Manners 2008; Manners 2002; Mayer and Vogt 2006; Whitman 2010). Traditionally, the EU sought to implement its value-rational foreign policy through civilian means such as development aid. Yet the shock of brutal warfare in the EU neighborhood in Bosnia and Kosovo in the 1990s and the inability of the EU to put an end to the conflicts is said to have prompted a change in the EU's foreign policy role conception. The EU has made itself into an ethical power ready to use the CSDP as a force for good in world politics—a humanitarian power with teeth.

The constructivist focus on the ideational dimension of social reality tends to downplay material factors as causes of the CSDP (but see Mérand 2010; Meyer and Strickmann 2011). One expression of this analytical predisposition is the absence in constructivist accounts of threats as drivers of the CSDP. Indeed, for many constructivists the security enjoyed by the EU has been one of the structural conditions enabling the creation and development of the CSDP. In contrast to realists, constructivists stress that intra-EU and transatlantic relations are characterized by the absence of any traditional interstate security concerns. Relations among EU states and between them and the United States take place in a security community. In it there is "neither the expectation of nor the preparation for organized violence as a means to settle interstate disputes" (Adler and Barnett 1998: 34).

Realist Approaches:
The Balance of Power and Domestic Politics

During the first decades of the history of European integration, realist international relations theory was one of the principal theories in the conceptual toolkit of students of the EU. Its strength was explaining the limits of integration, notably in the field of security and defense policy (Hoffmann 1995). Yet in recent decades realist accounts of the EU have been few and far between (Grieco 1996; Loriaux 1999; Pedersen 2002; Rynning 2005). One of the most prominent realists predicted the imminent disintegration of the EU when the bipolar Cold War structure disappeared, which he believed had sheltered the European construction (Mearsheimer 1990). The creation of the CSDP has confounded such realist predictions and, paradoxically, revived the fortunes of realist accounts of the EU. Neorealism or structural realism has been at the forefront of this revival, though other variants of realism have been applied to the CSDP as well. Whatever the strand, realist approaches are united in their belief that states are the main actors in the security realm. They are primarily concerned about their survival because this is a precondition for all other values that nations may wish to pursue. States exist in an anarchical international environment, in which there is no higher authority to look after their security and well-being. This creates uncertainty about the intentions of other states and makes the international realm a self-help system centered on the balance of power.

Realist accounts of the CSDP argue that it is the EU's spearhead in the international struggle for power. However, realists disagree among themselves over how best to conceptualize the EU and the CSDP. Is the EU an international organization made up of sovereign states, which would make the CSDP a traditional balancing tool? Or is the EU a state in the making, which would make the CSDP its fledgling federal defense policy? The former view has been adopted by neorealists and is the best-developed realist account of the CSDP. The latter view has been propounded by neoclassical realists.

Some neorealists argue that only powerful states that have both offensive military capabilities and aggressive intentions will be balanced by other states (Walt 1987).[4] Balance-of-power theorists disagree. States balance against any concentration of power in the system. "Unbalanced power, whoever wields it, is a potential danger to others" (Waltz 2000: 28; 1979). States have to worry about superior power in the hands of another state, irrespective of its current intentions. At worst, a dominant state may pose a direct threat to the security and vital interests of other states. At best, concentrated power may decrease other states' autonomy and generate unintended consequences that negatively affect their policies and goals. Hence, fear and uncertainty drive second-ranked states to engage in hard balancing against the dominant power. They strengthen their military forces, form alliances, or pursue a mix of the two policies. Through alliances or other security institutions, second-tier states aggregate or pool their separate power resources. This enhances their security, increases their autonomy vis-à-vis the dominant power, and improves their capacity to project power abroad (Jones 2007). Yet international institutions are good not only for balancing nonmember states, but also at containing or "binding" powerful members of the institution. They provide less powerful states participating in the institution with a "voice opportunity" to shape the conduct of the powerful members (Grieco 1996). Neorealist scholars have argued that the CSDP is a case of hard balancing. EU states use the CSDP to modernize and build up their military forces and to pool them in order to check US power. Moreover, they use the CSDP to contain Germany and gain influence over its foreign and security policy.[5]

Balance-of-power neorealism identifies the changes in the international power structure brought about by the end of the Cold War at the end of the 1980s as the reason behind the creation of the military

CSDP. The collapse of the Soviet Empire affected both the global and European balance of power. Globally, the collapse of the Soviet Union left the United States as the sole power with truly worldwide power projection capabilities. Only the United States can do forced-entry operations anywhere on the globe on short notice. In Europe, the disappearance of the Soviet Union removed the main threat against the EU, lessened its security dependence on the United States, and returned the regional system to multipolarity. With the CSDP, the EU responded to the opportunities and risks engendered by these changes in international and European politics.

When considering the implications of the US global military supremacy, EU states do not fear for their survival or territorial integrity (Mearsheimer 2010). The United States and the EU are allies, and most EU states are members of the US-dominated NATO. Hence, for the time being the CSDP is not directed against the military unipole. However, it is motivated by the concentration of military power that it represents. Through the CSDP, the EU builds up its own punching power to narrow the gap in military power vis-à-vis the United States. The EU does so because it does not know how Washington will use its superior power assets. First, Europeans do not trust the United States to always be there to address security problems in their neighborhood. Also, they often do not like the way Washington manages international security (Posen 2006: 150–151; also Art 2006). Such concerns about US unreliability and capriciousness are rooted in Washington's policy in the Western Balkans in the 1990s when EU states often disagreed with the United States on how to stop the war in Bosnia. With the CSDP, the EU broadens its range of security policy options to deal on its own with civil wars and regional conflicts in Europe and Africa (Hyde-Price 2006). Second and closely related, the CSDP strengthens the EU's hard power to promote its economic and strategic interests abroad. Third, by developing its power projection capabilities, the EU enhances its bargaining leverage vis-à-vis the United States on global security issues (Art 2004, 2006; Jones 2007). Finally, the CSDP is a basic insurance policy against a turn toward predatory behavior on the part of the United States (Layne 2007: 147). It is an investment in a limited war-fighting capability that the Europeans can build up should a strategic need for deliberate balancing against the US arise.

As regards the regional balance of power, neorealists emphasize that post–Cold War Europe has reverted to multipolarity. This multipolar system is balanced because no European state has the capacity to impose its will on others. The absence of a regional contender for hegemony in Europe limits fear and suspicion among the main players. Balanced multipolarity has thus been a crucial facilitator of the creation of the CSDP at the turn of the millennium (Hyde-Price 2006). Russia's power has precipitously declined in the wake of the collapse of the Soviet Union. Since the beginning of the new millennium, Moscow has worked hard to reverse the decline by investing in rebuilding Russia's military power. However, for the time being, Moscow's regional power projection capabilities remain limited. Germany is the fulcrum of the European balance-of-power system because of its economic strength and geographic position. Initially, EU governments such as France and Britain were worried about German reunification at the beginning of the 1990s. A reunited Germany would have the raw power to impose its will on its neighbors. Would it seek to dominate European politics to advance German interests? To guard against the security threats emanating from the growth of German power, EU states opted to contain the reunited Germany through strengthening the institutional corset of the EU, including in the area of foreign and security policy (Grieco 1996; Jones 2007). This binding strategy was an important shaper of the 1992 Maastricht Treaty, which had as one of its key elements the creation of the CFSP. Germany agreed to containment by its EU partners in order to facilitate reunification and because it was at the time a status quo power.

Neorealist accounts of CSDP policymaking emphasize that central state decisionmakers shape the CSDP. National governments jostle with each other as they seek to utilize the CSDP strategically to advance their national interests. There is no room for supranationalism—EU-level institutions that trump national interests and competencies—in the high politics of national security. The defense pool is run along purely intergovernmental lines. The supranational European Commission, European Parliament, and European Court of Justice are kept at bay by governments. Moreover, intergovernmental decisionmaking is by consensus. Yet not all countries are equal. The military and financial powerhouses—Britain, France, and Germany—set the CSDP's agenda and shape its institutional trajectory, capability development, and deployment decisions. They are able to do so because their power assets allow them to drive a hard bargain and enable them to constrain or induce other member states to follow their lead.

Recently, a distinct neoclassical account of the CSDP has been put forward. In contrast to neorealism, neoclassical realism emphasizes that domestic factors, notably the states' extractive capacity, mediate the impact of the balance of power on states. To succeed in power politics, states must "reallocate societal resources otherwise spent on consumption to security and war-making functions" (Rathbun 2008: 302). Not all states have the same capacity to do so (Taliaferro 2006). Throughout most of its existence, the EU did not possess this ability, but, as it has become ever more statelike in the new millennium, this has changed. In this view, the CSDP "is the result of an organic process related to how federal systems evolve as they consolidate power across their Member States and then seek to have greater influence beyond their borders" (Selden 2010: 413; see also Kupchan 2004–2005). From such a neoclassical perspective, the CSDP policy process is increasingly EU-centric rather than intergovernmental. EU foreign and security policy is increasingly made by EU decisionmaking bodies, whose authority in this policy domain has grown at the expense of the member states. The EU is evolving into a traditional great power, with security and defense policymaking increasingly centralized in Brussels.

Liberal Approaches: International Interdependence and Intergovernmentalism

Liberal theories have long been a fixture in international relations scholarship and EU studies. Liberal intergovernmentalism is one of the best elaborated and most sophisticated approaches available to students of the EU. Yet liberal approaches have played a rather limited role in analyses of the CSDP and have been eclipsed by constructivism, which stresses the role of ideational factors in accounting for the CSDP. They have even been eclipsed by realism, which focuses on the role of the balance of power within the EU and more broadly in European international affairs. Arguably, the limited contribution of liberal approaches to the study of the CSDP has to do with the fact that the main liberal contender in EU studies—liberal intergovernmentalism—has more to say about EU policies driven by the economic interests of substate actors than by the geopolitical and security interests of states (Moravcsik 1993, 1998b).[6] Few scholars have shown an inclination to analyze EU defense policy from the perspective of economic interests (Moravcsik 1991, 1993a). Even though liberal intergovernmentalism has been sidelined in CSDP studies, two of its components have been widely, albeit often unsystematically and separately, employed to make sense of the CSDP: interdependence theory and intergovernmental bargaining theory.

The concept of policy interdependence is at the heart of liberal intergovernmental explanations of the demand for cooperation among EU states. Cooperation is a means for governments to regulate the pattern of policy externalities that link them in a web of interdependence. Through cooperation, states can limit the impact of negative policy externalities on themselves and reap mutual benefits. The EU is the most successful example in history of interstate cooperation designed to manage interdependence through institutionalized policy coordination (Moravcsik 1993b: 474). From this perspective, the CSDP can be understood as a response to security interdependence or security globalization.

Liberals argue that, after World War II, the United States built and managed a rule-based international order that promoted international cooperation for the purpose of creating mutual gains (Ikenberry 2001; Keohane 1984). In the wake of the end of the Cold War, the United States has taken the lead in expanding liberal order across the globe. This process involves the transformation of liberal internationalism (Ikenberry 2009). The emerging order is more inclusive, with a larger number of nations involved in global security management. Also, the policy agenda that governments have to deal with in this new order is broader, with novel security threats having been added. Post–Cold War liberal internationalism is influenced by the considerable growth in security interdependence (Kirshner 2006). Security interdependence has weakened the capacity of nation-states to provide for their national security by policing their borders and has created newly potent transnational security threats such as pandemics, climate change, and energy scarcity. And it has empowered nonstate actors such as terrorists to become significant security actors in world politics. To tackle the new threats and threateners, states have to organize collective action, which requires strong international institutions. The CSDP is such a security institution. Through it, the EU contributes to international security management by capitalizing on its strengths—addressing the root causes of conflicts and threats. The CSDP does so through its contribution to conflict prevention, peacekeeping, crisis management, and postconflict stabilization and reconstruction (Ikenberry 2007; Moravcsik 2003).

The CSDP serves three principal purposes. First, it is a means for the EU to protect itself more effectively against the security risks associated with security interdependence. The EU is faced with transnational security threats such as organized crime, terrorism, and illegal migration—threats that often originate or find shelter in frail or failed states embroiled in civil wars or regional conflicts. The CSDP gives the EU an additional tool to tackle these threats at the source. Second, the CSDP is a means to relieve the US from lower-level military tasks and equips the EU with capabilities to deal with low-intensity conflicts and post-hostility stabilization and reconstruction (Nye 2002: 32, 151; Moravcsik 2009: 418). This, in turn, allows the United States to concentrate on doing the high-end work of global order management: high-intensity war fighting. Third, the CSDP is a capability that has been built up in response to the human rights revolution, which has given rise to the Responsibility to Protect.[7] The CSDP enables the EU to contribute to the liberal project of intervening in weak and rogue states to protect basic human rights (Ikenberry 2009; Shaw 2000). Liberal explanations of the CSDP thus reject realist claims that the CSDP is about balancing US power. US leadership and military superiority are not a concern to Europeans but are crucial for regulating security interdependence for the benefit of the international community.

If liberal approaches disagree with realism on the causes of the CSDP, they agree that the CSDP is run along intergovernmental lines. EU states, not Brussels-based actors, manage the CSDP. For realists this is simply a reflection of where real power lies—with member states, especially those who have the most power resources (military and economic). With a more nuanced understanding of the CSDP policy process, liberals regard Brussels-based actors as playing some, albeit a subordinate, role in shaping the CSDP. They explain CSDP negotiations and their outcomes in terms of rational choice institutionalism and preference intensities. Rational choice institutionalism explains the actions of institutional actors such as Brussels-based CSDP diplomats and soldiers in terms of principal-agent relations. (In addition to the institutionalist literature cited in the "Constructivist Approaches" section, see Klein 2011; Pollack 2009.) Governments are the principals, who need agents to take care of the day-to-day management of the policies they adopt. They instruct their agents what to do and monitor and control their actions. But these are costly activities, which means that governments often do less than is needed to keep full control over their agents. This generates agency slack, giving agents some leeway to pursue their own preferences. Yet if their actions deviate too far from the wishes of their principals, threatening to bring about a situation of agency loss, governments will intervene and put their agents on a tighter leash. Liberal approaches thus adopt a middle position between realism, which sees EU institutional actors as marginal, and constructivist approaches, which stress that institutions provide a context that enables agents to emancipate themselves from their principals. While liberal approaches thus argue that Brussels-based actors play a nonnegligible role in CSDP policymaking, they claim that EU governments remain the ultimate decisionmakers. Moreover, a key factor in explaining CSDP negotiation outcomes is the intensity of governmental preferences. Governments that have strong preferences on a given CSDP issue are willing to "offer the most significant compromises or side-payments in order to achieve" what they want (Moravcsik 1998: 66).

Governance Approaches: New Security Threats and Networked Responses

Governance approaches sit at the intersection between liberalism and constructivism and combine insights from both theories. They have recently made considerable inroads into the study of European foreign and security policy (Balzacq 2009; Kirchner and Sperling 2007, 2010; Krahmann 2003, 2005; Lavenex and Schimmelfennig 2010; Schimmelfennig and Sedelmeier 2004; Wagnsson et al. 2009; Webber et al. 2004; Weber et al. 2007). The term "governance" refers to a form of political ordering that is situated between hierarchy and anarchy. The traditional state represents hierarchical rule and possesses the legitimate monopoly of the use of force and rules by fiat. Markets represent anarchical rule in which order emerges from and behind the back of the decentralized decisions and actions of self-interested individuals. Governance differs from both forms of ordering. It is premised on the fragmentation of state authority. Public and private actors work together in policy networks that are based on shared interests and/or norms and contribute to the formulation of public policy.

Security governance approaches highlight four interrelated features of post–Cold War European security affairs. In doing so, they build on liberal insights and at points radicalize them. Notably, their claims regarding the erosion of sovereignty in world politics and the role of nongovernmental actors in global security governance go further than what most liberals are ready to accept. First, governance scholars argue that EU states cannot anymore be thought of as authoritative allocators of values such as security. This is a radicalization of liberal interdependence theory. EU states no longer build a protective shell around their national territories but have abolished their internal borders and have allowed their external borders to become porous. Governance scholars refer to this development as the transmutation of the Westphalian state, which tries to defend its policy independence in international affairs. In contrast, post-Westphalian states are no longer committed to upholding their sovereignty but are ready to trade it for greater problem-solving capacity through institutionalized security cooperation with other states and nonstate actors. The EU is the state of the art of post-Westphalian security governance (Ross 2009; Sperling 2009). Second, insecurity in most parts of Europe is no longer linked to military threats against the territorial integrity and political survival of states. The post-Westphalian EU states have a considerably broader security agenda, which includes the security of societal identities and social cohesion, liberal-democratic governance (domestic and international), the market economy, the environment, and human security. Third and closely related to the previous point, threats by one state against another have, with a few exceptions, lost their salience in Europe. The principal threats faced by the EU no longer stem from enemy states but are transnational threats. On the one hand, they derive from hostile networks such as terrorists or organized crime groups operating within and outside the EU. Networked nonstate actors find in fragile states that have not completed the transition to democracy a launch pad for their criminal activities in the EU. On the other hand, the threats faced by EU societies stem from unintended negative externalities such as illegal migration or pollution that are generated by the actions of individuals, firms, and public authorities in third countries. Fourth, the primacy of efficiency over sovereignty concerns in EU security governance leads to geographical and functional specialization in the provision of security among states, international organizations, and nonstate actors.

From a governance perspective, the CSDP is about EU external security governance, which is concerned with the transfer of EU rules and policies to third countries. The EU has evolved a number of instruments to govern external polities, including the EU enlargement policy and policies of conditionality without the carrot of membership, such as the European Neighbourhood Policy (see, for example, Lavenex and Schimmelfennig 2009). The CSDP is one more tool in the EU's arsenal to promote external governance and is a cost-efficient way to deal with transnational security threats and the associated blurred boundary between internal and external security (Lutterbeck

2005). On the one hand, civilian CSDP missions are an instance of the externalization of domestic law enforcement functions. EU police officers replace, train, or support their local counterparts in postconflict societies. They may be supported by other criminal justice system experts operating under the CSDP flag, such as EU judges and lawyers. On the other hand, military CSDP operations are an instance of the "politicization" of soldiering. Troops may be asked to carry out civilian tasks as peace builders and security sector reformers. CSDP missions contribute to the stabilization and reconstruction of postconflict societies by extending to them EU rules, norms, and practices. They do so not just to make less fortunate societies better off but also to secure the EU by promoting "a ring of well governed countries to the East of the European Union and on the borders of the Mediterranean" (European Council 2003).

Governance scholars agree with constructivists that the circle of key actors in CSDP policymaking goes well beyond national executives. However, they differ from constructivists in terms of the toolkit of concepts they employ to study CSDP policymaking. Whereas constructivists draw on research on socialization and social learning to analyze the cognitive dynamics engendered by the CSDP policy process, governance approaches emphasize its networked character.[8] Yet their conclusions concur. Presidents, prime minister, and ministers play an important role in the CSDP but do not run it. Governance approaches stress that Brussels-based transgovernmental networks influence CSDP agendas and predecision deliberations.[9] Network interaction is characterized by a spirit of problem-solving rather than conflictual bargaining based on national utility calculi. In contrast to constructivism's focus on Brusselization, governance approaches emphasize the networked character of the broader European security scene. The overlapping and intersecting transgovernmental networks centered on different European security organizations—the EU, NATO, and the Organisation for Security and Cooperation in Europe (OSCE)—influence CSDP decisionmaking (Krahmann 2003; Hofmann 2009, 2011). Moreover, governance approaches expect that transnational networks—networks that include private actors—have similar effects. Defense firms, security think tanks, and nongovernmental actors are likely to have access to and influence the CSDP policy process through channels in Brussels. Incidentally, this view of the role of transnational actors differs from liberal intergovernmentalism, which regards the state as the main contact point for private actors who want to influence EU policy.

Notes

1. As students of the CSDP have become more theoretically sophisticated in recent years, a number of nonmainstream approaches have been used or have been recommended for use to examine EU security and defense policy. These alternative approaches include, notably, Marxism (Oikonomou forthcoming), poststructuralism (Merlingen 2007, 2011, and forthcoming-a), and neofunctionalism (Ojanen 2006). For an interesting social theoretical approach to the CSDP, which does not fall easily into any of the existing EU studies theory boxes, see Bickerton (2011).

2. Historical institutionalism explains the development of institutions in terms of path-dependency. In this view, "past lines of policy condition subsequent policy by encouraging societal forces to organize along some lines rather than others, to adopt particular identities or to develop interests in policies that are costly to shift" (Hall and Taylor 1996: 941). Institutional change is conceptualized in terms of critical junctures—that is, moments of abrupt institutional change that are caused and shaped by factors either internal or external to the institution. Sociological institutionalism explains institutional development in terms of the gradual buildup of pressure for change within institutions. It stresses that institutions seek to enhance their broader legitimacy by adapting to their cultural environment even at the expense of efficiency and functionality concerns. This quest for legitimacy leads to institutional isomorphism. Also, sociological institutionalism differs from historical institutionalism, which is a structural theory, by paying great attention to the mutual interaction of actors and the institutional structures in which they are embedded. Both these constructivist institutionalisms differ from rational choice institutionalism. They stress that institutions shape actor preferences and identities and the unintended effects of institutional choices on further institutional development.

3. For Mérand the proximate cause of the CSDP was an organizational crisis affecting both EU diplomacy and NATO. His structural constructivist perspective on the creation of the CSDP, which draws on the work of Pierre Bourdieu, goes beyond mainstream constructivism in CFSP studies. It brings into focus the practices and habitus of EU diplomats and soldiers who are embedded and act strategically within their respective social fields— European foreign policy and NATO defense (Mérand 2010) .

4. Balance-of-threat neorealism has given rise to the theory of soft balancing, which has been used to explain certain episodes in transatlantic relations, such as the opposition by France and Germany toward the US-led invasion of Iraq. Soft balancing relies on nonmilitary tools such as territorial denial, entangling diplomacy, and economic strengthening (Pape 2005: 36).

5. Some realists are skeptical about the EU's balancing capacity. "The European Union has all the tools—population, resources, technology, and military capabilities—but lacks the organizational ability and the collective will to use them" (Waltz 2000: 31; see also Brooks and Wohlforth 2008; Rynning 2011). From their perspective, the CSDP is a mirage or illusion.

6. Liberal intergovernmentalism is a bottom-up theory that explains state preferences in terms of the preferences of shifting domestic social coalitions.

7. The Responsibility to Protect, or R2P, refers to the protection of populations from genocide, war crimes, ethnic cleansing, and crimes against humanity. It was embraced by the General Assembly of the United Nations in 2005.

8. Most network analyses of European security are qualitative. For a recent quantitative contribution, see Mérand et al. 2011.

9. Transgovernmental actors comprise "government units working across the borders that divide countries from one another and that demarcate the 'domestic' from the 'international' sphere" (Slaughter 2004: 14).

PART 1

What Is the EU's Common Security and Defence Policy?

CHAPTER 3

The Development
of the CSDP

FOR CENTURIES EUROPEAN NATIONS HAVE BATTLED EACH other. The climax of this story of warring nations was World War II. Since then war has disappeared among those nations participating in European integration. The long peace has fueled Europe's desire and has given it a growing capacity for a greater role in international security affairs.

The ESDP was launched in 1999. (The 2007 Lisbon Treaty changed the name to *Common* Security and Defence Policy—CSDP.)[1] Yet European efforts to construct a European military power date to the end of World War II. This chapter recounts these efforts and explains why they failed. Furthermore, it shows that more modest policies aimed at coordinating Western European foreign policy succeeded where more ambitious policies had failed. Importantly, limited foreign policy coordination built up trust among European policymakers and put in place policymaking institutions that created the foundation without which European nations could not have turned themselves into a military power in the new millennium. Yet the creation of the ESDP was not the result of an inevitable historical process but required changes in the structure of the international system, the return of war to the heart of Europe, and political leadership.

The Western Union, NATO, and
the European Defence Community

Within a few years after the end of World War II, the anti-Hitler alliance gave way to the Cold War. A capitalist bloc of nations led by the United States confronted a Communist bloc led by the Soviet Union. In response to the perceived Communist threat, Britain, France, Belgium, the Netherlands, and Luxembourg created a defense pact: the Western Union. It was aimed against the Soviet Union and Germany, which was still perceived as an enemy nation by many in Europe so shortly after the Nazis had devastated many European nations. An important rationale for the creation of the Western Union was to persuade the United States to buttress Europe's faltering defenses. The countries forming the Western Union wanted to alleviate US congressional concerns about European free-riding. The Western Union was to demonstrate that the Europeans were ready to shoulder a fair share of the common defense burden of the North Atlantic community of nations. The maneuver succeeded.

In April 1949, the United States joined Canada and its European allies in signing the North Atlantic Treaty. Although the treaty's core function is collective defense, in 1949 no decision was yet taken on the creation of the multinational military machine that would later become the hallmark of NATO. The construction of collective defense capabilities only began toward the end of 1950.

In June 1950, Communist North Korea invaded South Korea. A US-led force became involved on the side of the South. The Cold War had become hot, which added urgency to the unresolved question of West German rearmament. Opposition to West German rearmament was strong in many Western countries, notably in France. Yet under the pressure of the war in East Asia, Washington began to press hard for a West German military contribution to Western Europe's collective defense. The United States called for the creation of a multinational military force under centralized NATO command headed by a supreme commander, which the allies accepted. Controversy arose over another point of the US proposal, which foresaw that German combat units, including at the level of divisions, would be part of NATO. The French balked at the idea of re-creating, as they saw it, the German Wehrmacht—the Nazis' military spearhead.

France's solution to the West German problem was the Pleven Plan for the creation of the European Defence Community (EDC). Named after the French prime minister, the plan called for the creation, within the framework of NATO, of a supranational European army. The force was to be composed of national contingents, including from West Germany, at the level of battalions. London welcomed the plan but decided not to join the EDC. Paris was disappointed, not least because it had been Winston Churchill who had earlier called for a European army.

Washington backed the plan. As the *Washington Post* put it at the time, a European army was "the best hope in Europe for building a meaningful defence quickly and for advancing the political unity for which the continent is crying" (cited in Fursdon 1980: 124). After difficult negotiations, France, West Germany, Italy, the Netherlands, Belgium, and Luxembourg signed a treaty in 1952 aimed at establishing the EDC.[2] At the same time, the EDC and NATO agreed on mutual security guarantees. Although Western European security seemed to stand on firm institutional grounds, France failed to ratify the EDC treaty. The French had second thoughts about giving up control over a large chunk of their armed forces while the British would keep full control over theirs. In addition, they feared that the EDC would sooner rather than later be dominated by an economically resurgent West Germany.

British foreign secretary Anthony Eden proposed a pragmatic way out of the crisis. West Germany's military contribution to NATO would be supervised by a modified Western Union, its residual anti-German bias would be abandoned, and West Germany and Italy would be invited to join. Without the supranational implications of the EDC, the Western Union would do the same job. It would provide an oversight mechanism for West German rearmament and thus make its military integration into NATO palatable to the French. France would retain its independent armed forces and partner with West Germany in a military arrangement in which Britain was a full member. Agreement on the plan and associated measures was quickly found. In October 1954, protocols were signed on the revision of the Western Union, which was renamed the Western European Union (WEU), and on West Germany's accession to the North Atlantic Treaty. Within a few years, Western European nations had moved from fighting each other on the battlefield to joining hands in military cooperation under US leadership.

From Security Community to European Political Cooperation

The post-1945 bipolar world kept traditional Western European security dynamics in check. The former European great powers were reduced to supporting actors in a confrontation that pitted the two new superpowers—the Soviet Union and the United States—against each other. This demotion was the background condition for European economic integration. In 1951 the six countries that would later sign the

EDC treaty formed the European Coal and Steel Community, and in 1957 they established the European Community (EC).[3] European economic integration was a powerful contributor to the creation of a pluralistic security community in Western Europe (Deutsch 1957; Wæver 1998). States rose above the relations of enmity and the multipolar balance of power that had governed their interactions for centuries. At the beginning of the 1960s, French president Charles de Gaulle sought the support of his fellow EC leaders for an intergovernmental political union. It was to be a means for cooperation in foreign and defense policy and for Western Europe's emancipation from US hegemony. A committee was set up to elaborate plans, but the foreign policy views of the EC states were too different and the project was aborted. At the end of the decade, the issue of European foreign policy returned. Detente among the superpowers transformed the tight bipolar international system of the 1950s and 1960s into a looser configuration. Second-ranked powers found they had more leeway to pursue independent foreign policies. EC governments seized the opportunity to raise their collective international profile and to create a mechanism to promote their common political interests and values. Without challenging US leadership in the transatlantic order, they expanded their international role repertoire by adding the role of diplomat to that of international trader and aid giver. The change was facilitated by new leaders in France and Germany. President Georges Pompidou, who succeeded de Gaulle, and West German chancellor Willy Brandt took the lead in strengthening European integration, partly by extending it into the field of foreign policy cooperation.

In 1969, the six EC states agreed to create a system of foreign policy cooperation: the EPC (Ifestos 1987; Möckli 2008; Nuttall 1992). Security issues were initially excluded. Intergovernmental in its nature, the EPC was an informal, consensus-based arrangement and was deliberately kept outside the EC legal and institutional framework to safeguard national sovereignty. The EPC quickly developed into a mechanism for the continuous exchange of information and national views on foreign policy. Joint communiqués were its main output, and critics called the EPC a "gentlemen's dining club" (Wallace and Allen 1977: 237). Yet on some issues, it produced more than declaratory policy. An early success was in the 1970s when EC countries managed to use the EPC to pursue a common policy in the negotiations during the Conference on Security and Cooperation in Europe (CSCE). Their united front was crucial in constraining the East Bloc to accept that human rights were a legitimate concern of interstate relations across the Iron Curtain (Thomas 2002). Over time, governments also evolved the capacity to coordinate intergovernmental political declarations and supranational economic instruments, notably sanctions and aid. This enhanced the clout of European foreign policy, for instance, in collective antiapartheid policies toward South Africa (Smith 2004a). Also, by 1983 the EPC's agenda had been enlarged to include the political and economic aspects of security policy.

The EPC was run by the foreign ministers, who kept their foreign policy gatherings strictly separate from their EC gatherings. They were supported by senior national diplomats, who met to discuss European foreign policy at least once a month in the newly set-up Political Committee. From 1973 onward, the day-to-day operation of the diplomatic system was managed by mid-level national diplomats who were called the European correspondents. They facilitated the exchange of information and the coordination of policy and monitored the implementation of agreed-upon policies. Over time, the European Commission became fully associated with the venture. A step toward bringing the EPC closer to the EC was the 1986 Single European Act, which paved the way for the single European market, although the act's foreign policy provisions were little more than an inventory of the EPC practices and norms. One of the few foreign policy innovations was the creation of a permanent, Brussels-based secretariat to assist governments in running the EPC.

Overall, the EPC was a small but successful move on the part of European nations to raise their profile and influence on the international scene. They branded themselves as a collective civilian power—an international actor that relies on nonmilitary tools and cooperates with other states rather than coercing them (Duchêne 1973). Yet at the end of the 1980s there were clear signs that the EPC had reached the limits of its development potential. Most notably, it virtually played no role in the most important foreign policy issue of the day: the Western response to the collapse of the Communist regimes in Eastern Europe.

The Maastricht Treaty and EU Security Policy

The end of the bipolar divide of Europe created powerful incentives to upgrade the EPC. During the Cold War, EC countries acted under the shadow of the perceived threat of the Soviet Union. Outside France, there was little appetite for an autonomous Western European security policy. Western Europe's safety depended on the capacity and political will of the United States to defend it. Hence, most Western European governments most of the time gladly accepted Washington's leadership in global and regional security politics. From the US perspective, there was a downside to its leadership role. The Europeans did not shoulder a fair share of the costs for ensuring the defense of the transatlantic security order. The collapse of the Soviet Union led Washington to become more insistent in calling for an end to European free riding in security matters, while the Europeans themselves were more receptive to these demands than in the past. They saw the disappearance of the Communist East Bloc as an opportunity to reinforce their collective international identity and influence in Eastern and southeastern Europe. Also, they realized that they would not always be able to rely on the United States to protect them. They wanted to be able to prevent conflicts in their neighborhood and to secure themselves against nontraditional security threats such as failed states and transnational organized crime. Another rationale for beefing up the EPC was that in many Western European chancelleries there was unease at the prospect of German reunification. A reunited Germany would have considerable economic and political weight and might be tempted to pursue a more nationalistic foreign policy to the detriment of its EC partners. These diverse push-and-pull factors and the skillful joint leadership of French president François Mitterrand and West German chancellor Helmut Kohl, who wanted to secure the support of EC nations for German reunification, persuaded EC governments to create the CFSP. It became one of the three pillars of the EU, which was created by the 1992 Maastricht Treaty (entry into force in 1993).[4]

The CFSP, which retained the intergovernmental character of the EPC, included "all questions related to the security of the Union, including the eventual framing of a common defence policy which might in time lead to a common defence" (Official Journal of the European Community 1992: 126). To placate the concerns of neutral Ireland and the EU members of NATO, the treaty stipulated that the CFSP was to be compatible with their specific security policies and international obligations. To stress the "S" in the CFSP, the Maastricht Treaty authorized the EU to call upon the WEU to "elaborate and implement decisions and actions of the Union which ha[d] defence implications" (Official Journal of the European Community 1992: 126).

The creation of the CFSP ratcheted up expectations among EU policymakers and the public about a new era of European foreign and security policy. The expectation that it would be more forceful and effective than the EPC shaped EU attitudes toward the violent disintegration of Yugoslavia in the early 1990s. In the summer of 1991, Luxembourg's foreign minister, who at the time held the rotating presidency of the Council of Ministers of the European Community, stated that this was "the hour of Europe . . . not the hour of the Americans" (cited in Riding 1991). Like many others he believed that the EC was powerful enough to enforce peace in the Western Balkans and did not need the United States. Yet, as Yugoslavia descended into violence, Europe's continuing diplomatic-strategic weakness was clear for everyone to see. While Brussels scored some early successes (Ginsberg 2001), it proved incapable of stopping civil war in Bosnia. The option of asking the WEU to intervene in the EU's backyard was never seriously considered. In the end, it was the United States, acting in the framework of NATO, that bombed the Bosnian Serbs and led them to the negotiating table. Washington subsequently used a combination of bullying and sweet talk to constrain the parties to agree to the 1995 General Framework Agreement for Peace in Bosnia and Herzegovina—commonly known as the Dayton Peace Agreement. The EU's extensively publicized project of transforming itself from a mere civilian power into an international actor capable of using military power was in shatters. Instead a wide capability-expectations gap had opened up (Hill 1993). The brand-new CFSP had turned into a public relations disaster.

The CFSP also suffered from other shortcomings. In particular, it did not galvanize EU states into making the strategic adjustments to their national armed forces that would enable them to engage effectively in foreign interventions. This was not immediately obvious. In 1992, the WEU states reached an agreement on the type of expeditionary operations they were prepared to undertake for the EU. These came to be known as the Petersberg tasks, based on the name of the mountain next to Bonn where the German government has its "Camp David." The Petersberg tasks comprised humanitarian, rescue, and peacekeeping operations and tasks of combat forces in crisis management, including peacemaking (Western European Union 1992). However, the Petersberg decision had little effect on national force postures. In many countries, notably Germany, the armed forces remained geared toward territorial defense and large-formation warfare. This considerably limited the military options available to the CFSP, even though NATO agreed in 1994 that it stood ready to make collective alliance assets available to WEU operations carried out by the EU in pursuit of its Petersberg tasks. Yet the WEU never approached NATO with a request for assistance.

Overall, then, the CFSP had a bad record, yet EU governments remained divided over whether to do something about this failure.

The Amsterdam Treaty: Muddling Through

In 1997, the EU nations agreed to the Amsterdam Treaty (entry into force in 1999), which grew out of a review of the accomplishments and failures of the Maastricht Treaty. The stated objective of the review was to improve the functioning of the EU. While this might lead one to expect that the Amsterdam Treaty made substantive changes to the CSDP, it did not. The reform that proved to be the most important one in the long run was the creation of the office of the high representative for the CFSP, who was tasked to assist the Council of Ministers in making and implementing the CFSP. The high representative injected considerable momentum into the development of the CFSP, but this was due less to the Amsterdam Treaty than to the fact that when the treaty entered into force, the EU was about to equip itself with its own military capabilities. At Amsterdam, the creation of an autonomous EU military machine was still politically unthinkable for key governments, as illustrated by the debate over the fate of the WEU.

The EU's impotent response to the Bosnian war had demonstrated that the institutional triangle among the EU, NATO, and the WEU did not empower the EU to turn itself into a military actor. Hence, France and Germany took the lead in advocating that the Amsterdam Treaty integrate the key WEU functions into the EU. They wanted the EU to be responsible for and have the means to carry out its own security policy. The Franco-German initiative was supported by a majority of member states but was blocked by Britain, with the backing of the Netherlands and those EU states committed to the principle of neutrality in foreign and security policy. London and the Hague feared a weakening of NATO and preferred the WEU to remain a bridge, however fragile, between NATO and the EU. The neutrals were concerned about a militarization of the EU. Hence, the WEU retained all its military functions, and the EU remained dependent on it for its military policy. Those nations wishing to turn the EU into a military power only achieved that the WEU's Petersberg tasks were incorporated into the Amsterdam Treaty, which was little more than a consolation prize. In addition, some minor linguistic changes related to defense were made. For instance, the Amsterdam Treaty empowered the EU to "avail itself" of the WEU, while the language of the Maastricht Treaty had been less forceful. It had stipulated that the EU "requests" the WEU to assist it in making and carrying out EU defense policy.

The Saint-Malo Accord and Its Aftermath: Working Toward the ESDP

At their bilateral summit in December 1998 in Saint-Malo, France and Britain finally drew the consequences of the failure of the hookup between the EU and the WEU. They agreed to what some observers called Europe's military revolution (Andréani et al. 2001). They asked the EU to develop "the capacity for autonomous action, backed up by credible military forces, the means to use them and the readiness to do so, in order to respond to international crises." For London, this was a major foreign policy change, made possible by the ouster of the Euroskeptic Tories from government and their replacement by a pro-European Labour government under Prime Minister Tony Blair. Yet there were also important continuities in British foreign policy. The convergence of views among Paris and London was limited to regarding autonomous EU military capabilities as a useful tool to tackle the nontraditional security threats that threatened the EU's security and prosperity. Beyond this, there was disagreement over what precisely the problem was that needed to be fixed by the transformation of the EU into a military actor. Under the new Labour government, London no longer saw the militarization of the EU as a threat to NATO but, on the contrary, as a means to solidify it politically and to reinforce its capacity to tackle higher-end international security threats. Conversely, for Paris, the militarization of the EU was primarily a means to solidify the EU's international political profile and to reinforce its role as an independent international security provider. (For details on their respective national views and the reasons behind them, see Chapter 7.)

Germany played no role in the Saint-Malo breakthrough. Indeed, Berlin was initially skeptical of the initiative. However, the government quickly came around to support it, realizing that it "offered a real chance to overcome the sometimes painful tensions that had in the past torn Germany between French and British views on European defense" (Andréani et al. 2001: 21). As the holder of the presidency of the EU Council of Ministers in the first half of 1999, Berlin played a key role in fleshing out the Saint-Malo declaration and built support for the project among the member states, some of which remained reluctant to see the EU move into military and defense issues. A consensus emerged that the ESDP was an opportunity to rebrand and relaunch the CFSP. Also, the German presidency advanced the debate on practical issues: the institutional machinery required for the intergovernmental ESDP and deployment scenarios. Two scenarios were outlined. In one, the EU would ask NATO to allow it to draw on alliance capabilities; in the other, the EU would go it alone.

During the Finnish presidency of the EU in the second half of 1999, London and Paris further concretized their ideas. In particular, they suggested the creation of a rapid reaction force, while the neutrals and smaller EU member states emphasized the importance of collective nonmilitary crisis response tools. Denmark and the Netherlands presented a proposal to make international police missions a priority for civilian ESDP deployments. Paris and London regarded the creation of civilian intervention capabilities as a distraction from their focus on military power in Europe. Germany supported the idea of giving the ESDP civilian capabilities. The Finnish presidency prepared separate reports on how to push ahead with a two-dimensional ESDP that combined military and civilian components. In November, the WEU Council agreed to prepare its "legacy and the inclusion of those functions of WEU, which will be deemed necessary by the European Union to fulfil its new responsibilities in the area of crisis-management tasks" (Western European Union 1999). The stage was set for the launch of the ESDP.

The Helsinki and Nice European Councils: The Birth of the ESDP and Its Codification

The EU Summit in Helsinki in December 1999 marks the formal birth of the ESDP. It agreed to "have an autonomous capacity to take decisions and, where NATO as a whole is not engaged, to launch and then to conduct EU-led military operations in response to international crises" (European Council 1999b: Annex IV, 1). Moreover, it agreed to equip the ESDP with a civilian stabilization and reconstruction capability. The centerpiece of the military ESDP was the military Headline Goal 2003, which stipulated the creation, by 2003, of a 50,000- to 60,000-strong European Rapid Reaction Force (RRF). Also, the EU states decided to establish a number of permanent Brussels-based bodies to plan and run military ESDP operations. The Helsinki Summit agreement on civilian capabilities was less far-reaching. EU states merely agreed on an action plan, which stipulated the creation of a database of national assets available for EU deployments. However, within a few months of the summit, the EU rectified its omission and created a Brussels-based body to guide and oversee the civilian ESDP. Also, it pledged national capabilities for ESDP police missions and agreed on additional priority areas for civilian missions (for details, see Chapter 6).

At the end of 2000, another European Council approved the Nice Treaty (entry into force in 2003). Its main objective was to prepare the EU for the accession of new eastern and southern European states in 2004. In CFSP matters, the treaty mainly codified previous decisions and introduced only minor changes in this area. The language was adjusted to reflect the fact that the EU had "devour[ed] the WEU to give birth to a European Security and Defence Policy" (Wessel 2001). More noteworthy, the treaty extended the procedure of "enhanced cooperation" to the CFSP. It enables a subset of member states to take the lead in implementing CFSP decisions and to make use of EU institutions and funds for this purpose. Policies with "military or defence implications" were excluded from enhanced cooperation. The EU summit that approved the Nice Treaty also decided to make permanent the interim ESDP bodies created in the wake of the Helsinki European Council. The presidency conclusions of the summit concretized their composition and functions.

The Lisbon Treaty: A Step Toward a More Ambitious and Coherent CFSP

The most far-reaching changes of EU foreign, security, and defense policy since the Maastricht Treaty were ushered in by the 2007 Lisbon Treaty (entry into force in 2009). It grew out of the draft European Constitution, which was aborted after having been rejected in referenda in France and the Netherlands. The Lisbon Treaty abolished the pillar structure of the EU and granted it legal personality, which allows it to conclude international agreements. For the first time, the treaty devoted a section to the renamed ESDP—now called the CSDP—and extended its scope (see Box 3.1). The main change in relation to foreign policy brought about by the Lisbon Treaty is the reform of what a former EU external relations commissioner called the "suboptimal institutional architecture" of European foreign policy (Patten 2005: 157). Without doing away with the divide between supranational and intergovernmental EU foreign policy domains, the treaty bridged the gap between

---

Box 3.1 The Lisbon Treaty and the CSDP Tasks

Joint disarmament operations

Humanitarian and rescue tasks

Military advice and assistance tasks

Conflict prevention and peacekeeping tasks

Tasks of combat forces in crisis management, including peacemaking
and postconflict stabilization

Support for third countries in combating terrorism

---

them. It created the post of high representative of the union for foreign affairs and security policy, which straddles the two domains and combines the beefed-up functions of the high representative for the CFSP and of the vice-president of the European Commission in charge of foreign policy. To support the new post of high representative, the treaty created a unified EU diplomatic service: the European External Action Service. These reforms promote the coherence and effectiveness of EU foreign and security policy.

Other important CFSP reforms ushered in by the Lisbon Treaty include the creation of the post of president of the European Council, the reinforcement of a differentiated Europe in which coalitions of the able and willing are given greater salience, and collective defense and solidarity clauses. The president of the European Council is appointed by the EU heads of state and government and prepares and chairs the summits of the European Council with a view to facilitating agreements on important issues, including the CFSP. Also, the post holder is entrusted, together with the high representative, to represent the EU on the international stage on matters falling under the CFSP. The Lisbon Treaty strengthened the principle of self-differentiation through a number of measures. "Enhanced cooperation" was extended to military and defense issues. In a codification of existing practice, coalitions of the able and willing were authorized to carry out CSDP operations on behalf of the EU. More importantly, the Lisbon Treaty established a procedure for "permanent structured cooperation." Whereas enhanced cooperation is open to all EU states who wish to participate, permanent structured cooperation is not but is reserved for those countries that meet certain military capability requirements.

Acting within the EU framework, eligible states can press ahead with deeper defense integration. In particular, they can cooperate to enhance the quality of European troops and military capabilities. A new collective defense clause, modeled on article 5 of the North Atlantic Treaty, obligates member states to assist, with all the means in their power, any EU country that is the victim of armed aggression. However, the commitment is qualified. The obligation neither prejudices the policy of the EU neutrals nor undermines the defense commitments of EU states that are also NATO members. This said, the defense clause is a step toward a European homeland defense. Finally, an equally new solidarity clause enjoins states to assist each other if one of them becomes the target of a terrorist attack or the victim of a natural or manmade disaster. Such assistance may draw on CSDP resources and structures.

To conclude this brief historical overview, throughout the second half of the twentieth century, Western European states have pursued the goal of forging a common foreign and security policy. As long as the Cold War existed, they did not dare go beyond limited foreign policy coordination. Since the 1990s, their readiness to take on an international security role has gradually increased. A comparison of the EPC and the CFSP in its Lisbon Treaty version highlights how much European nations have achieved on this front. This said, the CSDP still falls short of what Europeans aimed for when they envisaged the creation of the EDC in the early 1950s.

Notes

1. This chapter uses the terms "ESDP" and "CSDP" in a chronologically correct fashion. All the following chapters use only the term "CSDP," even when reference is made to a time when the policy was still called ESDP.

2. The treaty deviated from the Pleven Plan. Among other things, it codified the US view that the smallest national contingents to be integrated into the European force would be divisions.

3. To be precise, the 1957 Treaties of Rome established the European Economic Community and the European Atomic Energy Community. Together with the European Coal and Steel Community, the integrative arrangements established by the Rome Treaties were known as the European Communities.

4. The other pillars were the European Communities and the Justice and Home Affairs pillar. The main purpose of the Maastricht Treaty was the creation of the Economic and Monetary Union.

CHAPTER 4

Political Actors in the Policy Process

WHO RUNS THE CFSP? MEMBER STATES OR BRUSSELS? THIS IS a long-standing debate in international relations and EU studies. On the one side are scholars who regard the EU as a traditional international organization run by the states. On the other side are scholars who regard it as a novel political form that rises above traditional interstate politics. The debate is complicated by the sheer complexity of CFSP policymaking. The multiactor and multilevel policy system comprises national governments and numerous Brussels-based institutions. This chapter and the next cut through the complexity of CFSP policymaking by discussing the powers and functions of the various players populating this policy system.

Intergovernmentalism

This chapter covers the political actors at the apex of the CFSP. In this policy domain European nation-states have not been submerged into a supranational community but own the CFSP. Central national decisionmakers—presidents, prime ministers, and foreign and defense ministers—determine the development and functioning of the CFSP. They are motivated by different national interests and threat perceptions. The political influence of supranational actors—the European Commission and European Parliament—is limited, especially when it comes to military issues.[1] But principals of complex organizations

need agents who deal with day-to-day management issues. To prepare and implement the big CFSP decisions, central national decisionmakers rely on permanent EU civil servants and national representatives, who are temporarily posted to the EU institutions in
Brussels. These agents of governments are the topic of Chapter 5,
which will show that the CFSP agents have their own sources of
power and influence on which they can draw in their relations with
their principals. The agents inject an element of supranationalism
into the intergovernmental CFSP. A CFSP player that cannot be easily classified as either a principal or an agent is the high representative of the union for foreign affairs and security policy. The office is
covered in this chapter because the power resources available to and
the functions carried out by it make the officeholder more akin to a
principal than to an agent.

As old as European integration itself is the conceptual distinction
between intergovernmentalism and supranationalism. In supranational policy domains such as the Common Agricultural Policy, policy is
based on legislative acts proposed by the European Commission;
governments share the power to make legislation with the European
Parliament; legislative decisions are binding on the member states;
majority voting applies; and legal acts are subject to judicial oversight by the supranational European Court of Justice. The CFSP is
run not along supranational but along intergovernmental lines. It is
not about legislating and enforcing a single policy irrespective of the
national views of the member states. It is about enabling governments
to formulate and implement common policies on issues on which
their national views converge.

The principal formal norm of the CFSP is the obligation of EU
states to inform and consult each other on their foreign and security
policies. Because separate national foreign and security policies
coexist with common European policies, the EU often speaks with
more than one voice on the international stage, and EU states sometimes pursue contradictory foreign policies. In virtually all cases, the
making of CFSP requires consensus, which has opened up a consensus-
expectations gap (Toje 2008). High-flying aspirations and expectations
run into the procedural roadblock of a decisionmaking process that has
to take account of EU countries' national sensitivities and preoccupations, which makes it difficult to reach consensus. Sometimes policy
blockage or policies reflecting the lowest common denominator of
the interests of all states are the result. Thus, on some important
issues of foreign and security policy, the EU does not have a strong

and coherent position, say, on its relations with Russia. Instead of a bold and forceful CFSP that would be commensurate with its raw power, the EU's diplomatic-strategic behavior on the global stage often resembles that of a small power (Nuttall 2000; Toje 2010). In short, intergovernmentalism is the principal determinant of the CFSP's functioning, and it goes a long way toward explaining the EU's remaining limitations as a global security actor.

The European Council: Defining the CFSP

The European Council was established in 1974 and soon evolved into "the most politically authoritative institution" of the EU (Bulmer and Wessels 1987: 2). It is composed of the heads of state and government of all EU states, the president of the European Council, and the president of the European Commission. It meets at least twice every six months to discuss and decide the political priorities of the EU. Decisionmaking is by consensus, with some minor exceptions. Ever since the Maastricht Treaty, the Council has had the power to define the strategic lines of the CFSP and provides guidelines to foreign ministers on how to translate the treaty-based objectives into policies. The Lisbon Treaty considerably strengthened the role of the European Council in shaping the EU's international role, giving it an overarching steering power over all aspects of European foreign and security policy—the CFSP and EU external relations governed by supranationalism such as foreign trade and development policy. This reform enhances the coherence and effectiveness of EU foreign policy.

After each summit, the European Council issues "Conclusions," which often include statements and decisions on the CSDP. For instance, the decision to launch the CSDP was announced and given legal force by the Conclusions of the Helsinki European Council. Also, the European Council exercises important informal leadership functions, which are not derived from the treaties but from the fact that it is composed of the highest-level national decisionmakers (see, for example, Bulmer and Wessels 1987; and, more generally, see Hayes-Renshaw and Wallace 2006). For instance, it may act as policy arbitrator of last resort, which resolves contentious CFSP issues.

To give greater intertemporal consistency to the work of the European Council and to put a stable face on it, the Lisbon Treaty created the post of president of the European Council. When the proposal for the office was first made, it proved controversial among smaller countries and the European Commission. While the latter feared that it would strengthen the intergovernmental dimension of the EU, the former were worried about losing influence in the European Council. The president is elected by a qualified majority of the members of the European Council for a once-renewable period of two and a half years, during which time the post holder cannot hold any national office. With the new position, the Lisbon Treaty created an honest broker and facilitator of the deliberations and decisions of the European Council and a readily identifiable spokesperson. The president of the European Council adds to the European Council's stature on the international stage and its influence in EU policymaking.

Also, the new office is well placed to contribute to greater strategic coherence of the CFSP. In case of an international crisis, the president can convene an emergency meeting of the European Council to define the EU response. The functions of the president include representing the EU in CFSP matters on the international stage. In 2009 former Belgian prime minister Herman Van Rompuy was appointed as the first president of the European Council. Governments wanted a backroom fixer rather than a charismatic and well-known international figure who would steal the limelight from the heads of state and government. Van Rompuy has proven an adroit dealmaker. Moreover, he quickly established himself as the public face of not just the European Council but the EU as a whole. The president of the European Commission has had to accept a diminished role in EU policy, including in foreign policy.

The Council of Ministers: The Principal CFSP Decisionmaker

The Council of Ministers is the EU's principal decisionmaker. The European Commission takes part in its work. While the Council is legally one entity, it meets in different ministerial formations depending on the subject matter to be discussed. Initially, the Council of Foreign Ministers was the only formation. As the scope of EU policymaking increased and became more specialized, additional councils were established, including for transport, agriculture, and so forth. Foreign ministers continue to deal with foreign policy as well as general and politically sensitive EU business. The Foreign Affairs Council meets at least once a month, with more meetings scheduled as required. Twice a year it meets informally at so-called Gymnich meetings in the country holding the rotating presidency. This allows for frank discussions of sensitive policy issues.

The Lisbon Treaty has reduced the influence of the Foreign Affairs Council relative to the reinforced powers and visibility of the European Council and of the high representative. Yet the Foreign Affairs Council remains the main policymaking body of the CFSP. Based on the EU interests and objectives defined by the European Council, it makes all CFSP decisions.[2] The militarization of collective foreign policy has so far not led to the creation of a permanent Council of Defence Ministers. Because the idea proved too controversial, a compromise was found. Defense ministers meet periodically alongside foreign ministers in CSDP councils. The Foreign Affairs Council makes policy by adopting positions and actions. Positions define the EU's stance toward third countries, international events, or situations. Member states and the Commission have an obligation to uphold the positions, including in international organizations and conferences. Positions may require implementing measures. For instance, member states have to adopt separate national implementing measures to give effect to common EU positions on arms embargoes. Actions are the principal foreign policy tool of the Council of Ministers. Unlike positions, they involve measures that are administered jointly by governments and require the pooling of national resources and means to carry out specific actions. For instance, all CSDP deployments have to be authorized by actions. In addition, the Council engages in political dialogue with third countries and international organizations. To present its views on international issues of importance, it makes secret demarches and public declarations.

Ever since the Maastricht Treaty went into effect, EU treaties define the consensus principle as the default option in Council decisionmaking on the CFSP. Abstentions do not prevent the adoption of decisions and can be formalized through the procedure of "constructive abstention," freeing those who abstain from the obligation to apply the decision. In return, they accept that the decision commits the EU and refrain from interfering with it. In some matters, such as the appointment of EU special representatives (EUSRs), qualified majority voting applies, except when it comes to decisions having military or defense implications (for the functions and role of EUSRs, see Chapter 5). Also, the majority vote does not apply when a government declares that it opposes such a vote, because it risks negatively affecting a "vital" interest. This reference is a legacy of the 1966 Luxembourg Compromise, which reversed the trend toward supranationalism in the

EU by reasserting the primacy of the nation-state. Informal Council working lunches and dinners have come to play an important role in facilitating consensus-based decisionmaking. The foreign ministers meet without their delegations to engage in frank discussions on CFSP matters and to seek out compromises. The need for unanimous decisionmaking on most defense matters is an important part of the explanation as to why the EU has so far not deployed more robust military operations. Determined opponents can prevent the deployment of CSDP operations they do not like.

An important office of the Council of Ministers is the Council presidency, which dates back to the beginnings of European integration. When the EPC was created in 1970, the office was asked to run it. This has changed with the Lisbon Treaty, which excluded the CFSP from the brief of the presidency.[3] Prior to the Lisbon Treaty, each member state took on the role of chief executive officer of the CFSP for a period of six months. Diplomats and experts from the country holding the presidency chaired and steered all CFSP meetings, down to those of the lowliest CFSP working group. They organized, managed, and drove forward the agenda and were responsible for policy implementation. Last but not least, they represented the EU on CFSP matters, including in international organizations and in political dialogue with third parties. The Lisbon Treaty transferred the presidency functions to the high representative.

The presidency offered governments a platform for influencing the CFSP in accordance with their national interests. Countries that pushed too hard to inject their own interests into the agenda were likely to see their role as brokers diminished, with policy blockage as the likely result. Larger countries were more likely to be too ambitious in this regard, while smaller ones were more aware of the limits of their influence. Conversely, smaller countries often found it hard to lead on CFSP issues because the presidency overburdened their national administrations. Also, their national interests and preoccupations tend to be narrower than the CFSP agenda. Even well-defined presidency priorities could be derailed by fast-moving and unpredictable foreign policy events. At the same time, an international crisis could provide an unexpected window of opportunity to display leadership. For instance, when Russia and Georgia went to war in the summer of 2008, France held the presidency. French president Nicolas Sarkozy brokered a cease-fire, negotiated the withdrawal of Russian troops from Georgia, and agreed with Moscow to deploy European monitors to the crisis area. The French skillfully used their presidency to translate these national initiatives into CFSP measures. The Lisbon Treaty has made such exploits impossible.

The High Representative of the Union for Foreign Affairs and Security Policy

The 1997 Treaty of Amsterdam created the Office of the High Representative for the CFSP. The purpose behind this innovation was to streamline the management of the CFSP at a time when it faced institutional and policy challenges. To begin with, in 1995, three neutral countries (Austria, Finland, and Sweden) joined the EU. Also, there was pressure on the EU to do more to tackle the post–Cold War disorder in the Western Balkans and post-Soviet space and to step up its involvement in global security management. Together these developments confronted the CFSP with considerable challenges. On the one hand, they created a more diverse portfolio of national interests. This made EU policy coordination and the management of intra-EU disagreements more difficult. On the other hand, these developments created a more ambitious foreign policy agenda and a greater demand for negotiations and cooperation with third parties. To address these challenges, the high representative was mandated to assist the EU states in the formulation, preparation, and implementation of the CFSP and the representation of the EU on the international stage. While formally an agent of the Council of Ministers, the high representative, Javier Solana, succeeded within a short period of time in establishing himself as much more than that. The Lisbon Treaty has revamped the Office of High Representative, which has been renamed Office of the High Representative of the Union for Foreign Affairs and Security Policy. The overhaul makes the post holder even more akin to a CFSP principal than Solana ever was.

The EU states appointed Solana to the post because he had a number of assets that made him a natural for the job. A former Spanish foreign minister and NATO secretary-general, he had extensive expertise in matters of foreign and security policy. Also, he enjoyed high international name recognition not only among the cognoscenti but also among the attentive public. He was at the head of NATO during its much publicized war over Kosovo. Finally, Solana had good working relations with key governments and foreign policy officials in the EU and the United States. His reputation as an Atlanticist was important to soothe fears in Washington that the

CSDP might undermine NATO. In brief, by appointing Solana, the EU states showed that they were serious about upgrading the CFSP without abandoning the transatlantic security framework.

Solana did not disappoint EU governments. In more than one way he was to the CFSP what the European Commission has been to the European Community: a motor of integration. He provided continuous leadership to the CFSP and carved out a high-profile role for himself in international affairs, putting a face on the CFSP. In building up the CFSP, the high representative took full advantage of the significant institutional resources with which his post was endowed. He availed himself of the administrative services of the CFSP to influence the bureaucratic politics of EU foreign and security policy-making, which at the time included (besides the high representative) the EU governments, the European Commission, and the General Secretariat of the Council of the EU.

Solana proved highly effective in rebranding the CFSP. When he took office at the end of 1999, the reputation of the CFSP was severely damaged by the EU's inability to put an end to the bloody conflicts in the Western Balkans in the 1990s. The foreign policy chief did much to revive the tarnished reputation of the EU as a serious foreign and security policy actor. For instance, he played a key role in brokering a peace deal to end the armed conflict in Macedonia in 2001. His intervention in Ukraine in 2004 contributed to a peaceful outcome of the pro-Western Orange Revolution. On the initiative of Britain, France, and Germany, and with the blessing of the other member states, he carried out negotiations with Iran on the issue of nuclear weapons and uranium enrichment activities. In the Middle East, he ensured a greater role for the EU in the peace process between Israel and its neighbors. His leadership was important in persuading governments to deploy civilian CSDP missions to Palestine. Also, he helped convince member states to make a significant European contribution to the UN peacekeeping force in Lebanon after the 2006 war between Israel and Hezbollah. During Solana's stewardship of the CSDP, more than twenty CSDP operations were deployed. He strengthened and professionalized the CSDP management structure. His success in building up the CSDP occasionally led to angry outbursts by member states who accused him of empire building.

Although the Lisbon Treaty gave the new Office of High Representative of the Union for Foreign Affairs and Security Policy considerable powers, EU states chose not to make the most of this upgrade to enhance the EU's international role and impact. In 2009, they appointed Catherine Ashton, a little-known British politician, as the first post-Lisbon high representative. She got the job even though she had little foreign policy experience.

The Lisbon Treaty strengthened the CFSP competencies of the high representative and gave the officeholder the additional role of vice-president of the European Commission. This role extension makes the high representative responsible for external relations incumbent on the Commission. The redesign of the leadership of EU foreign policy was motivated by conflicting purposes. Key member states wanted to maintain intergovernmental control over the CFSP, while all governments wanted to limit dysfunctional turf battles between the Council and the Commission. They all wanted to enhance the efficiency of foreign policymaking and improve the coherence and effectiveness of policy output. Finally, the European Commission, certain EU states, and a number of nongovernmental organizations did not want the intergovernmental CFSP to intrude too far into supranational EU foreign policy. One fear was that this would subordinate the generous EU development aid to diplomatic-strategic considerations. The office of the high representative/vice-president is a compromise between these contradictory views. It reinforces the link between the supranational and intergovernmental dimensions of EU foreign and security policy but does not do away with the underlying divide.

High Representative Ashton has the right to submit CFSP proposals to the Foreign Affairs Council, a right that Solana did not have. More importantly, she takes on the CFSP responsibilities previously exercised by the Council presidency. Ashton chairs the Foreign Affairs Council, runs the CFSP, and represents the EU on the international stage. However, she shares this latter role with the president of the European Council, and this mandate overlap is a potential source of friction. Van Rompuy and Ashton have managed to sidestep dysfunctional turf battles and personal rivalries. Ashton's supranational foreign policy portfolio includes bilateral relations between the EU and third countries as well as relations with international organizations and the management of EU embassies around the world. The foreign policy briefs covering trade, development, enlargement, the European Neighbourhood Policy, and humanitarian aid continue to be managed by fellow European Commissioners. However, Ashton and the diplomatic service that supports her are tasked with ensuring that actions taken in these policy areas are consistent with overall EU foreign policy.

The high representative and her staff fulfill three important functions in relation to CFSP policymaking: agenda management, brokerage, and implementation monitoring. These functions are crucial in facilitating negotiations, deliberations, and decisions in the transgovernmental CFSP bodies and the intergovernmental Council of Ministers (see, for example, Tallberg 2006). Ashton and her representatives who chair CFSP committees and working groups have to structure the CFSP agenda so as to maximize the likelihood of reaching intra-EU agreement on as many issues as possible. They have to identify and appropriately sequence promising items and exclude overly controversial ones from the agenda. They have to broker intra-EU agreements by acting as consensus builders, mediators, and facilitators. Finally, they have to look after the implementation of Council decisions with a view to improving the consistency, continuity, visibility, and effectiveness of the CFSP.

Ashton has more competencies and resources to shape EU foreign and security policy than her predecessor Solana had. The Office of the High Representative effectively combines in a personal union what previously were three different jobs: European Commission vice-president, Council presidency, and high representative for the CFSP. As a result, EU foreign and security policy is set to become more coherent and effective. Yet at the same time, the continuing institutional separation of supranational and intergovernmental foreign policy ensures that the actions of the EU's foreign policy head will continue to be hampered by interinstitutional turf battles and divergent national interests and threat perceptions.

The European Commission: Playing Second Fiddle in the CFSP

Member states have relegated the European Commission to a secondary role in CFSP policymaking. This said, its influence has grown over the years, although it has never managed to achieve equality with the member states. Within a few years of the establishment of the EPC, it became clear that the artificial boundary between Commission-managed supranational foreign policy and intergovernmental foreign policy cooperation limited the effectiveness of the latter. The EPC was thus gradually opened to input by the Commission. The Maastricht Treaty further upgraded the role of the Commission by giving it the right to make CFSP policy proposals. The Lisbon Treaty has had an ambivalent impact on the European Commission's role in foreign policy. Some changes have clearly weakened the

Commission, while others may possibly strengthen it. The treaty has brought about a reversal of the gains the Commission has made over the years in shaping EU foreign policy. The new overall steering power of the European Council in relation to EU foreign policy comes at the expense of the Commission, as does the creation of the office of the president of the European Council. Also, the treaty removed the right of the Commission to submit CFSP proposals to the Council of Ministers. According to the new rules, the Commission can do so only jointly with the high representative. With regard to the creation of the beefed-up Office of the High Representative, it will take years before it becomes clear what its precise impact will be on the balance between supranationalism and intergovernmentalism in EU foreign and security policy. The high representative may either weaken or strengthen the supranational dimension of EU foreign policy, because the officeholder is double-hatted as vice-president of the European Commission. This creates two alternative institutional development trajectories. Either the high representative extends intergovernmental influence into Commission-run supranational foreign policy, or the vice-president extends supranational Commission influence into the CFSP.

Irrespective of these uncertainties, the Commission's formal powers in the CFSP are limited, but this does not mean that it cannot influence the CFSP, either directly or indirectly. The military sector has long been exempted from single-market legislation. Since the second half of the 2000s, the Commission has become more proactive in using its market-making powers to push for greater integration of the EU market for armaments. It has worked closely with the intergovernmental European Defence Agency (EDA) on this issue. The Commission's role in promoting a European military-industrial complex, which is crucial for a powerful and autonomous CSDP, is likely to grow in the future. Its activism is facilitated by increasing pressure on EU states to deepen their armaments cooperation to cut their national budget deficits. Also, the Commission has taken advantage of the nature of modern foreign and security policy to influence the CFSP. Today's world of globalized capitalism is characterized by extensive cross-border flows of people, goods, services, capital, diseases, organized crime, terrorism, and so forth. To be effective, foreign policy has to be holistic, bundling diplomatic, economic, military, and other measures to achieve the desired objectives. From the perspective of the EU, many of these challenges are horizontal issues that cut across the competencies of the Commission and the Council and call for close interinstitutional cooperation. The declaratory policy of the CFSP may rattle the windows of foreign chancelleries,[4] and the peace support operations carried out under the CSDP may make international news headlines. Yet their impact will be significantly reduced if they are not linked to other instruments, such as economic sanctions, trade agreements, foreign aid, and technical assistance projects. The Commission has treaty-based rights as policy initiator, budget manager, and policy implementer in relation to many non-CFSP instruments of foreign influence. Hence, the Foreign Affairs Council is constrained to listen carefully to the voice of the Commission and to take its advice to ensure the success of the CFSP.

In the military CSDP, the Commission adopts a low profile throughout the policy cycle, while, in the civilian CSDP, it plays an active role as the manager of the EU budget. Unlike military operations, which are financed by the participating states, civilian CSDP operations are funded by the EU. Yet there is also a more self-serving reason why the Commission takes an active interest in civilian operations. The Commission sees itself as well positioned to play the lead role in EU policies aimed at the stabilization and reconstruction of postconflict societies. When the Council began to build up capabilities in this field, the Commission was concerned because it saw the initiative as an attempt by the member states to step on its turf and to limit its foreign policy profile. This sentiment has remained and has predisposed the Commission to leverage its peace-building expertise, formal functions in the policy process, and its budgetary powers to exert influence on the mandate, activities, and termination of civilian CSDP missions. It does so in three ways. To begin with, it takes full advantage of the fact that it is an integral part of the Brussels-based management of civilian missions—from putting together the initial mission planning documents to elaborating lessons-learned papers after mission termination. For instance, the Council actively seeks out the opinions of the Commission when it defines mission objectives. Second, the success of civilian CSDP operations often depends on externally funded capacity-building projects, which gives the Commission some bargaining leverage in its interaction with the Council. It may be able to influence what missions do and how well they achieve their objectives. Take the case of the CSDP police mission in Bosnia, which elaborated about 120 police-related projects. To fund them, international donors had to be solicited. One of the most important donors was the Commission, which inevitably gave it some influence over mission activities. Third, CSDP operations may run concurrently with or be followed up by Commission-managed stabilization and reconstruction programs. To ensure cooperation, or a smooth transition between these different types of EU intervention, the Council has to take the Commission's views on board. For instance, the Commission successfully insisted on excluding penitentiary reform from the mandate of the CSDP mission in Georgia, which was tasked to assist the country in strengthening the rule of law, even though mission planners wanted to include penitentiary reform in the mission brief. The Commission had its own ongoing penitentiary reform programs and did not want them subordinated to the newcomer (Kurowska 2008). In Macedonia, a special CSDP police advisory team had to be established to bridge the period between the termination of the regular CSDP police mission and the onset of the Commission follow-up police reform project. The point is that while the European Commission plays second fiddle to the Council in the CFSP, it has ways to make its voice heard and to exert influence in this intergovernmental policy domain.

The European Parliament: Where Are the Checks and Balances?

The CFSP powers of the European Parliament have incrementally increased over the years. This said, compared to EU governments and even the Commission, the institution remains a weak player. When it comes to the CFSP, EU governments wish to keep the European Parliament at bay. A former director of the official foreign affairs think tank of the EU, the EU Institute for Security Studies, put it bluntly: Most EU governments are obsessed with excluding the members of the European Parliament from the CFSP in order to retain control of the policy (Gnesotto 2004: 19). The sidelining of the Euro-parliamentarians has engendered a pronounced democratic deficit of the CFSP.

The Lisbon Treaty slightly strengthens the role of the European Parliament in CFSP matters by giving the Parliament indirect influence over who becomes high representative. This is because the appointment of the Commission members is subject to a vote of consent by the European Parliament. By withholding its consent, it can prevent the high representative from putting on his/her second hat as Commission vice-president. Since the Lisbon Treaty stipulates that the high representative serves as Commission vice-president, such a rejection would effectively force EU governments to look for a new high representative. Equally, the right of Euro-parliamentarians to dismiss the Commission in a vote of censure extends to the vice-president function of the high representative. While vetoing the appointment of the Commission, and calling for its dismissal, are nuclear options that cannot be used in routine negotiations and interinstitutional power struggles, they do ensure that the opinion of the European Parliament on the (proposed) high representative is taken seriously by the member states. When it comes to day-to-day CFSP policymaking, the Euro-parliamentarians are limited to consultative and informational roles and to the indirect use of their budgetary powers. Sometimes they manage to punch above their weight.

The European Parliament relies on a number of channels to keep abreast of CFSP developments. The high representative regularly consults with and briefs Euro-parliamentarians on the CFSP. The officeholder is required to submit a detailed report to the European Parliament once a year on the basic choices and main developments of the CFSP. Also, Euro-parliamentarians take full advantage of their right to ask questions (oral and written) of the Council and hold regular plenary debates on the CFSP. They established two committees to shadow the CFSP: the Committee on Foreign Affairs and its Subcommittee on Security and Defence. The high representative and EU special representatives as well as a host of high-level national representatives from member states, third countries, and international organizations are frequently invited to come before the Committee on Foreign Affairs to discuss the CFSP.

The European Parliament has a number of means of influence available when it comes to the CFSP. To begin with, it uses the bully pulpit to put pressure on EU governments. It proactively uses public debates and press releases in an effort to shape the CFSP and regularly issues nonbinding communications, recommendations, and resolutions. Another means of influence is its power of the purse. As part of the annual EU budgetary negotiations, the Council and the European Parliament have to agree on the size and priorities of the CFSP budget. This gives the European Parliament leverage vis-à-vis the Council to shape the general financial conditions of the CFSP. However, this is a blunt instrument, especially when it comes to influencing CSDP deployment decisions and mission mandates. Yet, on occasion, the Euro-parliamentarians manage to wield their budgetary powers with precision. This was the case when it came to the creation of the EU diplomatic service in the wake of the Lisbon Treaty. Though formally the Council only had to consult the European Parliament on the issue, the Euro-parliamentarians used their budgetary powers and competencies in relation to EU staffing rules to wheedle concessions from the high representative. In particular, they insisted on the diplomatic service's political accountability vis-à-vis the Euro-parliamentarians, winning agreement from the high representative to hold informal confirmation hearings on senior officials who are scheduled to head important EU embassies. Also, they were assured that in briefings to the European Parliament, the diplomatic service is represented by the high representative, a fellow commissioner, or the foreign minister of the country holding the EU presidency. The Euro-parliamentarians were concerned that they would be briefed by a faceless bureaucrat, which would have prevented them from politically making the most of the event.

The powers of the European Parliament are most limited when it comes to the CSDP. Euro-parliamentarians do not have any formal competencies in EU decisions on the deployment of CSDP missions and their mandates. The marginal role of the European Parliament in this policy domain has been an issue of contention between it and EU governments from the inception of the CSDP. The European Parliament has unsuccessfully lobbied governments to give it a stronger voice in security matters. In addition to its limited treaty rights, it faces two more challenges when it comes to exercising influence and oversight over the CSDP. On the one hand, the requirements for confidentiality in security matters reduce the scope for parliamentary debate and scrutiny. On the other hand, the funding arrangements for military operations undermine the budgetary powers of the European Parliament. The ensuing democratic deficit of the CSDP is aggravated by the fact that many national parliaments, too, have limited powers in the security and defense field. However, their limitations tend to be less pronounced than those of the European Parliament.

According to the Lisbon Treaty, military operations must not be funded from the CFSP budget but are paid for by national governments according to the principle "costs lie where they fall." In the wake of the French-led EU military operation Artemis in the Democratic Republic of Congo, which was largely paid for by Paris, the Council agreed to beef up its limited burden-sharing arrangement. The so-called Athena mechanism, through which states participating in CSDP missions contribute to their costs, was agreed upon in 2004. While the coverage of the Athena mechanism has been gradually expanded, a breakthrough in mutualizing the costs of military operations has so far proved unattainable. Because big net contributors to the EU budget such as Germany want to avoid becoming the paymasters of the military CSDP, Athena covers only a limited amount—less than 10 percent—of common pre-deployment and operational costs. For instance, it covers the setup and operation of headquarters and the provision of medical services to the troops (General Secretariat of the Council of the EU 2007b). Euro-parliamentarians are highly critical of the Athena mechanism (Brok and Gresch 2004: 187) because it is a purely intergovernmental mechanism that remains outside their control and influence.

When it comes to the civilian CSDP, the European Parliament is in a somewhat better position to exercise influence. The default option for financing operations is that everything is funded from the CFSP budget, except the regular salaries of the mission personnel seconded by EU states. This enables the European Parliament to use its budgetary powers to gain some influence over the civilian CSDP, although member states can free themselves from this limited control. Discretionary payments by member states often play an important role in providing complementary funding for the start-up and operation of EU-financed missions. For example, a considerable amount of the funding for the Aceh Monitoring Mission in Indonesia completely escaped the control of the European Parliament because it came from individual contributions by states.

Turning to the European Parliament's consultative rights in CSDP matters, Euro-parliamentarians have limited access to sensitive information. This hinders their ability to scrutinize the CSDP decisions of the Council and hold it accountable. When the CSDP was launched, the issue of classified documents became a hot potato between the Council and the Parliament. As high representative, Solana signed a security agreement with NATO in 2000 to enable the EU to negotiate a strategic partnership with the alliance. The agreement excluded the European Parliament from access to the classified military information that the EU received from NATO. Also, it applied restrictive NATO rules to the handling of Council military documents. This incensed the parliamentarians, who saw their already limited influence in the CSDP further reduced, and took the Council to the European Court of Justice. The interinstitutional squabble was solved in 2002 when the Council and the European Parliament agreed on a procedure that allows the latter to get restricted access to sensitive information. A select group of Euro-parliamentarians is briefed *in camera* on classified material by the high representative. Moreover, they can request to see confidential documents on the Council premises.

The limited powers of the European Parliament in relation to the CFSP and especially the CSDP raise questions about the legitimacy of

European-level security policy. There are two broad concepts of legitimacy related to the input into and the output of governance. The former is concerned with democratic participation, accountability, and control, while the latter is concerned with the effectiveness of governance and popular support. Beginning with input legitimacy, as discussed previously, the European Parliament has limited powers to influence CSDP decisionmaking or to hold the Council to account. Although this does not hold true for national parliaments, their impact on the CSDP tends to be low. For instance, the British, French, and Italian parliaments were either legally unable or politically unwilling to shape national decisions regarding participation in military CSDP operations (Bono 2005, 2006; Wagner 2006b; for an overview, see Giegerich and Nicoll 2008). This lack of parliamentary control in CSDP matters is a manifestation of a more general phenomenon. EU decisionmaking strengthens national executives vis-à-vis national parliaments (Moravcsik 1994). Collective EU decisionmaking allows governments to exert control over the joint policy agenda. Also, it gives them privileged access to information about the bargaining process in Brussels and the preferences of fellow governments. National parliaments are often left with a take-it-or-leave-it option because they are not part of Brussels-based negotiations. In brief, CSDP input legitimacy suffers from a double democratic deficit. Both at the national and supranational levels, parliamentary control is limited.

At first sight it seems that the CSDP can rely on robust output legitimacy. Polls tracking European public opinion on EU policies and institutions consistently show that a stable majority of Europeans, country-specific differences notwithstanding, support the CSDP. Yet a closer analysis reveals that these poll figures should be taken with a grain of salt (Brummer 2007). The CSDP is not high on the agenda of citizens, nor do they know much about it. As long as the CSDP does not venture into politically controversial and militarily difficult operations, it is unlikely that true support for the policy can be tested. The CSDP ranks high in opinion polls because it ranks low in people's concerns. This does not make for strong output legitimacy. On neither definition of legitimacy, then, does the CSDP score well. This said, some commentators argue that such a legitimacy gap is inevitable. An effective CSDP will often require secret deliberations and fast decisions (Giegerich and Gross 2006). Parliamentary checks and balances do not easily lend themselves to such a policy process.

This chapter has shown that the CFSP is an intergovernmental policy domain. The European Council and the Council of Ministers, together with the high representative, define what the CFSP can and cannot do. The supranational European Commission and European Parliament are bit players who can influence policy at the margins but are excluded from the key decisions, such as whether or not to deploy CSDP operations. Yet central national decisionmakers rely on agents to prepare, formulate, and implement the CFSP. The next chapter shows that these agents do more than simply carry out the wishes of their principals.

Notes

1. With some minor exceptions related to procedural issues, the European Court of Justice of the EU plays no role in the CFSP and will thus not be discussed in the chapter.

2. CFSP decisions have to be taken by the Council but not necessarily by its foreign affairs formation.

3. In policy domains other than the CFSP, the EU presidency retains its functions.

4. This sentence paraphrases a statement of the former European commissioner for external relations, Chris Patten (2000).

CHAPTER 5

On Diplomats and Bureaucrats

THE PREVIOUS CHAPTER SHOWED THAT NATIONAL GOVERN-ments are the key actors in the CFSP. Yet analysts who look only at the intergovernmental dimension of the CFSP miss what goes on beneath the political summit of CFSP policymaking. The CFSP is more than the sum of national foreign policies. The very fact that policy is hammered out in numerous Brussels-based committees and working groups ensures that elements of supranationalism—EU-level views, rules, and norms—enter the CFSP. The Brussels-based bodies are composed of national representatives, notably diplomats and soldiers but also staff from other governmental units such as interior and justice ministries. They form transgovernmental networks—that is, cross-border networks of national officials who work for the same ministries and on the same issues. They either regularly meet in Brussels for meetings or are posted to the EU's capital for a number of years. Either way, they are influenced by their extensive exposure to the "Brussels scene" and influence national positions. Thus, paradoxically, national representatives are key carriers of supranationalism in the CFSP. EU officials, too, are carriers. Permanent EU civil servants and personnel who have a temporary work contract with the EU neither receive instructions from nor report to individual EU governments. They often identify more with the EU than with their home countries. Over the years the EU civil service has evolved from a provider of secretarial services to a policy adviser. This chapter discusses the competencies and functions of these actors.

Brussels-based CFSP committees and working groups are composed of one delegate from each member state, joined by staff from the EU diplomatic service. All committees and working groups dealing with the CSDP are chaired by members of the EU diplomatic service, who are appointed by and represent the high representative. Formally agents of their political principals—the member state governments—these transgovernmental and administrative players are the lifeblood of the CFSP policy process (see, for example, Westlake 1999: 303; and, more generally, Christiansen and Larsson 2007). Many issues are resolved within Brussels-based committees and working groups before they reach the political summit where all CFSP decisions are formally adopted. These predecided issues are the so-called A-Points on the agenda of the Foreign Affairs Council and are simply rubber-stamped by the ministers without any further discussion.[1] Committees and working groups play a similarly important role in the implementation of agreed-upon policies. In short, CFSP decisions are framed, prepared, often informally decided, and implemented by Brussels-based committees and working groups. In EU studies, this state of affairs is denoted by and analyzed with the help of the Brusselization concept.

Brusselization

Although the official task of national delegates is to carry out, not make, national policy in Brussels, in practice the principal-agent relationship is more nuanced. In general, Brussels-based representatives receive instructions from their governments about the line to take in CFSP committee and working group meetings. But the agents may well have shaped the content of the principals' instructions in the first place. As two seasoned EU officials observed, "Many national delegates will readily admit that they spend more time negotiating with their national capital to ensure they get the 'right' instructions, than with colleagues from other member states" (Westlake and Galloway 2006: 228). This does not mean that transgovernmental and administrative actors are the real masters of the CFSP. Nor does it mean that European interests trump national interests. It means that Brussels-based agents push the CFSP, especially on second-order issues, beyond the lowest common denominator formed by the divergent national interests of EU states. In this way, they contribute to making the CFSP gradually more coherent and forceful.

Brusselization has been defined as "the steady enhancement of Brussels-based decision-making bodies" (Allen 1998: 42). The influence of Brussels-based actors in the CFSP policy process is due to two phenomena: socialization and superior information and expertise. First, Brussels-based CFSP actors acquire their own intangible power resources. These nonmaterial resources enable them to influence national positions on the CFSP and the Brussels-based processes of formulating and implementing the CFSP. Being at the center of the collective CFSP decisionmaking machinery, national delegates in Brussels have more information and better knowledge about CFSP procedural rules, developments, and dossiers than their home-based colleagues in the EU states. Also, due to their regular interaction with their counterparts from other EU states, Brussels-based national representatives have an excellent firsthand grasp of the diversity of member state views. They know the particular sensitivities and preoccupations of other governments and the issues on which they are ready to compromise. As to EU officials, their CFSP competencies and resources have slowly but steadily grown since the beginning of the new millennium. This bureaucratization of the CFSP has strengthened professional CFSP administrators and managers at the expense of both EU governments and their national delegates in Brussels, although the latter retain their value for home ministries. Government officials back home depend on their insider information for formulating national positions and adjusting them according to the state of play of the deliberations and negotiations in Brussels.

The Brussels-based delegates of small and medium-sized EU countries are particularly well positioned to influence national policy. Smaller countries are likely to have insufficient administrative capacity and expertise to deal hands on with the permanent CFSP negotiations in Brussels. Moreover, their range of national interests is likely to be narrower than the range of European interests covered by the CFSP. This combination of lack of interest and expertise on the part of their principals gives the Brussels-based delegates of smaller EU states additional leeway in defining their countries' national positions. Yet even the big states do not always come to the Brussels negotiating table with firm national interests. On occasions, governments (big and small) do not know precisely what they want. Policy options may be unclear, and their opportunity costs may be impossible to estimate. The issue may not have been sufficiently "politicized" domestically to engender a strong national response. In such circumstances, CFSP decisions do not reflect convergent national interests but genuine European interests that have been defined by Brussels-based transgovernmental bodies.

A second feature of Brusselization is that it socializes national delegates into a distinct corporate identity. Many CFSP committees and working groups have at least two formal meetings per week. In addition, national delegates engage in intensive networking to exchange information, form alliances, and agree upon policy lines. Empirical studies have documented that these frequent contacts engender a club-like atmosphere, promote a "we" feeling, and generate informal norms (Glarbo 1999; Howorth 2010; Jørgensen 1997; Juncos and Pomorska 2006; Juncos and Reynolds 2007; Nuttall 2000; Smith 2004a; Tonra 2001, 2003). Of the informal norms that constitute the corporate identity of transgovernmental CFSP bodies, three are crucial in facilitating CFSP agreements that rise above the lowest common denominator predicted by intergovernmentalism. First, the "coordination reflex" predisposes diplomats to ask of every national foreign policy initiative: "what will our European partners say, what is the opinion in Europe" (EU diplomat, cited in Tonra 1997: 187). This reflex is closely linked to a second informal CFSP norm that emphasizes joint problem-solving at the expense of utility-maximizing bargaining. Threats and promises—the stuff of bargaining—play a limited role in CFSP decisionmaking. Instead, interaction based on argumentation and persuasion dominates, which facilitates agreements and the development of European interests. Finally, an important informal norm says that it is inappropriate to open CFSP deals reached at lower levels in more senior committees and the Council of Ministers. Socialization, then, is an important feature of Brusselization, but its identity-shaping powers should not be exaggerated. There "is little evidence of the emergence of an all-powerful European identity that trumps national affiliations" (Fouilleux et al. 2007: 115; see also Lewis 2000). The average tour of duty of national representatives in Brussels is three to four years, which does not suffice to replace national allegiances with European ones.

The Brusselization of the CFSP policy process constrains intergovernmentalism and blurs the boundaries between foreign and security policymaking at the national and EU levels (Duke and Vanhoonacker 2006; Smith 2004b). In general, CFSP meetings are not battlegrounds on which national delegates defend national interests until they get what they want or until the negotiations are bogged down in deadlock. Neither are the meetings team-building exercises in which common European interests are upgraded and imposed on national governments.

Although Brusselization has gradually increased the influence and role of Brussels-based national delegates and EU officials in the CFSP policy process, the key CFSP decisions continue to be made by central national decisionmakers motivated by what they consider to be in their nations' best interests. Within variable limits, they control their national delegates in Brussels and tell them what line to take in CFSP bodies. In short, Brusselization modifies intergovernmentalism but does not trump it. Jolyon Howorth (2000) refers to the hybrid nature of CFSP policymaking as supranational intergovernmentalism.

This chapter discusses the transgovernmental CSDP bodies and the EU diplomatic service—the European External Action Service. It explains the role that these actors play in the CSDP policy process and highlights the institutional limitations that so far have held the EU back from becoming a major international security actor.

The Transgovernmental Bodies in Charge of Preparing and Implementing the CSDP

The Political and Security Committee

The Political and Security Committee (PSC) is the centerpiece of the CFSP and the main conduit through which EU governments jointly control it. Composed of high-ranking national diplomats, usually of (near) ambassadorial rank, the PSC sits atop the CFSP committees and working groups, whose deliberations it directs. Lower-level bodies seek to reach consensus on as many aspects of a given CFSP dossier as feasible. Only if further progress becomes impossible is the dossier pushed up to the PSC. The PSC meetings, at least twice a week, are prepared by the Nicolaidis Group, which derives its name from its first chairman—a Greek. It previews the PSC agenda and identifies items that may be of particular interest or concern to member states.

The PSC is the principal adviser to the Foreign Affairs Council on CFSP issues. The PSC ambassadors are mandated to monitor and analyze international developments that may impinge on the EU and contribute to the definition of common policies. Once a common policy has been formally approved by the Foreign Affairs Council, the PSC monitors its implementation. Last but not least, the PSC is the linchpin in CSDP decisionmaking. It exercises political control and strategic direction of CSDP operations under the authority of the Foreign Affairs Council and the high representative. Crucially, the committee has evolved into the key institutional site in the EU where a European strategic culture is forged. Howorth (2010) has documented a number of supranational dynamics in the PSC that promote a convergence of strategic views among its members.

The PSC replaced the Political Committee that was created at the time of the EPC and inherited some of its problems, notably the turf battle with the Committee of Permanent Representatives (COREPER), the Council's most senior transgovernmental body. According to the treaty, it is responsible for preparing the work of the Council of Ministers and is thus entitled to vet CFSP files before they are passed on to the foreign ministers. This raises the question as to which Brussels-based committee—COREPER or the PSC—is ultimately in charge of CFSP issues. Based on a compromise between COREPER and the Political Committee dating back to the 1990s, the PSC is responsible for the substance of policy, while COREPER only evaluates the institutional, financial, and legal implications of CFSP agreements reached in the PSC. It does not second-guess the underlying policy judgments. To assist it in its task, COREPER relies on a special working party, the Foreign Relations Councillors (RELEX), who check and finalize all decisions in order to ensure they conform to EU rules.

In practice, the division of labor agreed on between COREPER and the PSC is not as clear-cut as it looks at first sight. For instance, the CFSP often draws on supranational foreign policy tools such as trade and aid. In institutional terms, this creates considerable overlap between the policy competencies of the two committees. According to established procedures, COREPER can reopen any CFSP file predecided by the PSC when this is necessary to ensure the coherence between intergovernmental and supranational aspects of a single dossier (Duke 2007: 131). This contributes to persistent tensions between the two committees. Some PSC ambassadors feel that their role as *the* experts on the CFSP is slighted by COREPER. As one EU official put it, the PSC is a "specific animal in the Council machinery; many PSC ambassadors see their committee as superior to COREPER."[2]

The Committee for Civilian Aspects of Crisis Management

The Committee for Civilian Aspects of Crisis Management (CIVCOM) briefs and advises the PSC on all aspects of the civilian CSDP. Its wide-ranging brief covers mission deployments from the planning process to the identification of lessons learned from completed operations. Also, it assists the PSC in giving impetus and direction to the improvement of civilian CSDP capabilities. The committee is made up of professional diplomats, most of whom tend to be generalists rather than experts in the stabilization and reconstruction of posthostility countries. Often committee members do not have any operational experience but are armchair strategists and tacticians. Some CIVCOM delegates readily admit that the composition of their committee has on more than one occasion been a handicap in guiding and supervising the planning and conduct of CSDP operations, especially in the early years of the CSDP.[3]

In its first years of existence, CIVCOM played a key role in elaborating the doctrines for civilian CSDP missions. When the blueprints were ready and the first missions were deployed, the committee became operations-focused and developed the bad habit of micromanaging missions and of second-guessing decisions taken by the mission leadership in theater. The creation of the Civilian Planning and Conduct Capability (CPCC) has changed this. The body acts as a check on CIVCOM's interventionist impulse and contributes to more professional and effective mission planning and support.

The EU Military Committee

The EU Military Committee (EUMC) is the chief military body of the EU and is composed of the national chiefs of defense, whose permanent military representatives conduct routine committee business in Brussels. In a departure from the procedures governing other committees and working groups, the chairman of the EUMC is selected by his or her fellow generals and appointed by the Council for a period of three years. The EUMC, which serves under the direction of the PSC, is the principal forum for cooperation on the military CSDP among member states. It oversees all military activities of the EU and is the collective bottleneck through which all military aspects of the CSDP are filtered and fed to the PSC. Thus, the EUMC is in charge of advising the PSC on the improvement of EU military capabilities and is the PSC's chief adviser on the launch, conduct, and termination of military CSDP operations. Finally, the commanders of military CSDP operations report to it. To carry out its tasks, the EUMC draws on the expertise of the EU military staff.

The Politico-Military Working Group

The Politico-Military Working Group (PMG) sits between the civilian and military bodies just discussed. Among all CSDP bodies, it is the one whose responsibilities and role are least clear. Initially, the body played an important part in elaborating the generic political-strategic planning and programming documents of the military CSDP. Once the blueprints were agreed on, the PMG had to be content with a lower profile. It is responsible for, among other things, liaising with the United Nations and NATO. Some national delegates complain that they are often reduced to "copying and pasting the advice of the Committee for Civilian Aspects of Crisis Management or of the EUMC into different documents."[4] Others insist that the PMG is a privileged interlocutor of the PSC and argue that its hybrid brief, which straddles political and military aspects of the CSDP, enables it to provide valuable input into the PSC's deliberations.[5] The actual role that the PMG plays in the CSDP policy process depends largely on the PSC chair. If the officeholder delegates issues to the PMG, this raises its profile. It can act as a sounding board and a preparatory body that facilitates and influences the PSC's work.

The European External Action Service

The EU diplomatic service was established by the Lisbon Treaty and is the administrative hub of the CFSP policy process. The service draws on EU officials from the Council General Secretariat and the European Commission and on personnel from the national diplomacies of the EU states.[6] National diplomats are assigned to the EU service for a limited tour of duty. The European External Action Service includes more than 120 EU embassies or, as they are officially called, EU delegations, which, prior to the Lisbon Treaty, were under the authority of the European Commission.[7] At the time of writing, the European External Action Service has about 3,650 personnel at headquarters in Brussels and in the EU delegations and an additional 4,000 people serving in the CSDP operations (O'Sullivan 2011). The main task of the service is to support the high representative, but it also assists the presidents of the European Council and of the European Commission in their foreign policy dealings. The European External Action Service represents an important rationalization of EU foreign and security policy. It cooperates with the European Commission to make sure supranational policy is in line with the EU's intergovernmental CFSP. The EU diplomatic service thus narrows the gap and limits the associated policy rivalries between the supranational and intergovernmental actors and institutions involved in making and implementing EU foreign policy. It enables the EU to better leverage its large foreign policy toolkit of civilian and military, short-term and long-term, conflict prevention and postconflict stabilization tools. At the same time, the service further reinforces the role of EU officials vis-à-vis home-based diplomats in the CFSP policy process.

The European External Action Service is unlikely, at least in the foreseeable future, to relieve the tensions between temporarily delegated national diplomats and permanent EU officials, because they have different views on the foreign policy process and even on the nature of diplomacy. EU civil servants, especially those affiliated with the European Commission, tend to approach diplomacy in a technocratic manner that emphasizes technical fixes for political problems. National diplomats tend to regard diplomacy as a political practice of mediating between and negotiating with actors whose views on a given issue diverge. The European External Action Service's composite nature makes it unlikely that it will anytime soon become as coherent and effective a body as the world's best national diplomacies.

The core of the EU diplomatic service is composed of the Crisis Management and Planning Directorate (CMPD), EU Military Staff, Civilian Planning and Conduct Capability, Joint Situation Centre, and EU special representatives. The CMPD takes the lead on the political aspects of the planning and conduct of CSDP operations and assists the PSC in ensuring civilian oversight over EU military operations.

The EU Military Staff and the Civilian Planning and Conduct Capability

The EU Military Staff (EUMS) comprises about 200 military and about 15 civilian personnel. Most of the staff is seconded by the member states. Headed by a general, it is the main repository of military expertise in the EU. It receives directions from the EUMC and reports to it. The EUMS has three broad functions: early warning, situation assessment, and the strategic planning of CSDP operations. Also, it keeps track of the national forces and capabilities declared to the CSDP and the gaps that remain. The EUMS developed and regularly revises the military doctrine and concepts of the EU.

Today's EUMS is a more substantive body than Britain and other Atlanticist governments had bargained for when they agreed to its creation. They wanted the EUMS to carry out only limited tasks. This was clearly expressed by a senior official of the British Ministry of

Defence in 2001, who described the role of the EUMS in the CSDP decision process. The body is

> a small-ish military staff, about the same size as the WEU had which has been abolished, which can frame the questions that will be sent off to the NATO planning staffs for preparing options for them to consider. Beyond that, it will depend on drawing on capabilities either from NATO or from the EU nations, so there will not be anything else independent being created for the EU as such. (Cited in Oakes 2001: 61)

Since then the EUMS has acquired advanced planning, command, and control capabilities. In 2005, a civil-military planning cell was set up within the EUMS and tasked with carrying out conceptual work, for example in the area of security sector reform. Furthermore, the cell assisted in the strategic planning and coordination of civilian and civil-military operations. For instance, its staff contributed to the planning of the civilian CSDP operations in the Gaza Strip and Aceh. Once the CMPD was created, the functions and key staff of the civil-military planning cell were transferred to the new directorate. Since 2007, the EUMS has had the capacity to set up an ad hoc operational headquarters (OHQ), the Operations Center,[8] which can plan and run CSDP operations. When the Operations Center is activated, its small permanent staff is reinforced by double-hatted EUMS staff and pre-identified augmentees (national and EU). The creation of the Operations Center was an important political step and represented a victory for the Europeanists.[9] When the CSDP was set up, the United States and the Atlanticist EU states insisted that the planning, command, and control of CSDP operations rely on NATO OHQ capabilities. By depriving the EU of its own OHQ, they wanted to keep the CSDP dependent on NATO. Yet while the creation of the EU Operations Center broke a political taboo, its operational significance is limited, because it suffers from severe planning, command, and control shortcomings (Simon 2010). At best, it can plan and run small operations of about 2,000 troops. The activation and call-up of EUMS augmentees would severely impede the functioning of the EUMS. Hence, while the overall competencies and capacities of the EUMS have grown considerably in recent years, it still falls far short of the powers and resources of the military staffs of countries such as Britain and France and of NATO's international military staff.

The CPCC, with a staff of about sixty, performs functions similar to those of the EUMS. However, there are important differences. The remit of the CPCC is significantly larger than that of the EUMS. It not only is involved in the planning of civilian missions but also functions as their OHQ. The creation of the CPCC in 2007 was the result of an effort to rationalize and professionalize the management of civilian operations. Until then a separate directorate in the Council General Secretariat was responsible for the planning of civilian missions and mission support but lacked the required staff and expertise to handle the rapidly growing number of CSDP deployments. With dedicated expertise in the area of postconflict stabilization and reconstruction and a capable mission support structure, the CPCC strengthens Brussels's strategic command and control over its personnel in the field. Mission commanders report to and receive advice and instructions from the CPCC head, who acts as civilian operations commander of all civilian CSDP missions while under the control of the PSC and the overall authority of the high representative. Last but not least, the CPCC evaluates missions to produce "lessons learned," which it then feeds back into the design and management of new missions.

The limited staffing of the CPCC is indicative of the so-far-limited commitment on the part of EU states to build up a more robust EU-level civilian stabilization and reconstruction capability for interventions abroad. The CPCC personnel strength is sufficient to deal with a limited number of mainly small missions that mostly operate in benign environments. CPCC resources would be overtaxed if the EU got serious in Afghanistan and Iraq and added thousands of police officers and justice system personnel to its current missions there in order to make a difference in how these countries' security sectors work.

The Joint Situation Centre

The Joint Situation Centre (SitCen) is the evolving intelligence arm of the EU and provides early warning of international crises and intelligence assessments of EU theaters of operation. SitCen comprises about 100 seconded staff from the national military and civilian intelligence agencies. Although some have a background as intelligence operatives, the majority are policy analysts. SitCen has a limited intelligence-gathering capability. By and large, it relies on open-source information and intelligence from the intelligence agencies of member states, NATO, and other international organizations. It cooperates closely with the intelligence branch of the EUMS. SitCen synthesizes the intelligence it receives into an all-source assessment, which is then fed into the CFSP policymaking process, in particular in the preparation for and during CSDP operations. SitCen's powers have incrementally increased over time. Prior to the September 11 attacks, it was, in the words of its first director, "a sort of empty shell" (cited in *Statewatch Bulletin* 2005), but the terrorist attacks on the United States transformed the sleepy body into a hub of EU foreign intelligence sharing and analysis. Another "power grab" occurred in 2004. After the terrorist attacks in Madrid (2004), the member states agreed to expand SitCen's brief, authorizing it to branch into the collection and analysis of domestic intelligence. Since SitCen established cooperation with the domestic security services of the member states and the European Police Office, it has produced strategic threat assessments of terrorism originating within the EU as well as abroad. Last but not least, SitCen has a limited operational capability. It can deploy, and has done so in the past, personnel alongside CSDP operations to beef up their situational awareness.

SitCen provides the CSDP with an in-house intelligence capability. The fact that over the years it acquired new responsibilities and functions shows that no serious international security actor can do without such a capability. By the same token, the continuing small size of SitCen and its dependency on external input underline how far the EU still has to go to become a major international security player.

EU Special Representatives

EUSRs are proposed by the high representative and appointed by the Council of Ministers. Council decisions on EUSRs and their mandates are one of the few occasions when the principle of qualified majority voting applies to CFSP matters. EUSRs carry out their mandates under the authority of the high representative, from whom they receive instructions based on operational guidelines, which concretize the official mandate.

Under High Representative Solana, EUSRs evolved into an important CFSP crisis management tool. On his proposal, EUSRs were appointed for post–civil war countries such as Bosnia, for conflict-prone regions such as the Southern Caucasus, and for countries with ongoing conflicts such as Afghanistan. EUSRs "promote European Union policies and interests . . . and play an active role in efforts to consolidate peace, stability and the rule of law" (General Secretariat of the Council of the EU 2007a). Their behavioral repertoire includes the whole gamut of diplomats' actions (Grevi 2007). To begin with, they provide information to CFSP stakeholders on developments on the ground, an informational function important for small EU states with limited diplomatic resources. Second, EUSRs are important channels through which the EU interacts and negotiates with local players and international actors on the ground in an effort to contain and defuse crises. They add a hands-on dimension to EU foreign policy. Third, given their intimate knowledge of the local situation, EUSRs are well positioned to provide input into the Brussels-based CFSP policy process. For instance, the EUSR for Macedonia played a decisive role in the decision to extend the EU police mission in Macedonia for one more year after its initial mandate expired at the end of 2004. Finally, EUSRs play an important role in enhancing the coherence and effectiveness of EU policy on the ground. They are empowered to provide local political guidance to civilian and military CSDP missions.

When High Representative Ashton assumed her position, she wanted to reduce the number of EUSRs and, by implication, their role in EU conflict prevention and crisis management. The political justification was that the creation of the European External Action Service has made EUSRs less important. The incorporation of the EU embassies into the EU's diplomatic service has enhanced their political status. The political upgrade of the embassies, which used to be outposts of the technocratic European Commission, has given them a greater capacity to carry out the highly political tasks engendered by crisis management. In the words of one Brussels insider, in the past, EUSRs had "political weight but no economic clout. The European Commission delegation on the ground [had] economic clout but no political weight."[10] With their incorporation into the European External Action Service, EU delegations added political weight to their economic clout. In short, EUSRs' value for the high representative and the EU as a whole has declined with the creation of the EU diplomatic service.

This said, Ashton's plan to axe EUSRs has been criticized on political and functional grounds. A number of EU governments believe that the termination of EUSRs sends the wrong political message to the concerned parties, namely that the tensions and conflicts afflicting their countries and regions are no longer a priority of the CFSP. Also, while EU ambassadors have gained political clout through being integrated into the European External Action Service, they are usually not in a position to address regional conflicts because their mandate responsibilities are mostly limited to dealings with their host countries. EUSRs, on the other hand, often have regional mandates.[11]

This chapter has discussed the role of Brussels-based national delegates in shaping the CFSP and the CFSP functions carried out by EU officials. The picture that emerges from the analysis is that of an incrementally thickening EU-level governance structure of the CFSP. Yet the structure still has important "holes" that hamper the policy process. These shortcomings notwithstanding, EU-level CFSP governance has introduced supranational processes into the CFSP.

Notes

1. B-Points are controversial dossiers on which working groups and committees are unable to reach consensus. They are discussed and decided by the Council of Ministers.

2. Interview with a senior official of the Council General Secretariat, Brussels, 13 July 2007.

3. Interviews with CIVCOM delegates, 16 November 2004 and 25 July 2007.

4. Interview with a senior Council official, Brussels, 17 October 2008.

5. Karsten Geier, EUCPCM, final conference, Brussels, 5–6 July 2007.

6. The Council General Secretariat dates to the beginnings of postwar European integration. Staffed by permanent civil servants and temporary agents, it provides a business management service to the Council of Ministers (Nuttall 2000). Initially, it was preoccupied with administrative tasks such as booking rooms, ensuring the right number of chairs, taking notes during meetings, and drafting and distributing reports afterward. Over time, it took on more political functions such as contributing to the framing of EU foreign policy and facilitating compromises among the member states (Christiansen and Vanhoonacker 2008; Dijkstra 2008, 2010; Westlake and Galloway 2006).

7. The EU calls its personnel in charge of delegations "heads of EU delegation" rather than "EU ambassadors."

8. Linked to the Operations Center is a Watchkeeping Capability, which monitors all CSDP missions and acts as a 24/7 point of contact.

9. The Operations Center grew out of the "chocolate summit" held by France, Germany, Belgium, and Luxembourg in April 2003. For a discussion of the controversial summit in the context of transatlantic relations, see Chapter 12.

10. Interview with a senior EU official, Brussels, 13 July 2007.

11. At the time of writing, it remains unclear to what extent High Representative Ashton will rely on EUSRs to conduct EU crisis management in the future.

CHAPTER 6

Military and Civilian Capabilities

THIS CHAPTER LOOKS AT THE POWER RESOURCES THAT underpin the CSDP. What capabilities does the EU have and which ones does it still lack? What does the EU do to reinforce its power? At this point it is important to remember what the EU is and what it is not (see Chapter 1). The EU is not a federal state and has neither a Euro-army nor a Euro–peace corps. The CSDP is a capability pool. EU states lend civilian and military capabilities to the EU when it calls for national contribution so that it can launch an expeditionary operation. States are not legally obliged to heed such calls, even when they have previously made pledges to do so. Hence, what power the CSDP can marshal depends on what capabilities EU states themselves have and which of their national capabilities they actually put into the pool to resource a given CSDP operation.

The chapter discusses both civilian and military CSDP capabilities, emphasizing the military—the defense budgets of EU states, the availability of expeditionary troops for CSDP deployments, and the achievements and gaps in relation to the development of EU firepower. The analysis shows that the EU has launched into building up its power projection capabilities and has started to plug its power gaps. Initially, the process was hampered by the fact that the EU agreed to acquire operational capabilities but failed to agree on a security strategy that would tell it what to do with them. In the absence of a shared strategic vision for the CSDP, capability development lacked impetus and purpose. The formulation of the European Security Strategy in 2003 and the creation of the EDA in 2004 have energized the buildup of EU capabilities, although improvements have proceeded slowly and unevenly, and serious shortfalls remain. In terms of capabilities, the EU is still considerably less than its composite parts—the EU states.

Civilian Capabilities

At first, the EU attached less importance to the development of civilian CSDP capabilities than to military ones. This is not surprising. When France and Britain made their CSDP proposal in 1998, they wanted to equip the EU with autonomous military capabilities. Civilian stabilization and reconstruction missions were only later added to the construction plan of the CSDP. Until about the mid-2000s, the development of civilian capabilities was secondary to the development of military power. By then it had become clear that in the post–September 11 international environment, nation building was an important element of international security policy, which raised the salience of civilian CSDP capabilities.

When the EU launched the CSDP, it had few concrete things to say about civilian capabilities. It agreed to set up a database on national capabilities and expertise available for CSDP operations. Further, it made it a priority to build up capabilities to deploy CSDP police missions to uphold and reform law enforcement in postconflict societies. Such operations can be dispatched to advise and train local law enforcement personnel or to take over law-and-order functions in crisis areas. A few months after agreeing to CSDP police capabilities, the EU agreed on three more priority areas for the construction of the civilian CSDP. First, rule-of-law operations strengthen the judicial system of countries in crisis or emerging from conflict. Second, civilian administration operations offer assistance on issues such as the organization of posthostility elections and the return of internally displaced persons and refugees. Finally, civil protection missions provide disaster relief in situations characterized by domestic instability and conflict.

By 2004, the EU had three civilian operations under way—in Bosnia, Macedonia, and Georgia. With international demand for further EU stabilization and reconstruction operations on the rise, Brussels decided it was time to improve its civilian capabilities. It began to use a needs-driven approach to develop CSDP capabilities. In the new approach, the EU identifies what sort of civilian operations it wants to carry out. These scenarios are then used to offer strategic guidance for resourcing the civilian CSDP pool. Previously, EU states had pledged national capabilities to the CSDP in the absence of any strategic EU-level guidance on what was actually needed. Furthermore, the EU added two more priority areas to the civilian CSDP: monitoring missions and support for EUSRs. Monitoring missions can be deployed to verify the terms of a disarmament or cease-fire agreement. Through their presence on the ground, they help prevent the resumption of conflict and deter spoilers of the peace. Support missions provide EUSRs with special expertise, say, in areas such as security sector reform or disarmament, demobilization, and reintegration. Toward the end of the 2000s, the EU further improved its support capabilities by creating a pool of national security sector reform experts who are available for rapid deployments both under the CSDP flag and for European Commission projects. Also, the EU began to develop dialogue and mediation capacities.

Initially, the civilian CSDP did not have the capability to respond rapidly to crises. Moreover, its single-priority missions fell short of international best practice that emphasizes a holistic approach to stabilization and reconstruction tasks. In response to these shortcomings, the EU established Civilian Response Teams. They enable the EU to put together small, tailor-made groups of experts.[1] Also, because they can be on the ground within five days of a request, Civilian Response Teams give the EU a civilian rapid response capability. More importantly, the EU developed the capacity to field integrated, multifunctional CSDP operations that allow for a comprehensive approach to security sector reform. For instance, CSDP police advisers may work with CSDP law advisers in order to ensure that criminals apprehended by a reformed police in a postconflict society are not subsequently released by an unreformed judiciary. The Lisbon Treaty further improved the EU's rapid response capability, notably through the creation of a start-up fund to provide the speedy funding for the preparation and launch of civilian CSDP operations.

An enduring challenge for the EU has been to recruit staff with the right expertise and training for civilian CSDP missions (see, for example, Jakobsen 2006; Korski and Gowan 2009). The willingness and ability of national governments to address this problem have been uneven. Some countries keep rosters of deployable personnel, while others do not. Of those who do, only a few regularly update the rosters. This means that many governments do not know precisely what expertise they can contribute to operations when a call is issued by Brussels. On a more structural level, many governments have undertaken reforms to create incentives for police officers, forensic experts, judges, educational reform managers, and so forth to serve abroad. Also, they have taken measures to enable sending institutions to make up for the absence of personnel working under the CSDP flag. However, these reforms remain insufficient to address the personnel gap in EU missions. A case in point has been the embarrassing inability of the CSDP police mission in Afghanistan to reach its authorized strength of about 400 police experts. Institutional inertia has proven a powerful force. Civilian institutions such as the judiciary have little to gain from organizational changes that enable them to respond quickly to foreign demands for their expertise. Also, the CSDP training regime remains patchy. The multilayered system comprises national premission training, EU-level training, and mission in-house training. But there is a lack of standardization, and the different layers are at best loosely integrated. In some countries, premission training is a requirement for being sent on mission, while in others it is not. One prominent proposal to tackle these shortfalls is to create a civilian reserve corps that would sign up, incentivize, and train qualified personnel who would commit to being available on short notice for deployments abroad (Korski 2008). If the EU fails to set up such a corps, it is in danger of falling behind the United States in an area in which it has prided itself on being the world's most capable actor—civilian stabilization and reconstruction missions.[2]

Defense Spending

National defense outlays in the EU have declined since the end of the Cold War, and critics argue that the EU does not spend enough on defense. In 2008, EU member states collectively allocated less than 1.7 percent of their gross domestic product to defense, which was less than the world average of 2.4 percent. The United States spent 4.3 percent of its gross domestic product on defense in 2008.[3] Although these numbers look bad for EU states, they are misleading. They do not take into account that the size of defense budgets differs widely across EU states. For instance, in 2009, little Malta spent about US$50 million on defense, which amounts to about 0.7 percent of its gross domestic product based on 2008 figures. Conversely, the main EU powers have consistently been among the world's top military spenders. In 2009, France allocated about US$64 billion, or 2.3 percent of gross domestic product, to national defense, more than any other country in the world except the United States and China. Britain was in fourth place in the global military spending league table, making about US$58 billion, or 2.5 percent of gross domestic product, available to its armed forces. Even pacifist Germany spent about US$46 billion on its military in 2008, making its defense outlay the sixth largest in the world, even though it spent only 1.3 percent of its gross domestic product on it. In 2009, France, Britain, and Germany allocated about US$168 billion to their military budgets (see Table 6.1). In the same year, EU states together spent about 2.6 times less on defense than the United States (European Defence Agency 2010b: 2).[4]

EU defense spending is impressive by any other than the US yardstick. On paper, the EU is a military heavyweight (Moravcsik 2009: 408). Yet this assessment, too, needs to be taken with a grain of salt. In recent years, EU defense spending has declined not only relative to the United States but also to newly emerging powers such as China and India. Moreover, national defense spending across the EU is only a rough indicator of EU military power. Military budgets are determined by national priorities. Most procurement funds as well as defense research and technology budgets are spent on national rather than EU projects (Stockholm International Peace Research Institute 2008: 272). Military role specialization and the development of niche expertise have become important guiding principles of defense planning in some

Table 6.1   Big Spenders: The 10 Countries with the Highest Military Expenditure in 2009 (in US$, at 2009 exchange rates)

Rank	Country	Spending (billions)	World Share (%)
1	United States	661.0	43.0
2	China	100.0	6.6
3	France	63.9	4.2
4	United Kingdom	58.3	3.8
5	Russia	53.3	3.5
6	Japan	51.0	3.3
7	Germany	45.6	3.0
8	Saudi Arabia	41.3	2.7
9	India	36.3	2.4
10	Italy	35.8	2.3

Source: Sam Perlo-Freeman, Olawale Ismail, Noel Kelly, and Carina Solmirano, "Military Expenditure Data, 2000–2009," *SIPRI Yearbook 2010: Armaments, Disarmament and International Security* (Oxford, UK: Oxford University Press, 2010), p. 203.

smaller EU countries. However, most EU states continue to maintain, or aim at, full-spectrum capabilities. The result is a great deal of duplication of capabilities. The EU has twenty-seven armies, twenty-three air forces, and twenty navies. The United States invests 11.5 percent of its total defense expenditure in research and development, which helps to ensure that its armed forces stay ahead of the rest. The EU countries spend only 4.3 percent on this crucial item. Conversely, a wobbling 50.7 percent of all defense spending in the EU goes to personnel costs. This compares with 20.9 percent in the United States, even though its troops are a considerably more formidable fighting force than their European counterparts (European Defence Agency 2010b: 9, 11). Also, whereas US arms procurement sharply rose in real terms after September 11 (Stockholm International Peace Research Institute 2007: 358), no equivalent growth spurt occurred in the EU. On the contrary, CSDP capability development has taken place in a context characterized by financial constraints. Unproductive spending and duplication combine to produce a situation in which each dollar spent on defense in the EU buys less usable firepower than each dollar spent on defense in the United States. If EU states were to allocate more of their available funds to joint projects—from research and development to procurement—they could give both the CSDP and national armed forces more firepower without having to increase their defense budgets.

Troops for Deployments Abroad

When the CSDP was launched, EU states agreed to set up a corps-sized RRF of 50,000 to 60,000 troops. The EU aims to be able to deploy the full force within sixty days of a political decision and ensure that the troops are sustainable in the field for one year. Taking into account rotation cycles as well as support functions, the EU envisages a force that comprises well over 200,000 troops. The RRF or components thereof are intended to enable the EU to carry out the full range of treaty tasks, from joint disarmament operations to peacemaking. The RRF is not a multinationally integrated standing force but relies on national troops, military hardware, and headquarters. To enable the deployment of the CSDP force, the EU states set themselves the goal of developing collective capabilities in the field of command and control, intelligence, and strategic transport. In 2001, the EU declared the RRF ready to conduct low-intensity stabilization operations. So far the force has never been deployed in a corps-sized operation. However, all military CSDP operations have drawn their troops from the RRF pool.

In 2004, the EU decided to stand up CSDP Battle Groups, which are battalion-sized forces of about 1,500 troops (Lindstrom 2007; Quille 2003). Since 2007, at least one Battle Group has been kept in a ready-to-go status at any given time. Countries volunteer to offer a national Battle Group or to contribute elements to a multinational one. Unlike in the case of the RRF, national contributions to Battle Groups have to be pre-identified and are thus not available for other missions. Battle Groups can be in theater within ten days of a political decision and are sustainable for up to thirty days. They include their own combat support, such as intelligence and reconnaissance, and combat service support, such as logistics. Battle Groups can be used in a variety of scenarios short of large formation warfare and large-scale peacekeeping tasks. For the time being, no Battle Group has yet seen action, although this has not prevented the EU from developing new ambitious targets for the military CSDP. Among other things, Brussels wants to be in a position to deploy concurrently two major postconflict stabilization operations of up to 10,000 troops, two rapid response operations using Battle Groups, a civilian-military humanitarian assistance operation, and a rescue mission extracting EU citizens from a conflict zone (European Council 2008).

So far, military CSDP operations have been small. With initially about 7,000 troops, the peacekeeping operation EUFOR (EU Force) Althea in Bosnia, which was deployed in 2004, has been the largest deployment. However, EU countries annually deploy about 60,000 to 70,000 soldiers abroad (Giegerich 2008). Some of them fight, while others keep the peace or advise and train the armed forces of their host countries. Most do so under their own national flags or under the banner of an international organization such as the United Nations or NATO, while a minority of these troops serve under the EU flag.[5] The ability and willingness of EU states to field annually 60,000 to 70,000 troops abroad, many in high-risk environments, are a considerable departure from the attitudes and policies prevailing at the end of the Cold War. Furthermore, national military reforms have enhanced the operational capabilities of European troops. There has been a trend across the EU to move from conscripted to professional armies. Today's European troops are better trained, better equipped for expeditionary operations, and better at cooperating with each other than yesterday's place-bound forces. Many have gained significant war-fighting experience. Battle Groups are so far the most visible European-level expression of this transformation of national forces. Yet these improvements in EU military manpower are balanced by some serious shortcomings.

Only between 10 and 20 percent of the just under two million men and women in uniform across Europe are deployable abroad. In comparison, the United States has about 250,000 troops deployed abroad, out of over 1.3 million soldiers. Germany, the most populous EU country, was a particular laggard throughout the first two decades after the end of the Cold War, because its short-term conscripts were trained and equipped for homeland defense. In 2010 the Bundeswehr had the capacity to send at most 10,000 troops to foreign theaters, even though it had about 250,000 soldiers (German Defence Minister zu Guttenberg, cited in Blitz and Studemann 2010). This made a wobbling 95 percent of German troops incapable of contributing to the CSDP and the key challenges facing international security management—from peacemaking to the war on terrorism and counterproliferation. Berlin finally started to tackle the problem. In 2011, it suspended conscription and moved toward a considerably smaller all-volunteer force. The reform makes a few thousand more German troops available for foreign deployments, which narrows but does not plug the gap of deployable EU soldiers. For the foreseeable future, the problems associated with the CSDP manpower gap will remain. The EU's inability to field more of its soldiers to face down global threats leads to overstretch, as deployed troops are not properly rested between their tours of duty;[6] generates competition between NATO and the EU for scarce combat soldiers; and makes EU states reluctant to deploy additional CSDP missions because they would further strain their armed forces.

Acquiring Firepower

At the beginning of the new millennium, member states pledged 100,000 troops, 400 combat aircraft, and 100 vessels to CSDP operations. Yet the numbers of this initial force pool and the updates since then are less impressive than they look on paper. The CSDP pool overlaps with the NATO pool, which creates uncertainty about the availability of forces in a contingency. An ongoing NATO campaign may limit the options for the launch of a CSDP operation. Even if NATO is not the obstacle, EU states are often reluctant to redeem their pledges and to make existing capabilities available to CSDP operations.

In 2004, the EU created the intergovernmental EDA to help plug the CSDP capability gap.[7] Yet disagreements among EU states meant that EDA was given limited powers. Money-savers reluctant to fund new European-level activities joined Atlanticists wary of a supranational armaments authority to prevent EDA from acquiring more powers and funds. Britain has been a particularly vocal opponent of a more powerful EDA. With one of the most competitive defense sectors in the world, Britain fears that a powerful agency tasked with strengthening the European military-industrial complex might undermine the privileged relations British arms manufacturers have with the world's largest buyer of military hardware—the Pentagon.[8] Its limitations notwithstanding, EDA has managed to establish itself as the undisputed hub of CSDP capability development. The agency has improved the EU's shortfall management and has taken measures to strengthen the fledgling pan-European defense industry. A competitive industry is crucial for the long-term success of an autonomous CSDP. Finally, EDA has turned itself into an effective advocate for the development of EU high-tech warfare capabilities.

In its efforts to rationalize the use of scarce capabilities, EDA has paid particular attention to strategic and tactical airlift. The EU's limited capability to get its troops rapidly to theaters of operation outside Europe has been one of the most crippling CSDP bottlenecks. EDA leads work on setting up a European Air Transport Fleet. Through the program, a number of EU member states will pool their lift capabilities, including the Airbus 400M once it becomes operational. However, the development of the European air transporter has run into a number of technical problems. Initially, the first deliveries of the heavy airlifters to European armed forces were scheduled to take place at the beginning of 2009. Subsequent delivery estimates were changed to 2013–2014 (Steinmann and Hegmann 2010). Also, under the umbrella of the European Air Transport Fleet, fleet service, support functions, and training will be pooled. To address the shortfall of in-theater airlift in CSDP operations, EDA developed a European program that trains pilots on helicopter tactics, which narrows the gap between the availability of helicopters in national armed forces and the lack of personnel qualified to fly them in expeditionary operations.[9] EDA's long-term plan is to develop a new EU heavy transport helicopter.

Also, EDA has taken measures to strengthen the EU's arms industry. In the United States, the industry underwent a significant consolidation between 1993 and 1997 (Stockholm International Peace Research Institute 2006: 399–401, 2007: 355). In Europe, the defense market has remained more fragmented, even though three major players emerged—the British BAE Systems, the Franco-

German-Spanish EADS, and the French Thales (Darnis et al. 2007; Giegerich and Nicoll 2008). This fragmentation has political reasons. Many European governments are eager to protect national defense firms and to buy national defense products even if imports would provide better quality. Defense procurement nationalism and the lack of cross-national defense industry integration have held back the CSDP. In a small but important step toward a European defense market, EDA established a European defense procurement regime, which regulates how national procurement contracts exceeding €1 million (about US$1.4 million) are handled. National tenders have to be publicly announced on an electronic bulletin board administered by the agency, which enables firms across the EU to participate.

More importantly, EU governments passed directives on defense procurement and intra-EU arms transfers to open up the EU defense market (O'Donnell 2009). Closely related, EDA brokered an agreement among EU states to raise the share of arms procurement expenditure on collaborative European programs from the existing 21 percent to 35 percent. The target for collaborative military research and technology was raised from 1.4 percent to 2 percent of defense spending (Stockholm International Peace Research Institute 2008: 272). To strengthen the EU defense technology base, EDA and the European Commission agreed to establish a European Framework Cooperation for Security and Defence Research, which enhances the synergy between civilian and military research activities across the EU. Finally, all this work by EDA is underpinned by collective strategic objectives, which are laid out in the Capability Development Plan and a series of specific strategies aimed at reinforcing Europe's defense industrial base. Their premise is that not even the biggest EU countries are any longer able to sustain national armament industries that can provide a comprehensive range of cutting-edge weapons systems at affordable prices.

EDA is the linchpin of EU efforts to coordinate CSDP capability development and to manage CSDP capability shortfalls. Yet there are multilateral capability-related programs outside the EU that benefit the CSDP. For instance, two consortia handle the growing demand for European troop transports to CSDP and NATO theaters of operation around the globe. First, NATO has set up a permanent European airlift pool called the Strategic Airlift Capability, which includes the United States. The states participating in the pool jointly bought and manage Boeing C-17 Globemaster airlifters, which are stationed on an air base in Hungary and are available for CSDP operations. Second is the Strategic Airlift Interim Solution, a temporary pool led by Germany. The consortium running the pool has leased six Antonov 124-100 Condor transport aircraft from Ukrainian and Russian partners. The outsized aircraft are available for the airlift of both CSDP and NATO troops.

As late as 2004, observers of the CSDP argued that "[w]here military capacity is to be required, it will probably be for long-term peacekeeping activities rather than 'shock and awe'" (Leonard and Gowan 2004). The EU has proven the pundits partly wrong. Edged on by EDA, the EU has begun to develop common network-enabled (as opposed to more powerful US network-centric) warfare capabilities. Although they do not equate to "shock and awe," they are designed to equip the EU with the capabilities for small to medium-scale, full-spectrum operations based on information superiority. Complementing measures taken by Britain, France, and other member states, the EU has started to build up its own (limited) C^4 ISTAR capabilities (command, control, communications, computers, intelligence, surveillance, target acquisition, and reconnaissance). Network-enabled capabilities have been defined as a critical priority for the EU by EDA's Capability Development Plan and its annual work plans. The agency prioritizes, among other things, projects on space-based intelligence, surveillance, and reconnaissance platforms; the elaboration of C^4 support for CSDP operations; and the integration of common capabilities into an EU ISTAR architecture. In the same vein, the EU reaffirmed its belief that space-based assets are crucial for the development of the CSDP (Council of the European Union 2008b). In line with this strategic thinking, France, Italy, and Germany agreed to give the EU Satellite Center, which interprets and analyzes satellite data for EU states in order to support national and CSDP operations, improved access to data from their respective military or civilian-military Earth-observation satellites. Also, in 2009, Belgium, France, Germany, Greece, Italy, and Spain agreed to develop a common satellite for surveillance and reconnaissance under the aegis of EDA.

EDA has done more to shake up European capability development and acquisition than many observers thought possible when it was created. Yet the big breakthrough in defense integration has escaped it. Many of its initiatives remain in the project preparation and planning phase. Actual progress in deepening defense cooperation has been real but limited. EDA has not been able to persuade EU states to make a strong commitment to joint development and procurement and the pooling of capabilities. In 2009, EU states spent €24 billion (about US$35 billion) on national defense procurement, and only spent €7 billion (about US$10 billion) on European collaborative defense procurement (European Defence Agency 2010a: 14). Since then, the numbers have only marginally changed. In this policy domain, EU states continue to act as twenty-seven sovereign states rather than as a collective actor. This state of affairs perpetuates a number of important CSDP capability gaps. According to the EU's own assessment, the CSDP still suffers from critical shortfalls in the area of information superiority, troop deployability, and force protection, including theater missile defense. To these gaps have to be added insufficient capabilities for maintaining situational awareness in theater, limited advance planning capabilities, and the lack of a permanent and secure communications and information system for autonomous CSDP operations (Simon 2010; Witney 2008). Yet these gaps in EU capabilities and cooperation may soon become a luxury beyond the means of Europeans.

First, rising military powers such as China, India, and Russia put additional pressure on the EU to plug its capability gaps so as to be able to play in the major league of military powers. Second, security interdependence is likely to increase demand for military interventions abroad in order to safeguard European interests. The anti-piracy EU naval operation off the coast of Somalia, which was deployed in 2008, is a case in point. Finally, national budgetary constraints across the EU have become tighter in the wake of the global financial crisis of the late 2000s. Its repercussions have threatened to send some states of the EU's Economic and Monetary Union into sovereign default. EU governments have had to cut their budget deficits in order not to upset global financial markets, which has already started to affect national defense outlays. In response, EU states have shown a new willingness to pool national capabilities and to work together on weapons development and procurement. Thus, in 2010, France and Britain signed an unprecedented defense cooperation agreement, which covers, among other things, cooperation on nuclear warhead research, an integrated carrier strike group, and the joint procurement of missiles. While this agreement remains outside the EU framework, it is likely that pooling will become an increasingly important part of resourcing the CSDP (see, for example, Biscop and Coelmont 2011).

European Intervention Capabilities Beyond the CSDP

The EU is not the only European organization through which EU states can deploy forces abroad. The two most important other organizations are Eurocorps and the European Gendarmerie Force, which were created and are jointly run by some EU states outside the EU framework. These states have pledged that they will make these forces available to CSDP operations if needed. Neither Eurocorps nor the European Gendarmerie Force is a standing force. The European Gendarmerie Force was launched by France, Italy, the Netherlands, Portugal, and Spain in 2006, with Romania joining in 2008. The force's core element is a rapid reaction capability of up to 800 gendarmes and can mobilize more than 2,000 gendarmes. The force can be deployed in EU as well as NATO operations. By carrying out law-enforcement tasks in theater, it can fill the enforcement gap that may open up in stabilization and reconstruction operations. Military firepower is often ill-suited to deal with low-level violence, while unarmed international police advisers cannot snuff out local violence. For these public order jobs in semi-permissive environments, armed gendarmes are best suited. From 2007 to 2010, the European Gendarmerie Force served with the military CSDP operation in Bosnia. It has also served in Afghanistan, where it has worked with NATO to train the local police.

Since Eurocorps was established by France and Germany in 1992,[10] Belgium, Luxembourg, and Spain have joined as full members. A number of countries assign liaison officers or troops to the force, which acquires operational command over earmarked national contingents only during operations and only with the agreement of participating states. In 1999, the participating states agreed to make Eurocorps available for CSDP assignments, and it was transformed into a rapid reaction corps. Eurocorps troops have served in NATO missions in Bosnia, Kosovo, and Afghanistan but the corps has not so far been deployed in any CSDP operation.

Conclusion

In 1991, Belgian foreign minister Mark Eyskens described the EU as "an economic giant, a political dwarf, and a military worm" (cited in Whitney 1991). Since then the EU has built its military muscles and now has sizeable expeditionary forces. It has begun to plug important capability gaps, to reinforce cooperation on research and development, to construct a common defense industrial base, and to build a common defense market. Evidence does not support critics who claim that the EU's "feverish attempts to devise capabilities improvement schemes have failed to deliver much practical progress" (Menon 2009: 233). Yet though there has been real practical progress, European defense transformation remains incomplete. The fact that only 10 to 20 percent of European armed forces are deployable in stabilization and reconstruction missions speaks volumes. So does the fact that Europeans still have over 10,000 main battle tanks in their armories. Some EU countries are still better prepared for the threats of the past—defending the homeland against a massive invasion by the Soviet Union—than for the expeditionary wars of today. The US National Intelligence Council (2008: 33) has predicted that "the EU will not be a major military power by 2025." The EU already today has the raw power to prove this forecast wrong. To transform its potential power into CSDP capabilities, it needs to considerably deepen and enlarge existing arrangements for defense cooperation.

Notes

1. Civilian Response Teams can carry out fact-finding missions in crisis areas, act as a bridging measure prior to the launch of a full-fledged CSDP operation, and offer urgent additional expertise to EU actors in theater.

2. In 2010, the number of responders of the newly created US Civilian Response Corps reached 1,000.

3. These and the following data on defense spending mentioned in this paragraph are drawn from Perlo-Freeman et al. (2010).

4. This statistic excludes the defense spending of Denmark.

5. At the "end of 2009, approximately 51,700 troops of EU member states were globally deployed to multilateral peace operations [of which] 7 percent were deployed to CSDP missions, 15 percent to UN missions and 78 percent to NATO missions" (Soder 2010: 2–3).

6. This has been a particular problem for British forces; see, for example, Rayment 2009.

7. With the exception of Denmark, all EU states participate in the agency.

8. In 2005, British BAE Systems became one of the largest contractors of the Pentagon with the purchase of the US defense firm United Defense (Stockholm International Peace Research Institute 2006: 405).

9. The lack of training and interoperability is only one problem. According to a former chairman of the EU Military Committee, only 50 percent of the helicopters in the arsenal of EU armed forces are actually available and operational (Henri Bentégeat, cited in European Security and Defence Assembly of Western European Union 2010).

10. The maritime counterpart of Eurocorps is Euromarfor (European Maritime Force). It was set up in 1995 by Spain, France, Italy, and Portugal and has been declared available for CSDP operations. So far Euromarfor has carried out an autonomous operation and served in UN and US operations. The twin brother of Euromarfor is Eurofor (European Operational Rapid Force), which participated in the CSDP operation in Macedonia.

CHAPTER 7

Grappling with Varying Perceptions of Threat

THE EU IS MADE UP OF TWENTY-SEVEN STATES THAT DIFFER IN their organization of foreign and security policymaking, national interests, and threat perceptions. Yet they also have many foreign policy commonalities. For instance, they are all allies of the United States and committed to multilateralism and upholding international law. The pattern of convergence-divergence among EU states is a key determinant of the strength of the CFSP. The greater the convergence on key foreign and security policy issues among EU states, the stronger the CFSP is likely to be. This pattern of cross-national convergence-divergence can be analyzed with the help of the concept of Europeanization. It refers to

> processes of (a) construction, (b) diffusion and (c) institutionalisation of formal and informal rules, procedures, policy paradigms, styles, "ways of doing things" and shared beliefs and norms which are first defined and consolidated in the making of EU decisions and then incorporated within the logic of domestic discourse, identities, political structures and public policy. (Radaelli 2000: 4)

The concept captures the reciprocal processes through which changes at the national and EU levels mutually affect each other. On the one hand, EU-level CFSP governance is shaped by member states, who upload their preferences and values to the EU level. More powerful states and states whose domestic political institutions and norms are similar to those already existing at the EU level have an advantage in diffusing and institutionalizing their preferences and values at the EU level. On the other hand, elements of EU-level CFSP governance trickle down to the national level. The ensuing domestic change is the result of either deliberate downloading choices or the unintentional side effect of the socialization of national delegates in Brussels-based CFSP committees and working groups. If there are no codified EU ways of doing things, the cross-national convergence of policies and institutions may result from policy emulation and policy learning among EU states and indirect pressures related to, for instance, the financial constraints imposed on national budgets by the EU's Economic and Monetary Union. In such instances of cross-loading, the EU is the frame for domestic changes rather than their source (Irondelle 2003; Major 2005).

This chapter explores the pattern of convergence-divergence of EU states in the field of foreign and security policy. The first part of the chapter focuses on three key elements of convergence. First, the EU states have constructed and institutionalized an EU strategic framework for thinking about and tackling threats facing them collectively. While the ESS remains patchy, it defines an EU way of maintaining international security. Second, EU-level security governance exerts adaptation pressures on EU states. Because the CFSP does not impose legally binding and enforceable obligations on EU states, the pressures are limited. Still, cross-loading and downloading processes in combination have resulted in an appreciable cross-national convergence in the policy domain covered by the CFSP. Third, the CFSP provides an opportunity structure for states to upload their policy preferences and values to the EU.

The second part of the chapter discusses persistent cross-national divergences in threat perceptions, security identities, and interests among EU states. These divergences generate cleavages among member states that hold the CFSP in check. At the same time, they bind states together in different like-minded groups that compete with each other in trying to upload their views to the EU. The chapter looks at the most salient cleavages among or "camps" of EU states. Although these cleavages remain powerful obstacles standing in the way of a more forceful CFSP, they have not prevented EU states from becoming increasingly supportive of the CFSP.

The European Security Strategy: Toward Shared Threat Perceptions and a Grand Strategy

It is a curiosity of the CSDP's creation that the EU did not at first identify the security threats and challenges that it wanted to tackle with the CSDP. What is more, once the CSDP became operational, EU governments started to dispatch military and civilian operations without having agreed on an EU security strategy. The initial reluctance of EU states to discuss common security threats and an EU-level strategy to counter them was primarily due to the concern that such talk would hamper rather than facilitate the buildup of the CSDP. It would lead to insolvable "theological" debates over the CSDP between different camps. The result was that for years the CSDP remained a capability in search of a strategy.

At the end of 2003, four years after the CSDP was launched, the EU finally established a basic strategic framework for its foreign and security policy. Governments agreed on a common definition of the security threats faced by the EU and on how to tackle them. The backdrop against which the ESS was formulated was the transatlantic and intra-EU controversy over the US-led invasion of Iraq in 2003. The controversy pitted the United States and its closest EU allies such as Britain against EU dissenters such as France and Germany (for more, see Chapter 12). After the overthrow of the Iraqi regime, EU governments realized the damage they had caused to transatlantic relations and their project to establish the EU as a credible international security actor. The elaboration of a common strategic vision was now reframed as a team-building exercise—a savior rather than wrecker of the CFSP. The ESS was intended to be what the high representative for the CFSP called the EU's "strategic identity card" (Solana 2004b: 6) that would demonstrate to EU citizens as well as the world at large that the CFSP was alive and well. Moreover, it would make it easier for EU governments to forge a consensus on security issues in the future. At least, this is what policymakers hoped. Also, the ESS offered an opportunity to mend transatlantic relations, which it did. Its reception inside the Washington beltway was largely positive. In the words of one Pentagon insider, the ESS was "something we could work with, something that had some handles" (cited in Kelleher 2008: 151; see also Asmus 2006).

The ESS is structured around three headings. Under the first, the ESS describes global security challenges and threats. It frames security as a precondition for development, which reverses the causal understanding that had informed EU foreign policy for decades. The ESS emphasizes global challenges against human security such as pandemics and global warming. It lists economic challenges faced by the EU such as competition for natural resources and energy dependency on third countries. The main security threats against the EU that the ESS identifies are terrorism, the proliferation of weapons of mass destruction, regional conflicts, failed states, and organized crime. The latter is further subdivided into trafficking in drugs, women, illegal migrants, and weapons. These phenomena are described as an internal threat to the EU that often has external sources. Some nuances notwithstanding, the ESS list of clear and present dangers, and their prioritization, is similar to US threat perceptions. This was one of the reasons why the George W. Bush administration welcomed the ESS even while it was skeptical of the CSDP. Another common thread running through the security strategies of both the EU and the United States is that they downplay traditional state-based threats against the homeland. As the ESS puts it, "large-scale aggression against the EU is highly improbable," although this assessment has not prevented EU states from including a collective defense clause in the Lisbon Treaty.

The threat assessment of the ESS is informed by a broad or non-traditionalist understanding of security. It appeals to state security but also to the security of collective identities and societal integrity, of liberal European and international governance (political and economic), of the environment, and of individuals. Many of the threats faced by these referent objects of security are unintentional by-products of the activities of nonstate actors and of the absence of functioning states. Moreover, the threat assessment reflects the understanding that European and to a lesser degree international security are indivisible. Dense interdependent relations among European states and societies provide multiple, difficult-to-control channels through which security threats travel across borders. Geographic proximity further enhances the mutual vulnerability of states and societies.

Under its second heading, the ESS outlines the EU's three strategic objectives. The first is to counter the identified threats and challenges, although the ESS gives few specifics about how the EU wants to do this. Noteworthy is the argument that "the first line of defense will often be abroad." There is nothing unusual about this claim when judged against the yardstick of a traditional great power. For the EU, it constitutes a new departure and suggests a readiness to intervene abroad to safeguard European interests and values. Still, compared to the United States, the EU downplays the role of military force in countering threats. A persistent feature of the US foreign policy role conception is the goal of being the world's best war maker. Conversely, the ESS expresses the EU's aspiration to be the world's best stabilization and reconstruction operator. It stresses that the EU is particularly well equipped to bring both civilian and military tools to bear on security problems and underlines the EU's comprehensive toolkit for tackling international security issues.

The second strategic objective of the EU is to build a secure neighborhood. Many of the main threats the ESS identifies are most dangerous to the EU when they occur in its backyard. Regional conflicts, failing states, and organized crime in the Middle East, northern Africa, and Eastern and southeastern Europe are too close for the EU to ignore if it values its security and prosperity. Hence, like any powerful actor, the EU is committed to the goal of pacifying its neighborhood and of remaking it in its image. The third strategic objective is to build a global rule-based order of effective multilateralism. The ESS envisions a world of well-governed democratic states whose relations are regulated by international law, the United Nations, and other international institutions. Trade, development aid, and the principle of conditionality are seen as important tools to spread good governance. The world the EU seeks to build is similar to the world the United States seeks. The US national security strategy routinely speaks of the importance of promoting democracy and an open liberal international order. However, in contrast to the ESS, the US strategy emphasizes that US leadership is crucial to the functioning and the modernization of international order. Moreover, it asserts the right of the United States to use military force unilaterally—that is, outside the UN framework.

A common thread running through the EU's three strategic objectives is the belief that to make itself secure the EU cannot simply reinforce its border protection. It has to cooperate with other states, international organizations, and nongovernmental actors in order to shape the international environment in which they all exist. It has to promote good governance in foreign countries and at the global level to reduce or eliminate the root causes of nonstate threats and to enable the international community to jointly police the channels through which the remaining threats cross borders.

Under its third and final heading, the ESS spells out four general recommendations. First, it calls upon the EU to become more active in pursuing its strategic objectives. This requires developing a "strategic culture that fosters early, rapid, and when necessary, robust intervention." As part of this new culture, the EU needs to be ready for "preventive engagement" abroad (European Council 2003: 17, 18). This is a toning down of the language in the ESS draft, which referred to "preemptive engagement." "Preemption" has a stronger military meaning than the fuzzier term "prevention." The linguistic change was introduced because some EU states were unhappy about the realpolitik implications of the term "preemption." Also, these states did not want the ESS to be viewed as supporting the principle of preemption, which was pronounced by the Bush administration in its 2002 National

Security Strategy. The second recommendation of the ESS is for Europeans to become more capable in military and civilian stabilization and reconstruction missions. The third is to make EU foreign policy more coherent, which refers to closer coordination of EU and national foreign policies and better EU-level coordination of different EU foreign policies such as the CFSP and the European Neighbourhood Policy. Finally, the ESS calls for greater cooperation between the EU and its international partners, singling out the United States as a strategic partner. The EU wants to have a "balanced partnership" with it and describes the buildup of the CSDP as a means toward this goal. Some observers have read this as meaning the EU is dissatisfied with being a strategic follower of the United States and is ready to employ the CSDP to balance US military supremacy (see Chapter 14). The EU-Russia relationship is described as developing toward a strategic partnership, while other countries such as Japan, China, and India are framed as potential strategic partners. The ESS ends on a high note, promising "a fairer, safer and more united world." This can be achieved if the EU becomes a more active and capable international player.

Clearly, the ESS cannot be accused of lacking vision. However, it can be criticized for lacking specifics. The ESS is best described as an "inspirational sketch" (Bailes 2004: 26). From a political view, its principal shortcoming is that many Central and Eastern European countries do not feel it sufficiently reflects their primary security concerns. The former Communist states, which only joined the EU a few months after the adoption of the strategy, see little sense in defining the resolution of the Arab-Israeli conflict as an EU priority while placing Russia's policy in Eastern Europe outside the scope of the ESS. In a similar vein, they believe the EU is naive when it refers to Russia as a strategic partner in the making. In their view, this underestimates the element of strategic rivalry between the two international actors (Edwards 2006; Osica 2004).

At the end of 2008, the EU issued the "Report on the Implementation of the European Security Strategy—Providing Security in a Changing World." The document, which records the evolution of EU strategic thinking, is not a replacement of the ESS, which remains in force. Coming in the wake of the short war between Russia and Georgia in 2008, the document takes a noticeably cooler view of Russia than does the ESS. It warns Moscow of the risks of flouting international norms and standards such as democracy, respect for the territorial integrity of states, and the peaceful settlement of disputes. The EU puts Russia on notice that without a more accommodating foreign policy, it will lose Europe's confidence and harm the bilateral relationship. The report on the ESS implementation also makes veiled references to Russia in its enlarged threat list. In addition to the five major threats identified in 2003, new or newly potent threats are highlighted in the new document—cyber security, energy security, climate change, and piracy. The first two items on the list are dear to the former Communist members of the EU, which consider Russia to be a threat to the EU's cyber security and energy security. Closely related, the report takes a more forceful line on the Eastern neighborhood and makes clear that the EU wants to draw the countries of the region closer into its orbit—and by implication reduce Moscow's influence in Eastern Europe.

The report on the ESS implementation is an important step in the development of common threat perceptions across the EU. It puts the CFSP on politically firmer ground, because it resonates better with the national security preoccupations of the former Communist EU states. Yet from an operational point of view, a number of weaknesses remain unaddressed. The report speaks of the "need to prioritise our commitments, in line with resources." However, neither it nor the ESS orders the identified challenges and threats according to their severity. Nor do they delineate the capabilities required to tackle them. Also, EU strategic objectives do not stand in any relationship of proportionality to Europe's current and potential power (hard and soft), which gives them the appearance of a wish list. Hard choices are avoided when it comes to the trade-off that may be necessary in the pursuit of EU objectives. For instance, the EU may find itself in a situation in which it must choose between its strategic objectives of enforcing international peace and promoting an international order centered on the United Nations.[1] The ESS does not provide any decision criteria for such situations. Last but not least, the ESS does not specify how to achieve the goals it lays out. In particular, it does not list the conditions under which the EU is ready to use its Battle Groups and the RRF, which has resulted in a lack of clarity as to under what situations the EU will deploy military CSDP operations.

A number of factors explain why both the ESS and the report on the ESS implementation are partial and imprecise. Of particular importance are differences in grand strategies among EU states and the consensus rule in EU security policymaking, including in the making of the ESS and the ESS report. In addition, two features of the ESS are important to note. First, it is generally easier to be precise about homeland defense than about out-of-area operations. The ESS is centered on foreign interventions of choice rather than on defensive wars of necessity. It is not about territorial defense[2] but is a postnational, deterritorialized security strategy for the projection of power and values abroad. Second, the construction of an EU-level strategic culture—shared strategic norms and ideas that define attitudes toward the use of force—is a slow process. When the ESS was agreed upon, no shared European strategic culture existed, and this lack was not conducive to the formulation of a forceful and precise security strategy. Since then, a fledgling EU strategic culture has emerged (Cornish and Edwards 2005; Howorth 2010; Meyer 2006; Toje 2008). Yet it continues to lack robustness and is characterized by risk aversion, a reluctance to get involved in military operations without the United States, and a low opinion of the efficacy and morality of military force (see, for example, German Marshall Fund of the United States 2007). This "soft" strategic culture goes some way toward explaining the continuing gaps in the ESS implementation report.

The shortcomings of the ESS notwithstanding, it is misleading to describe it as "a recipe for masterly inactivity" (Toje 2005: 131). It constitutes an appreciable convergence of national security perceptions. Despite their different national situations and histories, all EU states agree on the major security challenges and threats that confront them as a club. Also, the ESS defines an EU approach to international security, albeit a broad one. Based on the notion of comprehensive security, the ESS acknowledges the importance of a multidimensional understanding of security that addresses military, political, economic, social, and ecological aspects. To solve multidimensional security problems, it advocates varying mixes of civilian and military tools. It deliberately blurs the distinction between internal and external security and puts a premium on multilateral cooperation governed by international law. It emphasizes the importance of combining long-term foreign policy centered on conflict prevention and political and economic development and shorter-term interventions centered on the stabilization and reconstruction of postconflict societies. Closely related, the ESS expresses the EU's self-conception as a normative power. The EU sees itself as pursuing an ethical foreign and security policy (Biscop 2005; Lucarelli and Manners 2008; Manners 2002; Mayer and Vogt 2006; Whitman 2010). It wishes to use military force sparingly and only to be a force for good in the international arena. The ESS implementation report further strengthens this self-image, calling on the EU to advance the doctrine of the Responsibility to Protect (for a definition of the R2P, see Chapter 2, endnote 7).

The approach to international security delineated by the ESS gives the EU the character of a small power (Toje 2010). The ESS resonates strongly with the security strategies of small and medium-sized powers of secondary importance in world politics such as Sweden, the Netherlands, and Canada. Incidentally, the small power identity defined by the ESS is one of the reasons why the United States began to embrace the CSDP. Washington realized that its initial concerns that the CSDP signaled the EU's resolve to refashion itself into a diplomatic-strategic equal of, perhaps even a rival to, the United States were for the time being unsubstantiated. Yet the small-power strategy of the EU will come under increasing strain in coming years. As the EU builds up its military power, it will have to develop a more robust grand strategy to guide its use. Failure to do so would raise doubts about the rationale of the military CSDP, especially about the need to invest in autonomous military capabilities and assets. If the EU were to stick to its small-power security strategy, it would risk that the CSDP would "gradually lose its military component to NATO, which would become the sole military intervention body, with the possibility of development of a European defence pillar being integrated within it" (Gnesotto 2009: 34).

The Europeanization of Security and Defense

The construction and institutionalization at the EU level of a security strategy and strategic culture and of formal and informal rules and procedures regarding EU security policy have led to gradual and uneven domestic changes across the EU (Archer 2008; Dover 2007; Gross 2009a; Jokela 2011; Miskimmon 2007; Rieker 2006; Watanabe 2010; Wong 2006). The pressure in EU states to adapt to EU expectations and the cross-national emulation of best practice has facilitated the EU-wide modernization of national security policies and institutions. Also, it has helped governments sell costly or unpopular defense-related changes to their voters—changes they wanted to pursue in any case—because the CSDP allowed them to blame the changes on the EU. Moreover, the Europeanization of security policy has provided opportunities for EU states to upload their policy preferences and values to the CSDP, which has empowered them to punch above their individual weight in international affairs. It has enabled them to pool their national capabilities with those of fellow EU states in the pursuit of common objectives and to act with more international legitimacy than if they acted on their own. The CSDP has been a force multiplier and legitimacy provider for EU states.

The deployment of civilian CSDP operations has put pressure on EU governments to put in place and coordinate national mechanisms for identifying, training, and deploying police officers, judges, prosecutors, and so forth. Europeanization pressures in the military field have led to more far-reaching domestic changes. The buildup of the military CSDP has encouraged some governments to adapt their national security identities. For instance, successive German governments have successfully used CSDP operations in the Western Balkans, Africa, and Afghanistan to whittle away at the country's pacifist reluctance to deploy troops and civilian security personnel in war zones. The Nordic EU states have adjusted their security identities, to a varying degree, to the EU's comprehensive security approach (Rieker 2006). Neutral Austria modified its constitution to allow its troops to participate in the full range of CSDP tasks laid out in the EU Treaty. The EU's political commitment to the Battle Groups has pressured governments to curtail the role of conscription in favor of professional soldiers who are trained and equipped for expeditionary operations. Multinational Battle Groups have contributed to increased interoperability among EU forces (Bentégeat 2008; Witney 2008; and, on the transformational effect of Battle Groups more generally, see Jacoby and Jones 2008). In general, the CSDP has "led to a permanent state of benchmarking among European defence ministries" (Mérand 2008: 149).

A unique feature of the Europeanization of national military policies and institutions is that it is embedded in and constrained by powerful pressures of "NATO-ization." Through its collective force-planning system and its integrated military commands, the alliance downloads reforms to participating states. This results in cross-national convergence around common military policies, organizational forms, and practices. States that are not full alliance members but participate in its Partnership for Peace, such as the EU neutrals, face the same downloading pressures. While difficult, it is not impossible to disentangle the impact of NATO and the CSDP on national security policies and structures through careful process tracing (Gross 2009a).

Europeanization and NATO-ization in combination with the geopolitical constraints and opportunities of the post–Cold war era account for a key change in military institutions and doctrines across the EU. In response to international pressures, states have reformed their armed forces to enable them to participate in expeditionary warfare. Processes of downloading and cross-loading have been mediated by how states organized their military power in the past. The interaction of external factors and the stickiness of national institutions have resulted in an uneven convergence around a postterritorial model of warfare. Forster (2006) found that within the overall trend toward professional armed forces and enhanced deployability, four distinct military models in the EU remain. Since then there has been further convergence among these models. In particular, a number of countries have decided to abandon or suspend conscription.

In Britain and France, the expeditionary warfare model dominates in its pure form. Both countries see themselves as great powers with global reach. To defend their interests and to project their visions of order abroad, they rely on volunteer forces and emphasize the capacity for high-technology, high-intensity warfare. In the case of France, Europeanization was a major factor in shaping the national defense reforms that led to the institutionalization of the expeditionary warfare model (Irondelle 2003). In line with their national visions, both Britain and France advocate a high-tech CSDP. London wants to ensure that EU states can plug in to US-led war-fighting operations, either through NATO or US-led coalitions of the willing. France wants to have a CSDP that can take on higher-intensity missions on its own. In the absence of perceived state-based threats to their countries' political and territorial integrity, France and Britain regard national defense as a second-order objective of their armed forces.

In the former Communist EU countries, adaptation pressures by the EU and NATO have only partially modified the traditional territorial defense model. Many armed forces in the EU's East remain geared toward making an invasion by Russia as difficult as possible. However, the ex-Communist countries have fallen into line with international expectations engendered by Europeanization and NATO-ization. To enable troops to participate in CSDP and other international security missions, they have made the necessary changes to their armed forces. Also, the number of former Communist countries holding fast to conscription has recently further dwindled, with countries such as Poland and Lithuania suspending it in favor of professional forces. The third military model is the late modern model, mainly used by Germany, Italy, and Spain. Although it retains a residual territorial defense function, it puts the emphasis on the deployment of military forces abroad in line with the ESS and NATO strategy. Finally, the neutral model, found in Austria, Finland, Ireland, and Sweden,[3] is a close cousin of the late modern model and combines a commitment to territorial defense and peace support missions. The former remains crucial to how the neutral countries conceive of their security policies. However, the relative importance of the latter has increased in the post–Cold War era, as reflected in the declining importance neutrals such as Sweden and Austria attach to conscription. Sweden ended conscription in 2010, and at the time of writing, Austria is discussing plans to follow suit. The Europeanization of security and defense policy has been a key factor pushing neutrals toward greater military engagement abroad. In addition to UN peace support operations, CSDP missions have become an important reference point for the armed forces of the EU neutrals, which are supporters of the CSDP because their small-power security strategies conform to the ESS.

The Europeanization of national security policy is a multiplier of national capabilities and influence, achieved by those EU states that manage to upload their policy priorities to the CSDP. The cumulative effect of uploads has been to push the EU toward greater international security activism, which accounts for the fact that most CSDP missions so far have been in Africa. Former colonial powers have acted as policy entrepreneurs, dragging their often reluctant partners along. For instance, without the advocacy of Portugal, the security sector reform mission to its former colony Guinea-Bissau—EU SSR Guinea-Bissau—would probably not have been deployed. Another case is France, which succeeded in pushing its European partners to engage in humanitarian interventions in the Democratic Republic of Congo, Chad, and the Central African Republic (Gegout 2009; Olsen 2009). It also provided most of the troops for these military operations. This said, the CSDP missions in Africa did not only promote the national interests of their promoters but also enhanced the EU's visibility on the continent and demonstrated that the EU has become a security provider.

National Cleavages and Divergent Security Interests

Europeanization pressures are mediated and held in check by cross-national differences among EU states. The stronger these national cleavages are, the less potent Europeanization is likely to be. In foreign and security policy, national cleavages among EU states are pronounced. EU-level CFSP governance remains patchy and the trickle-down effects of Europeanization have produced only a limited convergence of national security policies and institutions.

Membership in some CFSP camps is seemingly permanent and may be rooted in a country's economic or military power. Take the Big

Three—France, Britain, and Germany—which form the EU's exclusive top powers club and have been the major framers of EU foreign and security policy. As a former European commissioner for external relations put it, "there is no European policy on a big issue unless France, Germany and Britain are on side" (Patten 2005: 160). As far as the military CSDP is concerned, the triumvirate *entente cordial* has been responsible for shaping its key features, including the RRF and the Battle Groups. This is not surprising given the gap in military and/ or financial power, which is unlikely to disappear in the foreseeable future, between them and the rest of the EU countries. CFSP camp membership may also be related to national political institutions and cultures, which change only gradually and over a long time. For instance, the Big Two—Britain and France—are likely for the foreseeable future to remain the only EU states that regard the capacity for autonomous military action abroad as crucial to their identities and national interests. Germany's soft strategic culture, which fosters skeptical attitudes toward military power, has remained strong. After the end of the Cold War, some observers thought that Berlin would return to the international scene as a traditional great power. Yet German thinking on the use of force abroad remains closer to that prevailing in the neutral EU countries than to that in Britain and France. Finally, in some cases, a country may change its camp membership from one day to the next. For instance, the conservative Spanish prime minister José María Aznar pursued a pronounced pro-US foreign policy, joining British prime minister Blair in strongly backing the George W. Bush administration in its diplomatic quarrel with Paris and Berlin over weapons inspections in Iraq. He then ordered Spanish troops into Iraq alongside the United States in 2003. When the socialists regained power in the following year, they quickly realigned Spanish foreign policy with that of France and Germany. Relations with the Bush administration cooled, and Spanish troops were pulled out of Iraq.

Atlanticists vs. Europeanists: Divergent Rationales for the CSDP

The Spanish flip-flop on Iraq touches on one of the most widely discussed fault lines running through the CFSP. The quarrels between Atlanticists and Europeanists are the stuff of many news headlines. Although the division has become a cliché, in reality it is more complicated and nuanced. Moreover, it is less important than often

assumed. On many foreign and security policy issues, EU governments line up on the basis of criteria unrelated to their political proximity to the United States. What is more, the two camps manage to
cooperate on important issues. Thus, the creation of the CSDP was a
Franco-British initiative. The principal proponents of the Atlanticist
and Europeanist camps agreed to give the EU autonomous military
capabilities, albeit for different reasons.

Atlanticists are pro-American. They try hard to avoid being on the
wrong side of the United States on crucial matters of international
security. They regard their friendship with Washington as their best
security guarantee and show a willingness to join in its wars. They
view US-led NATO as the mainstay of European and global security.
In the wake of the end of the Cold War when NATO's future was in
doubt, they argued for maintaining the alliance as Europe's security
pillar. Later Atlanticists opposed equipping the EU with autonomous
military capabilities, fearing the creation of a military power in
Europe that would end up rivaling NATO. In the end, the leader of the
Atlanticist camp—Britain—changed its mind, and fellow Atlanticist
governments had little choice but to follow suit.[4]

Britain's Atlanticism is deeply ingrained in its political culture. It
remains a country whose population and politicians are on average
more Euroskeptic than those of the other major European countries.
Moreover, the special relationship between Washington and London is
underpinned by powerful material factors. Since World War II,
London has enjoyed a special intelligence-sharing relationship with
Washington, and its nuclear deterrent depends on considerable US
input. Also, Britain is the United States' most important European military supplier, and the arms industries of both countries have become
increasingly integrated (Stockholm International Peace Research
Institute 2008: 269). This gives British firms privileged access to the
huge US armaments market and to advanced military technology.
These ideational and material supports of British Atlanticism notwithstanding, London joined the leader of the Europeanist camp to initiate
the CSDP. It did not become an advocate of autonomous EU military
capabilities because it abandoned its Atlanticist convictions. Rather, it
changed its views on how best to act on them.

Toward the end of the 1990s, developments in international
security and domestic politics changed the way Britain pursued its
Atlanticist agenda. The government began to be concerned about the
consequences of the EU's continuing inability to get its military act
together. It feared that this failure might endanger the transatlantic

security relationship, both at the political and operational levels. Politically, the 1990s saw persistent demands on Capitol Hill for more balanced burden sharing in the management of European security. Worryingly for London, these demands were voiced in the context of a shift of US strategic preoccupations away from Europe. Britain feared Europe might be abandoned militarily by the United States unless it heeded Washington's call for doing more for its own security. Operationally, various US-led campaigns in the 1990s brought into focus the persistent gap in high-tech military capabilities between the United States and Europe. London was concerned that this gap threatened the interoperability of European and US forces and undermined Washington's interest in NATO as a force multiplier in coalitional warfare. Hence, for both international political and military reasons, Britain decided to utilize the EU to inject new momentum into the buildup and modernization of European military capabilities.

There was also a domestic political side to the British security policy turnaround. In 1997, a Labour government came to power, and the new prime minister, Tony Blair, did not share the Euro-skepticism of his predecessors. Moreover, after years of self-imposed marginalization in European politics under the Tories, the new government wanted to carve out a leadership role for London in the EU. It initiated an internal review aimed at identifying issue areas in which Britain could play such a role, which created a window of opportunity for a small group of Whitehall mandarins to change British security policy. Already during the preceding conservative governments, these senior officials had evolved a shared understanding that both the transatlantic security relationship and Europe's own security provisions had to be remodeled to make them more relevant for the new strategic environment. With the Labour Party in power, they acted as policy entrepreneurs and proposed that the government play a leadership role in EU security policy. Britain could capitalize on its military power and expertise to revitalize its bridge function between the United States and Europe. Also, leadership in EU foreign and security policy would enable London to shape the European agenda and keep it focused on NATO's primacy (Dover 2007; Howorth 2004; Whitman 1999). The government was persuaded of the soundness of the strategic case for making the EU an autonomous military player and enticed by the vision of exercising security policy leadership in the EU.

Britain and other Atlanticists regard the CSDP partly as a "sales tool for NATO's force goals" (Posen 2006: 168). If the CSDP delivers national defense reforms that improve Europe's capacity to fight alongside the high-tech military forces of the United States, it will have done its job. In addition, Atlanticists have come to acknowledge that in today's geopolitical context Europe needs its own autonomous military capability. They fully support the ESS analysis that instability and crises in the EU's backyard create negative externalities for the EU itself. Hence, the EU needs to be able to take care of smaller-scale emergencies in its neighborhood where the United States has few incentives to get involved. But the support of Atlanticist governments for the CSDP remains qualified by the priority they give to their relationship with the United States and the role they assign to NATO in their strategic planning documents. Thus, the 2008 British National Security Strategy does not mention the CSDP once, whereas it mentions NATO seventeen times. The 2010 Strategic Defence and Security Review emphasizes that Britain only supports CSDP operations when "it is clear that NATO is not planning to intervene" (Her Majesty's Government 2010: 62).

Where Atlanticists look to the United States for Europe's security, Europeanists look to Europe itself. The leader of the Europeanist camp is France. In the 1960s French president Charles de Gaulle wanted to establish Western Europe as a third pole in international affairs, beside the United States and the Soviet Union. While he saw the Soviet Union as the main military threat to the EU, he regarded the United States as a political threat to the independence of France and the EU and to their role on the world stage. Seeing NATO as a vehicle for the projection of US power into Western Europe, de Gaulle put some distance between France and the alliance by pulling the country out of the alliance's integrated military commands (for more on the complicated US-French security relationship, see Chapter 12). He and subsequent French presidents advocated a *Europe tricolore*, a French-led Europe (Gordon 1993). The Gaullist vision of an autonomous European power also influenced strategic thinking in other European countries, which opposed the US dominant diplomatic-strategic role in Western Europe. During the Cold War, Paris sought to achieve its goal through close Franco-German military cooperation. For instance, the two countries took the lead in the early 1980s to reinvigorate the Western European Union (see, for example, Western European Union 1984; Western European Union 1987; also, Duke 2000: 72–78). Also, bilateral security cooperation was enhanced in the 1980s. Among other things, a joint Commission on Security and Defence and a joint military brigade were created, and numerous joint military maneuvers were held. Yet in security matters Germany never joined the Europeanist camp, and France never got the strong support for its policy that it wanted from Bonn.

After the end of the Cold War, the Gaullist dream was given fresh impetus. In the new international environment, Europeanists hoped to transform the EU into Europe's key security actor. Once again, France cooperated with Germany in an effort to give the EU a security identity and policy. This time, in the new geopolitical context ushered in by the end of the Cold War, the efforts bore fruits. The Maastricht Treaty created the CFSP. However, in the years following the adoption of the treaty, it became clear that there was no political will in the EU to develop the "S" in the CFSP. Once again, the Europeanist dream remained unfulfilled, although it was not abandoned. When London signaled its willingness to replace Germany as Paris's partner in shaping European security cooperation, Paris was ready and willing. It jumped on the opportunity to transform the EU into a military power.

The Franco-British accord was politically enabled by the fact that Paris had previously toned done its critique of NATO and had started to cooperate with the alliance more closely (see Chapter 12). Without this rapprochement between France and NATO, it is hardly conceivable that Atlanticist London would have considered partnering with Paris in advancing EU security policy. Also, security cooperation between the two countries was facilitated by shared political-military experiences during the 1990s, including joint frustration over US policy. To begin with, both Paris and London learned the hard way that their Cold War armed forces were no match for the high-tech US military machine that was changing the way the United States was conducting its post–Cold War expeditionary wars. In 1991, a US-led international coalition defeated Iraq, which had invaded Kuwait. France and Britain, which took part in the campaign, were able to deploy only limited capabilities. Moreover, their effectiveness partly depended on US support, for example in the area of satellite-based intelligence. The experience strengthened Paris's and London's resolve to modernize their armed forces. They sought to emulate, albeit on a much smaller scale, US expeditionary warfare capabilities.

Yet, not long after the Gulf experience, their continuing diplomatic-strategic weakness was brought into focus again. They and their European partners were incapable of bringing the bloody conflict in Bosnia to an end. Finally, a US-led NATO air war forced the Bosnian Serbs to the negotiating table in 1995. Before, during, and after the military campaign, policy differences pitted the British and French, on the one side, against the United States, on the other (Silber and Little 1997; Woodward 1995). Washington refused to join London and Paris in committing ground troops to the UN peacekeeping force in Bosnia because it did not want to put its troops into harm's way in a country that is of little strategic importance to it. Toward the end of 1994, it withdrew unilaterally from multilateral efforts to enforce the UN weapons embargo against the belligerents, which it thought unfairly disadvantaged the Bosnian Muslim–Croat forces in their fight against the Bosnian Serbs. In the Bosnian peace negotiations in Dayton, Ohio, both the French and the British felt that the United States paid insufficient attention to their views. A few years later, in the fall of 1998, preparations were under way in NATO for a possible international military intervention in Kosovo to stop the ethnic fighting between Serbs and Kosovars. In the process, the planning showed up the persistent European dependency on US military capabilities (Pond 1999). On a more practical level, the operational experience of working together in the Balkans from the early 1990s onward contributed to improved Franco-British military relations. Good cooperation contributed to mutual trust. As one analyst succinctly put it, "Their soldiers dying together brought them together" (Gnesotto 1997: 40; see also Treacher 2004).

With French president Sarkozy, a new breed of Europeanists has entered the EU stage in the new millennium. Although they accept that the United States and NATO are permanent and important fixtures of European security, they insist that the United States treats Europe as a strategic equal and believe that this requires making the CSDP more capable and autonomous. Without being a powerful and autonomous military actor in its own right, the EU will never be able to forge a transatlantic security partnership founded on equality. Unlike Britain, France thus attaches great importance to the CSDP in its national military planning. The 2008 French White Paper on defense and national security envisions a reinforced CSDP as fundamental to French and European security. As to the security functions of the CSDP, Paris agrees with London that it is an important tool to stabilize the EU's backyard and to protect it from soft external security threats such as organized crime.

However, Europeanists and Atlanticists have different opinions when it comes to the nature of EU military interventions. Whereas Britain prefers more demanding out-of-area operations by EU states to be conducted in cooperation with the United States, France is an advocate of more robust autonomous CSDP deployments. To this end, it advocates a considerable upgrade of the EU's capability to plan, command, and control military operations, a development resisted by Britain. In the end, the differences between France and Britain boil down to this: Paris wants the CSDP to be primarily an instrument to strengthen its own and the EU's influence and role in international security affairs, while London wants the CSDP to be NATO's savior. Also, London regards it as a tool to leverage both its special diplomatic-strategic relationship with Washington in Europe and its security leadership in the EU in its relations with Washington. Some analysts see in the Atlanticist-Europeanist dispute over the security architecture of the transatlantic relationship a traditional great power game (Matlary 2009: 73).

An important tie that binds the leaders of the Atlanticist and Europeanist camps together is their joint aversion to supranationalism in the CFSP. Both Britain and France are staunch defenders of intergovernmentalism in this policy domain. This is not surprising, because they are the only EU countries with serious power projection capabilities, which provides them with a great amount of influence in EU decisionmaking on military matters. Supranationalism would dilute their influence. Also, both states regard it as self-evident that the most powerful EU countries should lead the CFSP. Their preferences for intergovernmentalism and informal leadership by the strong bring them into conflict occasionally with some of their fellow camp members. For instance, in the first half of 2004, Britain, France, and Germany began to engage Iran diplomatically on the issue of its nuclear program without prior consultation with their EU partners. It was only later in the year, after criticism by other EU countries, that they associated the high representative for the CFSP with their demarche (Crowe 2005: 15).

The diplomatic fallout among EU governments over the Iraq war was a dramatic reminder of the continuing Atlanticist-Europeanist cleavage. In general, the two camps are preoccupied by more mundane controversies and tensions that happen out of the public limelight. For instance, London wants EDA to have limited competences and funds in order to prevent the agency from interfering in national defense-industrial decisions and from undermining the close Anglo-American defense industrial relationship. Conversely, Paris prefers a well-funded agency capable of promoting common weapons development and procurement policies across the EU, not least in order to enhance the fortune of its own defense industry champions.

Germany: The Vanishing Mediator

A country that is not easily classified as belonging to either the Atlanticist or Europeanist camp is Germany. Sometimes referred to as a Euroatlanticist, it has traditionally sought to mediate between the two sides. Throughout its post-1945 history, the country has tried to reconcile a pro-US with a French-leaning foreign policy. Although it values its partnership with France in the EU, it has generally been reluctant, unlike Paris, to take a public stance against Washington on important international security issues. In the 1990s, Germany played the role of arbiter between divergent British and French visions of post–Cold War European security. It supported both the revitalization of NATO and the reinforcement of EU foreign and security policy cooperation. Having played no role in the Franco-British initiative to launch the CSDP, Germany was crucial in transforming the bilateral initiative into an EU project. At the beginning of the new millennium, Berlin formed an anti-war coalition with Paris and Moscow to prevent the US-led invasion of Iraq. This was the first time after 1945 that Germany pursued a foreign policy that actively opposed the United States on an issue of vital importance to Washington. The result was not only a particularly bad spell in transatlantic relations but also the weakening of the traditional German role of honest broker (Miskimmon 2007). Relations were repaired when a new government came to power in Berlin and returned to the old balancing act of steering a pronounced pro-US course while maintaining close relations with Paris. However, Franco-German security cooperation has become more challenging, a fact that was obscured by the close cooperation on the Iraq dossier. Germany's identity has been partly "de-Europeanized" since its reunification (Wagner 2006a). This development shows itself in a number of ways.

To begin with, for a long time Germany was unwilling to make radical changes to the Bundeswehr to adjust it to the new international threat environment. As a result, it lacked expeditionary troops. This shortfall, in turn, acted as a considerable brake on the CSDP.[5] Second, in the decades prior to reunification, the reflexive support for a federalist EU was a fixture of German foreign policy. Since reunification, Berlin has displayed a willingness to put its national, mostly financial interests before its commitment to a capable and active CFSP. This has brought it into closer alignment with London on some issues and made it less willing to back French plans for strengthening the CSDP. Third, Germany continues to regard itself as a civilian power even as national attitudes toward the deployment of the Bundeswehr abroad have become more permissive in line with the militarization of EU foreign policy and NATO out-of-area operations. Unlike both France and Britain, Germany remains uncomfortable thinking about and acting on international security problems in terms of forceful military solutions and material interests (both national and EU). When, in 2010, German president Horst Köhler publicly stated that German troops abroad served German national interests, he found himself at the center of a storm of criticism and he resigned. The upshot of these factors is that Germany has become one of the main obstacles standing in the way of the Europeanist goal of developing Europe into a powerful and autonomous military actor.

The Former Communist EU States: Atlanticist and Concerned About Russia

The Central and Eastern European members do not form a separate CFSP camp but are Atlanticists of a particular kind. As mentioned, they have the most traditional military model of all EU states and focus on territorial defense because of their perception of Russia as a security problem if not a national security threat. In addition to their distinct views on national security, their foreign and security policies converge around two further issues. They want to roll back Russian influence in post-Soviet space and see the United States and NATO as their best protection against a resurgent Russia. Although the intensity of these perceptions and preferences varies across countries, they all share them. The attitudes of the former Communist EU states have had an appreciable impact on European foreign policy, and they have managed to upload some of their views and preferences to the EU. This has resulted in shifting influence in the club in favor of those countries who are concerned about Russia's illiberal policies at home and its geopolitical and geo-economic policies in its neighborhood (Müller-Brandeck-Bocquet 2006; Valášek 2005).[6] The former Communist EU states have thus contributed to the recent hardening of EU policy toward Russia. At the same time, their attitudes toward the CSDP have been "Europeanized," evolving from skeptical to supportive.

The former Communist EU states are more inclined than most of their Western European counterparts to see Russia as a security problem. Security concerns are particularly pronounced among the "new cold worriers"—Poland and Lithuania—which "suspect Russia of waging a new cold war against the EU" (Leonard and Popescu 2007: 48). For instance, the former president of Lithuania, Vytautas Landsbergis, continues to argue that it is a mistake not to regard Russia as an enemy (cited by Pop 2010). Yet security concerns about Russia are also present in countries such as Estonia, Latvia, and Romania, which have a more pragmatic policy approach to their big eastern neighbor. While the political atmosphere between the Eastern European EU states and Russia has been influenced by politics and unexpected events,[7] there are deep-seated reasons for Eastern Europe's attitudes toward Russia, which have proved largely immune to change. The former Communist countries are strongly influenced by their physical closeness to Russia and to what Moscow considers its "near abroad"—the now sovereign countries that once belonged to the Soviet Union. Their exposed location translates into a sense of vulnerability (political, military, and economic) vis-à-vis their great Russian neighbor. Also, in all Central and Eastern European EU countries memories of repression by the Soviet Union remain intact, which makes them particularly vocal defenders of Western democracy and human rights in Russia and its near abroad. Many Eastern EU governments believe that key Western European countries such as Germany and France are too soft on Moscow. Emblematic of this sentiment is a statement by Estonian president Toomas Hendrik Ilves, who accused Western Europeans of having "gone much too far in their appeasement policy towards Russia" (cited in Vinocur 2007).

The Eastern European EU states, especially Poland and the Baltic states, have played an important role in persuading the EU to modify its policy toward Russia (see Chapter 13). They have successfully argued that Russia's resurgence in Eastern Europe and its drift toward autocracy at home pose not only a threat to them but a challenge to the EU as a whole. Their view that instead of accommodating a bullying and illiberal Russia, the EU has to defend its interests and values has found considerable resonance in Western Europe.

Criticisms of "old Europe's" softness on Russia goes hand in hand with security policies that are strongly pro-US and pro-NATO. The former Communist members of the EU highly value their alliance with Washington and often side with it in international affairs even if this comes at the expense of the coherence and profile of the EU's role on the international stage. There are a number of sui generis reasons for the pronounced Atlanticism of Central and Eastern Europe, which sets it apart from the Atlanticism of Western European states. First, there is a widespread belief in the countries that it was the US policy of strength vis-à-vis Russia, especially under the Reagan administration, that freed them from Communism. Conversely, Western Europe's policy of change through cooperation, which was institutionalized in the Conference on Security and Cooperation in Europe, is regarded as having prolonged Communist oppression. Second, the United States was an early champion of the integration of Central and Eastern Europe into the Euro-Atlantic structures, while many Western Europeans were latecomers to the cause. Third, a strong United States in Europe acts as a check on the influence of the major Western European powers, which gives the small and medium-sized countries of Central and Eastern Europe more room for maneuver in European international affairs. The largest country in the region, Poland, harbors foreign policy leadership aspirations in Europe. Just like Britain, Warsaw supports a strong United States in Europe to take advantage of what it regards as its "privileged and special relationship with the Americans" (Foreign Minister Adam Daniel Rotfeld, cited in Edwards 2006: 148). Fourth, in some cases such as Poland and Lithuania, Atlanticism is fueled by large and politically active diasporas in the United States. Finally and most importantly, the former Communist EU states regard close political and military relations with Washington and a strong NATO as their best insurance against Russian military power.

Another shared preoccupation of the Central and Eastern European EU governments is their Eastern neighborhood. The former Communist EU countries have shaped EU foreign policy toward the region, including the European Neighbourhood Policy, which is the EU's main instrument to achieve the objective of the ESS to promote "a ring of well governed countries to the East of the European Union" (European Council 2003: 13). Though they were only EU candidate countries when the European Neighbourhood Policy was agreed upon, the former Communist states were vocal advocates of the eastward expansion of the European Neighbourhood Policy beyond the countries initially targeted when the policy was announced. They contributed to the EU decision in 2004 to invite the countries of the Southern Caucasus to join the initiative. Later the former Communist EU states successfully lobbied for reinforcing the European Neighbourhood Policy by creating the Eastern Partnership, which draws the EU's Eastern neighbors closer into the orbit of the EU. Also, opposing the "enlargement fatigue" of many Western EU countries, the former Communist EU states back the integration of their neighbors into the EU. The Central and Eastern European EU countries regard the eastern and southeastern expansion of the EU as a powerful means to secure post-Communist space for the West, to protect themselves against soft security threats stemming from political and economic instability, and to promote beneficial cross-border economic exchange.

Initially, the former Communist countries regarded the CSDP with suspicion, believing it was bad for NATO and EU-US relations more generally. Their idea of the Europeanization of security and defense policy was to strengthen the European pillar within NATO and to keep it under firm US supervision (Missiroli 2004/5). Eastern EU states seconded Washington's demand that the CSDP complement, not duplicate, NATO capabilities. As late as 2001 the Polish foreign minister called for dropping the "D" from the CSDP (Longhurst and Zaborowski 2006).

Since then, however, attitudes have evolved. Skepticism has been replaced by (qualified) support. This change shows up in a number of ways. The former Communist countries actively participate in EU operations, even in regions that are of little geopolitical interest to them. For instance, Poland contributed a battalion to the humanitarian intervention in Chad/Central African Republic in 2008, while Lithuanians served in the Aceh Monitoring Mission in Indonesia in 2005. Also, Central and Eastern European governments have underwritten the buildup of CSDP military capabilities. For instance, they contribute to EU Battle Groups, even though they duplicate the NATO Response Force and make the EU militarily less dependent on the United States. While they often buy weapons made in the US, they have started to participate in the buildup of Europe's military-industrial complex. Thus they have joined collaborative EU research, development, and procurement programs, which are designed to preserve an autonomous military-industrial base in the EU. In a similar vein, the Central and Eastern European EU members have abandoned their skepticism toward the construction of Brussels-based CSDP institutions. Initially, they followed the United States in opposing such institution-building because it duplicates NATO capabilities, but later accepted it not only as inevitable but useful. For instance, they have backed the gradual buildup of autonomous EU strategic planning, command, and control capabilities.

Five reasons account for the Europeanization of the attitudes of the Central and Eastern European countries toward the CSDP. First, their support for the CSDP is related to the effects of socialization in Brussels-based committees and working groups. As the diplomats and soldiers of the former Communist EU states have become more familiar with and have learned to trust their Western EU partners, they have become less suspicious of the CSDP. They trust the claims of their

Western counterparts, including those of the Europeanists, that they do not seek to replace NATO with the CSDP. Second, Eastern Europe's reevaluation of the CSDP has been facilitated by its success in uploading its views to EU-level foreign and security policy. Third, in the wake of the invasion of Iraq, Washington became supportive of the CSDP, thus removing a principal reason for the coolness shown by the former Communist EU states toward the CSDP. Fourth, countries such as Poland have realized that there is a political cost for aligning themselves too closely with Washington. As Zbigniew Brzezinski put it, by showing an "excessive and divisive demonstration of loyalty" toward Washington early on, Warsaw and other Eastern EU capitals unnecessarily damaged their relationship with European allies (cited in Longhurst and Zaborowski 2006: 60; Zaborowski 2004). Finally, the EU governments in Central and Eastern Europe have learned to view the CSDP as a potentially powerful instrument in shaping the future of Eastern Europe by reinforcing the European Neighbourhood Policy and securing the Eastern neighborhood for the Western community of values and interests. Incidentally, a more forceful extension of the CSDP into post-Soviet space is also a vehicle for the former Communist EU states to raise their own foreign policy profiles. Not only do they have an extensive local presence and political support in the concerned countries, they also have special expertise, including Russian language skills and knowing how to overcome the legacy of the Soviet political and legal system. These assets have allowed Eastern EU governments to stake out a CFSP leadership role in the region. For instance, Eastern staff has played a proportionally greater role (numerically and politically) in CSDP missions in Georgia than elsewhere. The same has held true for the offices of the EUSRs for the South Caucasus, Moldova, and the crisis in Georgia.

The EU Neutrals: Strong Supporters of the CSDP

The camp of EU neutrals comprises Ireland, Finland, Sweden, Austria, and Malta. During the Cold War, the countries refrained from aligning too closely with either of the two rival blocs. For some, such as Austria and Finland, neutrality was primarily a response to the constraints of the geopolitical situations in which they found themselves: in the border zone between the capitalist West and the Communist East. Their neutrality was pragmatic and realist, though particularly in the case of Austria it became part of the country's national identity.

For others, such as Sweden and Ireland, neutrality was more of an ideological choice (Eliasson 2004). Irrespective of these differences, since the Cold War ended, all EU neutrals have adapted their neutrality doctrines and reduced them to their essential core—not to join a military alliance. The convergence of views among the EU neutrals around a hollowed-out notion of neutrality was shaped by the new geopolitical realities of post–Cold War Europe. They removed the previously existing matrix of threats and opportunities within which their different neutrality conceptions had flourished. Moreover, the neutrals were influenced by the post–Cold War push and pull factors associated with the EU and NATO. Austria, Finland, Malta, and Sweden followed Ireland's lead and joined the EU. As mentioned previously, all EU neutrals moved into the orbit of NATO by joining the alliance's Partnership for Peace. An important reason for the EU neutrals to align their foreign and security policies with those of the EU and NATO was their desire to ensure a say in post–Cold War European and international security (Ferreira-Pereira 2006).

Ireland joined the EU in 1973 and has been an active participant in EU foreign and security policy ever since. Austria, Finland, and Sweden joined the EU in 1995; Malta did so in 2004. None of the latecomers asked to opt out from the military dimension of the CFSP, nor have they opposed the continuing militarization of the EU since then. However, they reserve their most vocal support for reinforcing the civilian CSDP and do not want the EU to venture any further into the area of collective homeland defense. This issue aside, they are active participants in the CSDP and are members of EDA. Ireland, Finland, Sweden, and Austria are committed to participating in EU Battle Groups, though Austria has found it hard to build the necessary military capabilities. Due to its geographical position, Austria has shown a particular interest in using the CSDP to prevent any spillover of soft security threats such as organized crime and illegal migration from the Western Balkans into the EU. Austria, Sweden, and Finland deployed troops to the first-ever EU military operation in Macedonia in 2003—the peacekeeping force EUFOR Concordia. And while many nonneutral EU countries were reluctant to join France in the military CSDP operation Artemis in the Democratic Republic of Congo in the same year, Sweden volunteered to take part. In 2008, an Irish general was appointed operation commander of the EU humanitarian intervention in Chad/Central African Republic, and Ireland was the second largest troop contributor. Clearly, neither Sweden nor Ireland had any national interests in or security fears related to these theaters of operation in Africa. Their participation in the missions was connected with how they define their identity in international affairs—to be a force for good—and with their wish to strengthen their standing in the EU (see, for example, Matlary 2009: 97).

In addition to the previously mentioned general reasons for the turn to "neutrality-lite," a number of specific factors account for the Euro-neutrals' support of the military CSDP. First, with the establishment of a global liberal order after the end of the Cold War, the idea of military neutrality faced new criticism. Did EU neutrals really want to be neutral in humanitarian interventions when liberal states acted abroad to defend human rights—the rule of law and democracy against their illiberal foes? Second, the EU Treaty does not include a full-fledged collective defense clause, which would be incompatible with neutrality. The Lisbon Treaty obligation to assist fellow EU members that are the victim of armed aggression is tempered by the Irish clause. Advocated by Irish negotiators during the Maastricht Treaty negotiations, it says that the CFSP "shall not prejudice the specific character of the security and defence policy of certain Member States" (Official Journal of the European Union 2010: 39) Hence, EU neutrals are free to show their solidarity with an attacked EU state by other than military means. Third, the neutrals can bank on unanimous EU decisionmaking on virtually all aspects of the CSDP as well as on the option of (constructive) abstention. Hence, they can either block or opt out from any decision that they consider to be incompatible with their neutrality. Fourth, the neutrals have supported the military CSDP because the ESS frames it as a cosmopolitan force, which resonates with their commitment to international peace support missions. Fifth and closely related, neutral backing of the military CSDP has been facilitated by the EU Treaty commitment to deploy EU operations in accordance with the principles of the United Nations Charter. Last but not least, the neutrals see the military CSDP as an opportunity to upload to the EU their own views of the best use of military force in world politics. Just like other EU states, they see CSDP operations as force multipliers that enable their troops to accomplish missions that they couldn't accomplish on their own.

To conclude, Europeanization matters in the CFSP. Common threat perceptions have been constructed and institutionalized at the EU level, as have security policy templates and ways of doing things. EU-level security governance has prompted domestic-level changes, prompting greater cross-national convergence of views, policies, and institutions. Europeanization has resulted in a stronger CSDP. This said, Europeanization in the intergovernmental policy domain of the

CFSP has been considerably weaker than in supranational policy domains such as agriculture. On important foreign policy issues, including the use of force, considerable policy differences persist among EU states. Moreover, the German example shows that de-Europeanization cannot be excluded.

Notes

1. This was the strategic dilemma Europeans faced in 1999 when they decided, in the absence of UN authorization, to support a NATO intervention in Kosovo to stop the interethnic fighting between Kosovars and Serbs.

2. The new collective defense clause in the Lisbon Treaty has not added territorial defense to the brief of the CFSP. See the discussion of the Lisbon Treaty in Chapter 3.

3. Forster calls this model somewhat misleadingly the postneutral model. But its adherents remain committed to neutrality. Also, he argues that Finland and Sweden are adherents of the territorial defense model. However, the military structures and doctrines of both countries have more in common with those of other EU neutrals than with those of the users of the territorial defense model—the camp of former Communist EU states.

4. The Atlanticist NATO member Denmark is the only country that refuses to contribute to the military CSDP. In a protocol attached to the Maastricht Treaty, Denmark was allowed to opt out of those CFSP actions and decisions that have to do with defense.

5. The transition to professional armed forces discussed in Chapter 6 removes one obstacle standing in the way of more robust German military deployments abroad.

6. The natural counterpart of the eastward-looking Central and Eastern European EU states is the southward-looking southern EU countries. They want the EU to step up its political and security engagement in Africa, notably the Maghreb.

7. For instance, in recent years the political atmosphere between Poland and Russia has been influenced by a meat crisis and a plane crash. The Polish meat crisis (2005–2007) erupted when Russia banned Polish meat imports because of alleged low food safety standards. Moscow's ban led to a low point in Polish-Russian relations. Conversely, the empathy shown by the Russian government when the Polish plane carrying President Lech Kaczynski crashed in Russia in 2010 considerably improved the political atmosphere between the two countries.

PART 2

The CSDP in Action

CHAPTER 8

Planning and Conducting CSDP Operations

HOW DOES THE EU GO ABOUT PLANNING, LAUNCHING, commanding, and controlling its CSDP operations? Until the beginning of the new millennium, the EU had no institutional capacity, no standard operating procedures that would enable it to act strategically as an international player capable of mobilizing and projecting power abroad. It lacked what even the smallest EU states possess—a purposive defense organization that, by relying on organizational rules and routines, can define mission objectives and translate them into specific tasks and learn from its performance. Beginning in 2000, the EU built such an organization from scratch and did so at an impressive speed, compared to the snail's pace that often characterizes EU institutional and policy development. The former high representative for the CFSP, Javier Solana, often said half-jokingly that the CSDP was rendered operational at the speed of light. An important factor facilitating the speedy organizational setup of the CSDP was NATO. With the encouragement of the alliance, the EU copied and pasted from its blueprint. Many of the CSDP military bodies, procedures, and doctrines are copied from NATO. There is thus considerable isomorphism between the two organizations. Later, additional drivers started to play a role in shaping the institutional trajectory of the CSDP. As in any organization, they include intraorganizational jostling over competencies, budgets, and staff and lessons learned from CSDP operations. Interestingly, the civilian CSDP, too, has been influenced by NATO. Though less pronounced than in the case of the military

CSDP, the alliance's influence is visible in the use of military termi-
nology and procedures in the planning, command, and control of
civilian missions. This chapter describes the organizational actions,
decision rules, and coordination mechanisms that the EU calls upon
when it sends its troops and civilian advisers on missions abroad.

The Military CSDP

The PSC is at the center of the deployment decision process (see
Figure 8.1). With the assistance of the CSDP bodies of the European
External Action Service, notably the EUMS and the SitCen, the PSC
monitors and analyzes the international situation on a routine basis.
When something out of the ordinary shows up on its radar or is brought
to its attention, it initiates preliminary deliberations. The EUMC and
the CMPD are key players in these deliberations and bring their own
distinct organizational routines and views to the table. Political input is
provided by the high representative and national governments, which
determine how the crisis is framed and what solutions are envisaged. A
key determinant of the discussions is the distribution of preferences
among EU governments. Particularly important is how the EU's key
military powers interpret the situation. Also, it matters whether or not
individual players in the policy system, such as a particular member
state or the high representative, act as policy entrepreneurs who push
the collective deliberations in a particular direction. If at the end of this
phase a consensus emerges among EU states that a military operation is
desirable, then the PSC gives the green light for the launch of the military-strategic planning process (see Figure 8.2).

Based on the guidance offered by the PSC, the Crisis Management
Concept (CMC), an options paper that identifies different political-
strategic scenarios, is drawn up, led by the CMPD. Member states,
especially defense ministries, are consulted at this stage as well as at
every other major juncture in the CSDP planning process. The EUMS
takes care of the military planning involved in drafting the CMC and
is likely to organize a fact-finding mission to the potential theater of
operation in order to facilitate the planning. Each scenario in the
CMC includes a description of the mission objective, the envisioned
military posture and measures, the designation as an autonomous EU
operation or an operation that draws on NATO capabilities under the
Berlin-Plus agreement between the alliance and the EU (see Chapter
12 for details), a risk assessment, and an exit strategy. After the proposals have been evaluated by the EUMC, the PSC forwards them to

Figure 8.1 The Decision Process for Launching
a CSDP Operation (military and civilian)

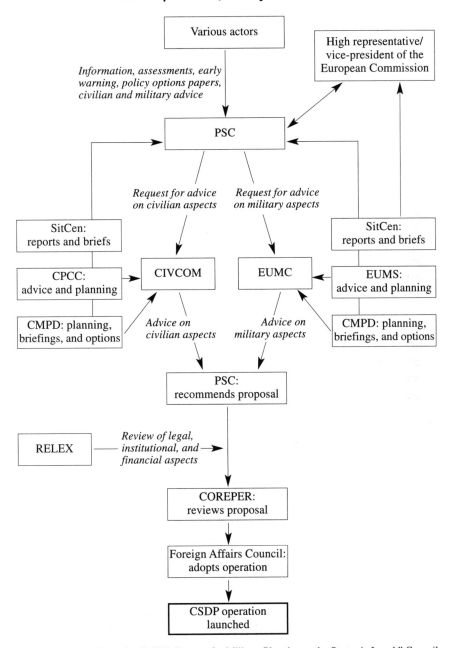

Source: EU Military Staff, "EU Concept for Military Planning at the Strategic Level," Council Document 10687/08, Brussels, 2008.

Figure 8.2 Military Planning Process for CSDP Operations

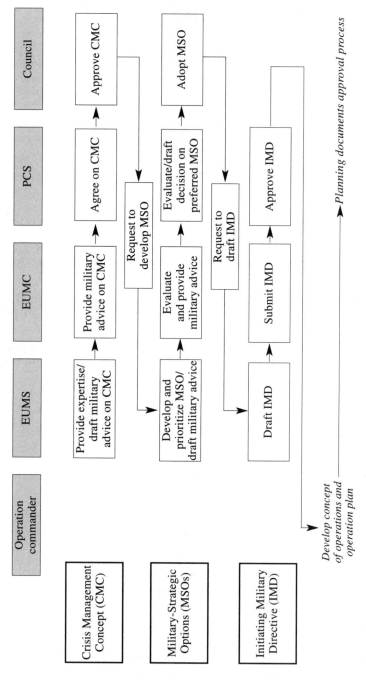

Source: EU Military Staff, "EU Concept for Military Planning at the Political and Strategic Level," Council Document 19687/08, Brussels, 2008, p. 11.

the Council of Ministers together with its own recommendations. On the basis of the CMC selected by the ministers, the EUMS draws up Military-Strategic Options (MSOs). The CMPD remains involved in providing input into and hands-on civilian oversight of the process. With the selection of an MSO by the Foreign Affairs Council, detailed operational planning starts.

In 2007, the EU states took a politically important step to enhance the capacity of the EUMS to plan operations, authorizing it to carry out advance strategic planning without prior authorization by the high representative or the PSC. The decision led to the creation of a small Military Assessment and Planning (MAP) branch, which is authorized to carry out generic and contingency planning on a routine basis—that is, without political intent or political tasking. The rationale of advance planning is that if a crisis becomes politically salient and the EU considers a military response, planners can draw on their preparatory work, which speeds up the actual crisis response planning. So far, however, the EUMS has not been given sufficient staff to carry out meaningful advance planning (Simon 2010).

In the framework of the CSDP, MAP is a controversial issue. Atlanticist EU states such as Britain are concerned that an advance planning capability reduces the control of governments over the CSDP planning process and, ultimately, the deployment of operations. The worry is that a powerful MAP capacity creates political pressure for military action later in the policy process. If the EU produced contingency plans for international crises on a routine basis, this might give additional ammunition to those inside and outside the EU who wish to see it take military action.

The EUMS translates the MSO into the Initiating Military Directive for the designated operation commander, who is the overall military commander of the EU force. The EU has three options with regard to the choice of operation commander and his OHQ (see Box 8.1). First, in a CSDP operation run under the Berlin-Plus agreement, the OHQ is provided by NATO's Supreme Headquarters Allied Powers Europe (SHAPE). The alliance's deputy supreme allied commander Europe, who is always a European officer, is the operation commander. In his capacity as CSDP commander, the deputy commander reports to the PSC and the EUMC, not to NATO.[1] Second, a CSDP operation may be run by a framework or lead nation. Five EU states—Britain, France, Germany, Italy, and Greece—have designated national OHQs for this purpose, which are capable of planning, commanding, and controlling military CSDP operations in accordance with EU standards and proce-

---

Box 8.1 CSDP Command Options

The EU has three command options for military CSDP operations. For each operation, the Council of Ministers chooses one of the following options:

1. CSDP operations may be run with the help of NATO planning, command, and control capabilities, and possibly other alliance assets (Berlin-Plus operations). The OHQ for such operations is provided by NATO's SHAPE.

2. Autonomous CSDP operations may be run by a framework or lead nation, which takes charge of mission planning, command, and control. Five EU states have offered OHQs: Britain, France, Germany, Greece, and Italy.

3. Autonomous CSDP operations may be run by the EU Operations Center within the EUMS. The OHQ can be activated and augmented on short notice.

---

dures. The operation commander is likely to hail from the framework nation but this is not a requirement. For instance, EUFOR Chad/Central African Republic was led by an Irish general in command of a French OHQ. Finally, when the operation is directed by the staff of the EU Operations Center, which so far has not happened, any member state may in principle offer to provide the operation commander.

The Initiating Military Directive provides the operation commander and his planning staff with the strategic parameters within which they draw up the Concept of Operations (CONOPS). Expressing the intent of the commander, the CONOPS details the objectives of the operation, the strategy to be pursued, mission support, and other relevant strategic-level aspects of the operation. The EUMS contributes to the development of the CONOPS. Once the technical work on the document is completed, it is vetted by the EUMC and the PSC before being submitted to the Council of Ministers. After the latter approves the CONOPS, it formally invites third countries to take part in the operation. In case of a Berlin-Plus operation, such an invitation has to be extended to non-EU European NATO members.

The adoption of the CONOPS sets the stage for the launch of a number of nearly parallel actions. To begin with, a Force Generation Conference is convened in which EU states and invited third states confirm their national contributions, which they indicated earlier in informal force contribution meetings. The Lisbon Treaty codified the practice that not every EU state always participates in CSDP operations (military and civilian) but authorized the EU to entrust the execution of missions to coalitions of willing EU states. In addition to organizing a Force Generation Conference, the EU sets up a Committee of Contributors whose members are given the opportunity to contribute to the finalization of the operational planning. If it wishes to draw on NATO means, the EU has to make an official request to the alliance. If it is accepted, a joint meeting of the PSC and NATO's North Atlantic Council specifies the conditions for the use of the borrowed capabilities and assets and for their monitoring and recall (European Council 2000; Oakes 2001). Last but not least, at a technical level the adoption of the CONOPS triggers work on the strategic aspects of the Operation Plan, which further concretizes the CONOPS. This task, too, is carried out by the operation commander. All nations contributing to the EU force are entitled to provide input into the process. The CSDP operation is formally launched by the adoption of an action by the Council of Ministers. In making the decision, the ministers act unanimously, with the possibility of (constructive) abstention.

The force commander is in charge of the troops on the ground and further elaborates the Operation Plan (OPLAN), transposing the CONOPS to the tactical level and allowing him to put his own stamp on the operation. For instance, the first force commander of EUFOR Althea in Bosnia, British general David Leakey, chose to make the fight against organized crime in the country one of his operational priorities.

The force commander reports to the operation commander, who reports to the EUMC, which advises the PSC. Under the authority of the Council of Ministers and the high representative, the PSC exercises political control and strategic direction of all operations. It is on the PSC's recommendation that the Council of Ministers extends an operation, changes its mandate, or terminates it. Through the Committee of Contributors, non-EU states can ensure that their operational concerns about in-theater developments are taken into account by the PSC (European Council 2000). In case a CSDP operation draws on NATO capabilities under the Berlin-Plus agreement, the PSC regularly informs the North Atlantic Council about the operation. The EUMS ensures the smooth exchange of information and coordination on operational matters between the EU and the alliance. Through the EU Cell at SHAPE, the EUMS works with its European NATO colleagues who are in the chain of command of the CSDP operation. This operational interface is facilitated by the NATO Liaison Team, which is permanently located in the EUMS.

The Civilian CSDP

The planning, launch, command, and control of civilian CSDP missions mirror those of military missions in most ways (see Figure 8.1). One big difference is that there is no civilian equivalent to the Berlin-Plus agreement and, more generally, to the complicated EU-NATO relationship, which facilitates and depoliticizes the civilian CSDP decision process. The planning of civilian missions follows the same iterative process as in the military field. The CMC, Civilian Strategic Option, which is the civilian equivalent of the MSO, and CONOPS—in this order—are drawn up by the CPCC and the CMPD. The division of labor between them mirrors that between the CMPD and the EUMS in the military decision process. In a modification of the military process, the OPLAN of civilian missions is elaborated by the designated head of mission—that is, by the civilian equivalent of the military force commander rather than by the operation commander. In this task, the head of mission is assisted by the CPCC. Just as in the military decision process, each of the civilian planning documents is evaluated by the PSC. To this end, it relies on the expertise of CIVCOM. All major decisions are formally taken by the Council of Ministers. Unlike military operations, civilian missions are financed from the CFSP budget, which is managed by the European Commission. This makes the Commission an important player in the deliberations about the mandates of civilian missions, their activities, and termination (see Chapter 4). As to the conduct of civilian missions, the heads of mission report to the head of the CPCC, who acts as their operation commander. As such, she or he is responsible for the strategic-level aspects of the mission. The CPCC provides mission support, assisting the mission leadership on issues ranging from medical evacuation provisions to procurement, recruitment, and budgeting. Just as in military operations, the PSC exercises political control and strategic direction of all civilian deployments.

To conclude, an elaborate array of Brussels-based bodies is involved in the process of planning, launching, and running CSDP missions. However, EU states remain the gatekeepers. Especially when it comes to military operations, the EU's military powerhouses are the key players. Their interests and concerns overlay the Brussels-based process. Without their expertise, troops, capabilities, and assets, the EU cannot launch any serious military operation. Big EU states intervene in the CSDP policy process through their PSC representatives, by lobbying the high representative or, if neither of these channels of influence yields satisfactory results, through a political intervention in the

Council of Ministers. When it comes to civilian missions, the high representative, the Brussels-based CSDP structures, and the smaller EU states have more leeway in influencing deployment decisions (see Chapter 11). Finally, both the military and civilian CSDP decision processes are characterized by a dearth of institutional access points for civil society actors and independent experts. This contributes to the democratic deficit of the CSDP while narrowing the knowledge base on which the planning and conduct of CSDP missions rely.

Note

1. However, he keeps NATO fully informed of all mission-related developments.

CHAPTER 9

EU Operations in Europe and the Middle East

SINCE THE INCEPTION OF THE CSDP, THE EU HAS DEPLOYED twenty-one operations (military and civilian). All have been stabilization and reconstruction operations that were deployed with the consent of the host country. This and the following chapter survey these operations. This chapter looks at the ten CSDP deployments in Europe and the Middle East.[1] For each operation, a brief background is provided on the crisis or conflict that prompted the CSDP deployment. Also discussed are the main reasons for each deployment, its basic objectives, the obstacles encountered by it, and its achievements. Some salient facts emerge from this survey. First, all operations have operated in permissive environments. Second, the military operation in Bosnia and the civilian operation in Kosovo have been the largest ever EU military and civilian operations, while the rule-of-law operation in Georgia was one of the smallest CSDP operations. The two military CSDP operations covered by this chapter have been Berlin-Plus operations—the EU planned, equipped, and commanded them with the help of NATO.

The impact of the missions on the ground has been uneven. In Bosnia and Kosovo, the CSDP has been a major contributor to international peace- and state-building. In most other theaters of operation in Europe and the Middle East, the symbolism of planting the CSDP flag in foreign soil has overshadowed the impact on conflict resolution and the promotion of good governance.

Operations in the Western Balkans

EU policy toward the Western Balkans has made full use of both supranational and intergovernmental tools. The key tools are the intergovernmental CSDP operations and the supranational enlargement policy (Merlingen forthcoming-b). The EU has committed itself to granting EU membership to all Western Balkan countries if and when they meet the EU accession conditions related to democracy, free markets, and national administrative capacity. The reasons for Brussels' heavy involvement in the region are twofold. First, the Western Balkans are a crucial test case for the credibility of EU foreign policy. If the EU fails to bring stability, peace, and prosperity to its immediate neighborhood, its reputation as a serious foreign policy actor will suffer a serious blow. Second, stability in the Western Balkans is crucial for the internal security of the EU. Civil wars, regional conflicts, failing states, and organized crime in the Western Balkans inevitably pose serious security problems for the EU. When Yugoslavia began to disintegrate in the early 1990s, the EU was full of expectations that this would be its hour. All the more profound was the political frustration that followed its failure to first prevent and then stop ethnic fighting in Croatia and Bosnia. While Europe was revealed as an emperor without clothes, its failure also created soft security threats for the EU, because organized crime could take root and spread in the anarchic environment of the former Yugoslavia. In addition, huge refugee inflows from the region taxed the labor markets and welfare systems of EU states such as Germany and Austria. Just over a decade after the implosion of Yugoslavia, the EU deployed its first-ever CSDP mission to the region. Its theater of operation was Bosnia. In short order, the mission was followed by CSDP deployments in Macedonia and Kosovo. The European Commission started (preparatory) negotiations with all countries of the region about their eventual accession to the EU. Within about fifteen years, Brussels had succeeded in turning the newly independent states of the former Yugoslavia from security liabilities and threats into prospective member states.

The CSDP operations have contributed considerably to this success story. They have kept peace in the region, which until recently was characterized by high levels of volatility rooted in interethnic and border conflicts. The security sector reforms carried out by the operations have improved public security and protected the EU against soft security threats such as organized crime and human trafficking. They have given Brussels additional leverage to guide the countries on the road to EU membership and have repaired the EU's reputation in the region, which was tarnished in the 1990s. Yet the missions had their fair share of problems, which hampered their impact.

The EU Police Mission in Bosnia (EUPM), January 2003–

The Bosnian secession from Yugoslavia in the early 1990s engendered the bloodiest conflict of all the conflicts generated by the violent disintegration of Yugoslavia. The three-year civil war (1992–1995) involved massive human rights violations, including widespread ethnic cleansing. The war, in which the police acted as an instrument of ethnic repression, was brought to an end by a US-led NATO air campaign. The 1995 General Framework Agreement for Peace in Bosnia and Herzegovina established an internationally supervised power-sharing arrangement among the three major Bosnian peoples—Bosniaks, Croats, and Serbs. To oversee the transition to democracy, the accords established the Office of the High Representative. The United Nations was asked to establish an International Police Task Force and to build a professional and democratic Bosnian police. While the UN police officers had achieved much by the time their mandate expired at the end of 2002, the international community felt that the Bosnian police needed further international control and guidance. The EU volunteered to take over from the United Nations.

The EUPM, launched in January 2003, had 540 internationals at its peak. It remains in Bosnia even though the country has enjoyed stable peace for a considerable period of time. The EUPM is tasked to reform the local police in accordance with best European and international practices. Police advisers assist locals in building a democratic, accountable, and effective law enforcement service. In its first three years of operation, the mission pursued a wide range of reforms. It ran seven capacity-building programs, comprising about 120 reform projects, which ranged from the introduction of new internal supervisory mechanisms that deal with police misconduct to the reorganization of how the Bosnian police conducts criminal investigations (Merlingen with Ostrauskaitė 2006; Mühlmann 2008). Many EUPM projects were funded by the European Commission. After 2005, the mission mandate zeroed in on two main objectives. First, the EUPM supported the centralization of the highly fragmented Bosnian police system. Success was limited because the country's quarreling ethnicities were caught in a political deadlock over how to proceed with the reforms. Second, to enhance the local capacity to combat organized crime, the mission tackled police-prosecutor relations, which were characterized by distrust and a lack of coordination that benefitted criminals. Not only did the EUPM help to build better police-prosecutor relations, it supervised the exercise of political authority over the police and the conduct of officers during crime-busting operations. Police corruption, misconduct, and political interference in operational policing decisions have been among the factors hampering the fight against organized crime. After 2009, the mandate emphasized the fight against corruption and organized crime.

The EUPM has experienced a number of internal challenges in its planning, start-up, and implementation phases. For instance, the final delivery of office computers for mission staff only arrived about a year into the mandate. Also, on more than a few occasions, EU police officers have lacked the experience and qualifications for advising local police leaders and managers. An important challenge initially faced by the mission was the narrow focus of its mandate. The EUPM's lack of powers in relation to the judiciary hampered its police reforms. This was partly rectified when its mandate was extended to include police-prosecutor relations among its reform priorities. The mission's main external challenge has been the legacy of the Dayton Peace Agreement, which saddled the country with a weak central state. Government functions, including law enforcement, are decentralized and ethnically divided. Organized crime can freely operate across the country, while law enforcement is hampered by jurisdictional and ethnic boundaries. Also, the persistent ethnic polarization fuels political interference in operational policing decisions. These problems hamper policing effectiveness, especially in relation to organized crime. This said, the Bosnian police force has come a long way since the days of the civil war, and the EUPM has played an important role in this development. Among other things, it has succeeded in making the local police more accountable (for example, by setting up, training, and mentoring internal control units that investigate police misconduct), in professionalizing police training (for example, through curriculum development), and in implanting modern human resource management in the Bosnian police apparatus (for example, by elaborating a gender- and ethnicity-blind recruitment and promotion system) (Juncos 2007; Merlingen 2009; for a critical perspective, see Merlingen and Ostrauskaitė 2005b).

The EU Military Operation in Bosnia (EUFOR Althea), December 2004–

In the wake of the Dayton peace deal, the United Nations authorized the deployment of a NATO-led peacekeeping force to Bosnia. Under Chapter 7 of the United Nations Charter, the 60,000-strong

Implementation Force was tasked to oversee the separation of Bosniak-Croat and Serb forces and their partial demobilization. Also, it was in charge of securing a zone of separation around the interethnic boundary line that cut the country into two. After one year, the Implementation Force was reduced to about 30,000 troops and renamed the Stabilisation Force, which stepped up second-generation peacekeeping activities such as providing security to returnees and tracking down and arresting war crimes suspects. As the security situation in Bosnia further improved, the Stabilisation Force was gradually reduced to 7,000 troops. In December 2004, EUFOR Althea took over the peacekeeping tasks from the Stabilisation Force, as authorized by the United Nations. Most EUFOR personnel previously served in the Stabilisation Force and merely changed the insignia on their uniforms on the day of the handover from NATO to the EU (Bertin 2008).

Starting out with 7,000 troops, EUFOR Althea is the largest ever military CSDP operation and has relied on NATO capabilities and assets under the Berlin-Plus agreement (on Berlin-Plus, see Chapter 12). The transition from the Stabilisation Force to EUFOR was relatively smooth, because EU military planners benefited from NATO's extensive experience on the ground. Also, the capabilities and assets the EU wanted to borrow from NATO were already in place. Cooperation between the two sides has been good ever since. Altogether, thirty-three countries contributed to Althea when it was deployed. Denmark, Cyprus, and Malta are the only EU states that have not participated in the force.

Althea's main function is to ensure a safe and secure environment in Bosnia. Initially, EUFOR focused on deterring possible spoilers of the Dayton Peace Agreement, notably the ethnically and institutionally divided armed forces. Another key focus of EUFOR activities was compellence—the initiation of military action (peaceful or violent) in an attempt to stop adversaries from continuing to engage in undesirable action (Art 2007). The first force commander used his troops proactively and at a high operational tempo, aiming to disrupt the local networks that obstructed the efforts of the international community to bring to justice individuals indicted by the Yugoslav war crimes tribunal. For instance, early on in its deployment, EUFOR conducted a large-scale operation to seize control of all underground military facilities in the country where war crimes fugitives hid (Bertin 2008). Also, the commanding general adopted a forceful approach to combating organized crime. Organized crime was linked to the support networks of indicted war criminals. Interpreting his mandate liberally, the general drew on EUFOR's own armed police force and regular troops to carry out country-wide operations against organized crime. Often he did not bother to inform either the local police or the EUPM, which resulted in confusion both in the EU family and among Bosnian authorities over who was in charge of improving local law enforcement. Also, it created bad blood between Althea and the EUPM. The latter complained that the "executive" approach of the military undermined its capacity-building approach based on local ownership. The disagreement was papered over, and Brussels designated the EUPM as the lead actor on the issue of combating organized crime.

By 2006, Althea's deterrence and compellence functions had become obsolete. The national defense reform at the end of 2005 established unified, democratically controlled armed forces. Responding to the evolving situation on the ground, the EU gradually reduced Althea to around 2,000 troops. The slimmed-down EUFOR has strengthened its reassurance function, mainly through the Liaison Observation Teams, which consist of small groups of soldiers who live and immerse themselves in local communities. They are used throughout Bosnia to build close relationships with locals and to reassure them that the EU will not allow a return to conflict. By 2008, even the new focus on reassurance seemed strangely out of sync, because the country had been peaceful for a considerable time. Yet encouraged by the United States, the EU soldiered on. In 2010, the EU reinforced Althea's contribution to the training of the Bosnian armed forces. Mobile Althea teams support training in areas such as medical evacuation, information systems, leadership, and weapons handling.

EUFOR operations have been complicated by national caveats. Because governments only "lend" their troops to the EU, they retain the power to exempt them from certain types of operational activities or roles. For instance, some member states did not allow the first force commander to use their soldiers for crime-busting operations. Others have objected to their contingents being included in Althea's tactical reserve force, which is designated to reinforce NATO troops in Kosovo in case of an emergency.

Althea was billed by Brussels as a "make it or break it" operation. Clearly, Althea has made it. Hiccups notwithstanding, it has demonstrated that the EU can successfully run a sizeable peacekeeping operation. Philip Gordon (2002: 92) said of the Balkans that they "arguably saved NATO from obsolescence in the 1990s." The region has played a similar role in the new millennium in keeping alive the EU's aspirations to become a serious military security provider.

The EU Military Operation in Macedonia
(EUFOR Concordia), March–December 2003

Unlike Bosnia and Croatia, the separation of Macedonia from Yugoslavia proceeded peacefully, but relations between the Slav-Macedonian majority and the ethnic Albanian minority subsequently deteriorated. Macedonian Albanians were underrepresented in the public sector and discriminated against in the fields of culture, education, and language (Brown 2000). When civil war broke out in neighboring Kosovo, Macedonian Albanians were radicalized. Kosovo Albanian refugees, fighters, and weapons streamed into Macedonia, and the resulting turmoil pushed the country into violence. Ethnic fighting broke out between government forces and the Macedonian Albanian National Liberation Army. Full-scale civil war was prevented by a joint NATO and EU diplomatic intervention. Under international pressure, the Slav Macedonians agreed to a peace deal, which gave the Albanian minority more rights and autonomy.

The Ohrid Framework Agreement, signed in August 2001, called for the voluntary disarmament and disbandment of the National Liberation Army. When NATO was asked to assist in this process, it deployed a 3,500-strong force code-named Essential Harvest. For thirty days the mostly European troops collected and destroyed the weapons handed over by the National Liberation Army. The alliance's follow-up operation—the German-led Amber Fox—was considerably smaller, with about 700 soldiers tasked to provide protection to international monitors. The latter monitored whether the Slav-dominated police force conducted itself properly as it reentered the Kosovo-Albanian villages from which it had withdrawn during the crisis. As the security situation in the country improved, the task force was reduced to 450 troops at the end of 2002. The renamed Allied Harmony monitored the former crisis area and advised the government on defense-related security sector reform. On 31 March, EUFOR Concordia took over the monitoring tasks from NATO.

Concordia was the first-ever EU military operation. All member states, except Denmark and neutral Ireland, took part, and fourteen non-EU states participated. It had the same number of troops as Allied Harmony. EUFOR could easily have been launched without recourse to NATO assets, and France had called for an autonomous CSDP mission. However, Atlanticist EU members and Germany insisted, for political rather than operational reasons, that the EU force be run in cooperation with NATO under the Berlin-Plus agreement. They wanted to signal to Washington that the CSDP was a supplement to NATO and not an ersatz alliance. Their view prevailed. Cooperation between Concordia and NATO was smooth, both during the transition from NATO to EUFOR troops and once Concordia was up and running.

EUFOR was tasked, initially for six months, to contribute to a stable and secure environment, and Concordia deployed Field Liaison Teams to patrol the former crisis area (Mace 2003).The operation was extended for three months until the end of December, which allowed for an uninterrupted transition from Concordia to the CSDP follow-up EU police mission (EUPOL) Proxima. EUFOR's significance was related less to its impact on the ground than to its symbolism. Concordia signaled to EU and international audiences that Brussels was finally ready to take on military security tasks. The EU peace-keeping force mattered because it was a successful test of the military CSDP and the Berlin-Plus procedures. The force's small size and the permissive environment made this an easy test.

The EU Police Mission in Macedonia (EUPOL Proxima), December 2003–December 2005

Police reforms were a central plank of the 2001 Ohrid peace accord. The Slav-dominated police had a record of misconduct, and its violence often targeted the Albanian minority (Abrahams 1998). Together with other international actors, the EU was asked to assist the country in modernizing its law enforcement. The EU thus deployed its second CSDP police mission.

EUPOL Proxima had a one-year mandate to contribute to the consolidation of law and order, the reform of the Ministry of Interior, the development of a civilian border police, and confidence-building measures between the police and the Albanian minority. Proxima's difficulties in the start-up phase mirrored those of the EUPM. For instance, three months into the mandate, some of the field offices still had not received basic office equipment. Yet the mission also had to struggle with challenges of its own making. In view of the short mandate, the mission leadership initially decided against a project-driven reform strategy. However, the resulting absence of a strategic focus threatened the achievement of the mandate. Also, personal frictions undermined the effectiveness of the mission. Relations between the head of Proxima, on the one hand, and the EUSR and the head of the EU embassy, on the other, were bad, with little coordination between them. Under pressure from Brussels, the mission was reengineered and established five reform programs, which together comprised twenty-eight projects (Merlingen with Ostrauskaitė 2006). They ranged from workshops to detect forged travel documents to policing manuals on the investigation of human trafficking. One innovative program was about law enforcement monitoring, which was designed to stretch the terms of the mission mandate to take account of the functional linkages between policing and the broader criminal justice system. Legal experts advised the government on how to improve the legal and procedural framework for police-prosecutor cooperation and organized workshops on how to facilitate the exchange of information and cooperation. Although the programmatic approach reinvigorated the mission, it came too late. Proxima only had six months to implement its reform projects, which was not long enough to have an impact on Macedonian law enforcement. To save the mission from failure, the EU Council decided to prolong it for one more year.

Proxima 1 (December 2003–December 2004), with a staff of about 180 international police officers, was deployed in more than twenty locations in the northwest of the country, where ethnic clashes had occurred. The follow-up operation Proxima 2 had its personnel strength cut to about 120 and was rolled out throughout the country. To make ends meet, the operation's new leadership was asked by Brussels to reduce the reform programs to three. The projects were for the most part a continuation of the uncompleted activities of Proxima 1.[2]

Proxima (1 and 2) had some success. For instance, it improved the accountability of police officers to citizens and upgraded the interface between law enforcement and the judiciary (Flessenkemper 2008; Ioannides 2007). In general, however, the mission was more about symbolic and intra-EU politics than about making a difference on the ground. Deployed about two and a half years after the Ohrid peace deal had been signed, numerous international actors in the meantime had successfully engaged the local police in reforms, and there was no real need for yet another police aid donor descending on the country (Merlingen and Ostrauskaitė 2005a). Yet the EU Council decided to maintain a CSDP presence in the country after EUFOR Concordia was terminated. On the one hand, it wanted to underline the EU's continuing political commitment to Macedonia. On the other hand, it wanted to signal to the European Commission that it intended to take a broad view of civilian crisis management. It staked out a large policy space for the CSDP on what the Commission has traditionally considered its turf.

The EU Rule of Law Mission in Kosovo
(EULEX Kosovo), December 2008–

Kosovo is a poverty-stricken corner of Europe mainly populated by ethnic Albanians. In 1989, the Yugoslav government abolished the limited autonomy the province had previously enjoyed. Martial law was proclaimed, but, instead of quelling ethnic unrest, this move fueled it. Within a few years, Serb security forces and the Kosovo Liberation Army battled each other. At the beginning of 1999, an international conference was held in Rambouillet, France, to find a peaceful settlement. The conference ended in deadlock, which the West blamed on the intransigence of the Serb participants. To stop the continuing bloody repression of Kosovars by Serb forces, NATO began bombing Serb targets in the province as well as in Montenegro and Serbia proper. After an air campaign of about two and a half months, operation Allied Force achieved its objective. Serb president Slobodan Milošević agreed to withdraw his military forces from the province. In June 1999, UN Security Council Resolution 1244 transformed Kosovo into an international protectorate, although it explicitly upheld Yugoslavia's "territorial integrity." The UN Mission in Kosovo was, among other things, responsible for the justice sector, including policing. About 50,000 NATO-led peacekeepers (Kosovo Force) took charge of establishing a safe environment.

In 2006, the UN Secretary-General appointed a special envoy to find a solution to the future status of Kosovo. Within a year, former Finnish president Martti Ahtisaari introduced a proposal to grant Kosovo independence. It provided a detailed road map on how to achieve it, included the establishment of an international civilian representative in charge of implementing the transition to independence, and referred to the deployment of a CSDP rule-of-law mission. However, Ahtisaari's proposal was rejected by Belgrade, and international mediation aimed at overcoming the deadlock between Serbia and Kosovo failed. In February 2008, Kosovo unilaterally declared its independence and was recognized by the United States, the majority of EU members, and assorted other countries. The EU states Cyprus, Greece, Romania, Slovakia, and Spain did not recognize Kosovo because they did not want to encourage or embolden separatist movements in their own countries. Although EU governments failed to agree on a common position on Kosovo's independence, they did agree to dispatch a CSDP rule-of-law mission to the country. Failure to do so might have resulted in a mission composed of a coalition of willing EU states led by the

United States (Koeth 2010), which would have been a severe blow to the newly established credibility of the CFSP. Also, the EU appointed a EUSR for Kosovo, who was later double-hatted as the international civilian representative by pro-independence Western countries. The mandate of the CSDP mission mirrors Ahtisaari's recommendations.

In 2010 the International Court of Justice issued a nonbinding ruling that declared that Kosovo's unilateral declaration of independence did not violate international law as Serbia and its international supporters had claimed. Both Belgrade and Moscow rejected the judgment and reiterated that they would not recognize the country. Kosovo's contested status is, and likely will remain, the major challenge facing the mission.

Although elements of EULEX Kosovo were deployed in June 2008, mandate implementation was delayed until the end of the year when the mission finally acquired initial operational capability. The delay was primarily due to two reasons, both having to do with Kosovo's contested statehood. First, with Resolution 1244 still in force, the United Nations was forced to reconfigure its presence in Kosovo rather than leave it, which complicated the handover of its equipment, premises, police cases, and legal files to EULEX. Second, Serbia and Russia insisted that the mission be status neutral, that is, that it refrain from taking any position on whether Kosovo was to remain a province of Serbia or become a sovereign country. The EU agreed with the United Nations that it would "operate under the overall authority and within the status-neutral framework of the United Nations" (Council of the European Union 2008a; United Nations Security Council 2008: 11).

EULEX is the largest civilian CSDP mission and has an authorized strength of nearly 2,000 internationals and 1,200 locals. Like other civilian CSDP missions, it has experienced problems in filling the authorized international posts. The first civilian operation with executive competencies, it has the power to run independent police investigations, to conduct trials, and to annul decisions taken by local authorities. Last but not least, it is the first CSDP mission with US participation. In early 2007, an informal deal was struck between Brussels and Washington to have US personnel serve in EULEX, while Brussels agreed to deploy a CSDP police mission to Afghanistan. About eighty US police officers, judges, and prosecutors joined EULEX. Many previously served in the UN mission in Kosovo.

The integrated rule-of-law mission EULEX is tasked to construct an independent and multiethnic justice and law enforcement system in Kosovo. It has three main components—police, justice, and customs. The police component is the largest. In addition to general police development work, EULEX police investigate war crimes, corruption, and financial crimes, especially money laundering. Mission justice experts are involved in drafting legislation prior to their submission to the Kosovo Assembly and provide comments on draft laws. EULEX judges and prosecutors took over cases from the UN mission in Kosovo, including on war crimes, organized crime, and corruption. Case management is handled jointly with local judges and prosecutors. The customs component, which focuses on monitoring and advising activities, is the one least involved in executive tasks.

The mission has faced some of the usual CSDP management problems. There were significant procurement delays due to the slow Commission process of approving tender files, while the mission has struggled to recruit and retain sufficient qualified personnel. Also, the task of coordinating its activities on the ground with those of the other members of the EU family (the EUSR and the EU embassy) and the many international actors has proven taxing. Yet the main challenge for EULEX is without doubt Kosovo itself. The country is likely to remain an EU protectorate for the foreseeable future. Challenges abound. For one, Kosovo remains awash in weapons, and the government in Priština has limited authority over the rule-of-law sector in the Serb-dominated North Kosovo. Crime throughout the country is rampant, especially money laundering, corruption, and human trafficking (European Commission 2008a, 2009). As in other former Yugoslav territories, political interference in operational policing decisions is common, and the justice system is regarded by the international community as the weakest of all of Kosovo's institutions (International Crisis Group 2010; Organisation for Security and Cooperation in Europe 2008). For instance, in 2008 the overstretched court system had a backlog of nearly 40,000 criminal cases, while the backlog of civil cases, many of which are related to property claims, was even larger.

Arguably the main long-term challenge for the mission will be to handle the different expectations addressed to EULEX by Serbs and Kosovars and the lack of a coherent EU position on Kosovo. For the Serbs, EULEX is there to protect endangered ethnic Serbian communities in a Serbian province. For the Kosovars, the mission is to help the Kosovo government build a functioning sovereign state. Reflecting these different expectations, the mission juggles with contradictory objectives. On the one hand, its mandate is to help build a viable, effective, and democratic justice and customs system in Kosovo. On the other hand, it is committed to being status neutral, which is ultimately incompatible with its state-building tasks. How the mission deals with the divergent public expectations and mission objectives will have a crucial impact on mandate implementation and mission impact. Yet the mission's room for maneuver is limited as long as EU states fail to develop a coherent strategy toward Kosovo. The stakes are high. As the ESS puts it, the EU's credibility as a foreign policy actor depends on the consolidation of its achievements in the Western Balkans.

The CSDP in Georgia

Throughout the 1990s and the beginning of the new millennium, EU involvement in Georgia was low-key. Financial and technical assistance to Georgia and its neighbors in the Southern Caucasus was limited compared to the largesse displayed in the Western Balkans. Although the region was initially not included in the plans for the European Neighbourhood Policy, by 2003–2004, the EU had become visibly more active, and the Southern Caucasus was incorporated into its Neighbourhood Policy. An EUSR for the region was appointed and a CSDP mission was dispatched to Georgia.

The EU Rule of Law Mission in Georgia (EUJUST Themis), July 2004–July 2005

In the wake of the breakup of the multiethnic Soviet empire, Georgia regained its independence in 1991, but failed to complete the transition to democracy and capitalism. There was widespread corruption and poverty. After rigged parliamentary elections, mass demonstrations forced the incumbent president out of office in 2003. In the wake of the Rose Revolution, new presidential and parliamentary elections were held and brought to power a pronounced pro-Western president—Mikhail Saakashvili. This was an opportunity for the West to limit lingering Russian influence in the country and to place it firmly in the Western zone of influence. Georgia has considerable geostrategic importance. Because the country borders Russia, it is an important asset in any Western contingency plans for containing a resurgent Russia. Furthermore, it is an East-West energy corridor. Oil and gas from Azerbaijan and, potentially in the future, from Central Asia can be pumped through Georgia to the EU without going through Russia. Against this background, US and European advisers, consultants, and NGO personnel flocked to the country to rebuild the state along the lines of a market democracy based on the rule of law. Particular attention was paid to the modernization of the country's armed forces and justice and home affairs.

At the beginning of 2004, Lithuania proposed dispatching a civilian CSDP mission to Georgia to strengthen the rule of law. Other member states responded positively to the initiative, seeing an opportunity to score an easy public relations success for the CSDP. The deployment of the CSDP mission would raise the political salience of the EU in the country. Also, the member states wanted to demonstrate that the CSDP was more than a Western Balkans crisis manager and could do more than police reforms. This broad consensus notwithstanding, mission planning was characterized by bureaucratic politics and its associated power games (Kurowska 2008). Although the European Commission agreed with the Council that the EU should reinforce its activities in Georgia, it wanted to expand ongoing Commission programs and thus opposed the launch of a CSDP mission. The member states decided to ignore these objections. However, in the deliberations about the mission mandate that followed, the Commission was able to mobilize its structural power as CFSP budget manager and succeeded in overruling CSDP mission planners and in excluding penitentiary reforms from the mission mandate. (For more on the Commission's purse power in CSDP policymaking, see Chapter 4.) The Commission was bent on preserving its policy leadership in this issue area, even at the expense of the overall EU impact on Georgia's justice system.

EUJUST Themis, which had a one-year mandate, was the first-ever CSDP deployment in post-Soviet space and the first-ever CSDP rule-of-law mission. Eight rule-of law advisers, colocated with Georgian authorities, were tasked to assist the locals in evaluating the justice system, in drafting a criminal justice reform strategy, and in elaborating an implementation plan. The advisers had to accomplish their assignment in an institutionally difficult environment, because the Saakashvili administration launched a massive purge of personnel associated with the old regime, including judges and prosecutors. At the same time, US and EU advisers vied for influence on how to restructure the justice system. Given their divergent legal cultures and philosophies, they frequently gave conflicting advice to their Georgian interlocutors (Helly 2006). Last but not least, the fact that penitentiary reforms were excluded from the brief of the operation hampered the development of a coherent criminal justice reform plan. In view of these internal and external challenges, Themis did reasonably well. For one, it drafted a criminal justice reform strategy that was accepted by Tbilisi. However, the operation ran out of time and left the elaboration of a plan on how to implement the strategy to the EU embassy and the Office of the EUSR for the Southern Caucasus.

Themis had few resources and little time to meet its objectives. It was not designed to maximize the EU's impact on the judicial reforms of the new government in Tbilisi. EU states left the inevitably lengthy process of capacity-building to the Commission-run European Neighbourhood Policy. Nor was the mission designed to maximize the EU's political influence in a geopolitically important country. The small size of the mission ensured that Brussels's political sway over Tbilisi remained limited compared to that of Washington. The EU's Georgia policy was further hampered by the fact that some EU states were less supportive of Georgia's pro-Western policies than was the United States. Countries such as Germany and France balanced their support for Georgia with efforts not to antagonize Russia, which has regarded Georgia's integration into Euro-Atlantic structures as a threat to its security.

The EU Monitoring Mission in Georgia (EUMM Georgia), October 2008–

During Soviet times, two ethnic minorities living on Georgian territory enjoyed autonomous status. In 1991, the South Ossetians and Abkhaz refused to be incorporated into the newly sovereign Georgia, and civil war ensued. Russia brokered an end to the fighting between Tbilisi and the secessionists and agreed to deploy peacekeepers to South Ossetia and Abkhazia. The territorial conflicts were "frozen," and there was no real progress toward a peaceful resolution. At the beginning of August 2008, the Saakashvili administration ordered its troops to retake South Ossetia by force. Moscow's response was harsh. It pushed Georgian troops out of South Ossetia and then expanded the war into Georgia proper (Cornell and Starr 2009). At the same time, Abkhaz troops drove out Georgian forces from Abkhazia. As Russia systematically destroyed Georgia's military hardware and infrastructure, the French presidency of the EU intervened. President Sarkozy saw an opportunity to upgrade the geopolitical profile of France and the EU in the region. As the drama unfolded, Washington stood on the sidelines because of the pending presidential elections, which condemned the George W. Bush administration to inaction. Appointing himself as the West's point man for bringing the conflict to an end, Sarkozy successfully brokered a cease-fire between Russia and Georgia. However, Russian troops remained deep within Georgia in a self-declared security zone around South Ossetia and Abkhazia. Moreover, toward the end of August, Moscow officially recognized the self-declared sovereignty of South Ossetia and Abkhazia. At the beginning of September, the EU and Russia agreed that Russian forces would withdraw from the areas adjacent to the breakaway republics within ten days of the deployment of an EU Monitoring Mission (EUMM). The agreement designated the EU as de facto guarantor of the peace in Georgia. Virtually overnight the EU considerably enlarged its geopolitical footprint in Georgia.

The EUMM became operational at the beginning of October 2008 and quickly put about 200 unarmed monitors on the ground. To circumvent lengthy European Commission procurement procedures, EU states dispatched preequipped national teams, which had their own vehicles, communications equipment, and so forth. The mission initially focused on verifying the implementation of the withdrawal of Russian forces from Georgia proper. Once the Russians had, by and large, pulled back into the secessionist territories, the mission focus shifted toward "prevention through monitoring." Through its 24/7 day- and nighttime patrols, the EUMM monitors the freedom and security of movement of civilians to and from the secessionist territories and along the administrative boundary line separating them from Georgia. Also, it pays attention to the humanitarian situation in the conflict area, especially to the treatment of internally displaced persons. In addition, the mission investigates arms movements, shooting incidents, and kidnappings along the boundary line. It facilitates the peaceful resolution of localized problems and intervenes to avoid misunderstandings among the conflict parties. For instance, the EUMM dissuaded the Georgian police from using unmarked armored vehicles in the areas adjacent to the breakaway territories, which could have led to misperceptions and misunderstandings on the part of the secessionist militias, increasing the risk of confrontation across the boundary line. Last but not least, the EUMM has played a central role in the principal conflict-prevention and confidence-building mechanisms established in the wake of the war. It is one of the conveners of the incident prevention and response mechanism set up to deal with the most serious security problems along the boundary lines between Georgia and South Ossetia and is an observer in the same mechanism for the boundary line between Georgia and Abkhazia. Finally, the EUMM staffs the crisis hotlines, which are attached to the mechanisms and through which the parties to the conflict can contact each other in case of serious incidents.

In short, through its activities the EUMM contributes to alleviating the security dilemma between Georgia and the secessionist territories. It contains tensions and reinforces stability. The major challenge it faces is the refusal of South Ossetian and Abkhaz authorities, and their Russian backers, to grant it access to the territory under their control. Hence, it is not able to act on its mandate to monitor the situation on both sides of the administrative boundary line. This is indicative of a more general limitation of the mission and the EU's role in postconflict management in Georgia. Because the mission has no enforcement powers, the EU's influence on the parties to the conflict remains limited. Russia does not appreciate Brussels's nonrecognition policy toward Abkhazia and South Ossetia, and Georgia criticizes the EU for not taking a tougher line on what Tbilisi considers Moscow's illegal occupation of its territory. Divisions among EU states and a lack of sticks and carrots appropriate for the situation have prevented the EUMM and the EU from acting as peacemakers rather than mediators and confidence-builders in Georgia.[3]

The EU Operations in Palestine

The Israeli-Palestinian conflict has been a stumbling block on the road to peace in the Middle East. In the wake of the 1967 Six-Day War, Israel occupied the mostly Palestinian-populated territories of the West Bank, the Gaza Strip, and East Jerusalem. Although the 1993 Oslo peace accords raised hopes for a breakthrough in the Israeli-Palestinian standoff, no permanent peace settlement could be agreed upon. Instead, in 2000 another intifada (Palestinian uprising) began, and Palestinian terrorist attacks against Israelis intensified. So did Israeli extrajudicial killings of Palestinians and military strikes against Palestinian targets. In response to the worsening security situation, the Middle East Quartet (the United States, UN, EU, and Russia) proposed the Road Map to Peace in 2003. It asked the Palestinian Authority—the government of the Palestinians—to stop the violence and to carry out fundamental democratic political reforms in return for a two-state solution. The security apparatus of the Palestinian Authority was to be restructured and made "free of association with terror and corruption" (Middle East Quartet 2003). In the following year, Prime Minister Ariel Sharon announced that Israel would pull out its troops from and dismantle Jewish settlements in Gaza and parts of the West Bank. The process was completed in September 2005.

The Middle East is the EU's southern backyard. The EU is dependent on oil from the region and vulnerable to security threats emanating from it, including terrorism and illegal migration. To promote its security and prosperity, the EU has been eager to advance peace and good governance in the Middle East. It has paid particular attention to the Israeli-Palestinian peace process and is the largest provider of aid to the Palestinians. The EU has cooperated with both the Palestinian Authority and the Israeli government in the framework of the Union for the Mediterranean and, previously, the Euro-Mediterranean Partnership. As a member of the Middle East Quartet, it has had an EUSR for the Middle East peace process.[4] The high representative for the CFSP, Javier Solana, made the Middle East peace process one of his main agenda items, and his successor, Catherine Ashton, continues the tradition. Yet the EU's political influence in the region has never been commensurate with its multifaceted involvement.

In the aftermath of the Israeli pullout from large chunks of the occupied Palestinian territories, the EU saw an opportunity to raise its political profile. In April 2005, it set up a small Co-ordination Office for Palestinian Police Support (EU COPPS) to act as adviser to the Palestinian minister of interior and the police commissioner. Together with their local counterparts, the EU advisers developed a Police Development Programme. In November 2005, the EU agreed to beef up its police assistance through a considerably bigger CSDP mission. Moreover, it launched another CSDP mission to monitor the cross-border flows of goods and persons through the Rafah Border Crossing Point between Gaza and Egypt. Both missions were severely handicapped by the victory of the radical Islamic Hamas in democratic elections of the Palestinian legislative council in 2006. Following the lead of the United States, the EU demanded that any Hamas-led government meet a number of conditions: accept the right of Israel to exist, abjure violence, and respect previous peace agreements. When Hamas refused, the EU boycotted its government of the Gaza Strip.

The EU Police Mission for the Palestinian Territories (EUPOL COPPS), January 2006–

Launched in 2006 with a staff of about fifteen police advisers, COPPS got off to a bad start, coinciding with the Hamas election victory. COPPS was paralyzed until the creation in 2007 of a government of the Palestinian Authority in charge of the West Bank that excluded Hamas, which took charge of the Gaza Strip. Since then, COPPS has provided assistance only to the West Bank component of the Palestinian Civil Police—the Palestinian law enforcement agency (European Commission 2008b).[5]

The objective of the mission is to assist the local authorities in transforming the Palestinian police into a sustainable and effective service in accordance with best international standards. Some EUPOL experts are collocated with senior local police managers, while others carry out daily visits to police stations in the West Bank. Monitoring, mentoring, and advising activities cover the whole gamut of police work—from crime scene management to budgeting and tackling sexual violence. In addition, COPPS helps European and international donors to identify and implement police assistance projects, for example, donations of police vehicles. Also, COPPS runs police training courses, supervises training delivered by local police trainers, and facilitates international training provided by a number of donors. In the summer of 2008, Brussels agreed to expand the mission's rule-of-law brief. COPPS recruited new international staff—judges, prosecutors, prison personnel, and so forth—in order to systematically improve the functioning of the whole criminal justice system. Since then, its personnel strength has increased to more than fifty. The mission cooperates closely with US-led security sector reform. The United States is in charge of training and equipping the local military—the Palestinian National Security Forces and the Presidential Guard.

Although the mission has faced a number of EU-related difficulties, including turf battles with the European Commission, its main limitations have been its small size and the difficult political and security environment in which it has operated, though the political and security situation is set to improve in the wake of the April 2011 reconciliation agreement between Fatah and Hamas. The mission has been too small to have a major impact on Palestinian law enforcement. The lack of manpower has been aggravated by the volatile security situation, which has made the work of the unarmed COPPS advisers and trainers dangerous. Threats to mission security have stemmed from Israeli settler violence and intra-Palestinian political and family feuds. Also, under pressure from Brussels, the mission had to adjust to how it carried out its mandate. Instead of staying neutral in the power struggle between Fatah and Hamas, it worked exclusively with the security forces of the Palestinian Authority. Hence the mission had to downplay the mandate objective of building a nonpartisan and inclusive police service that does not discriminate against any of the major Palestinian political groups (Bulut 2009; Sabiote 2008). Incidentally, this has made the mission a potential target for attacks by Hamas sympathizers disgruntled with the Palestinian Authority and Fatah. Despite these and other challenges, the mission contributes to a better-trained and -equipped Palestinian Civil Police. However, the sustainability of the reforms depends on a breakthrough in the peace process between Palestinians and Israelis and on intra-Palestinian reconciliation. The dependency of mission success on the political context is even more pronounced in the case of another CSDP deployment in Palestine.

The EU Border Assistance Mission for the Rafah Border Crossing Point (EUBAM Rafah), November 2005–

The mandate for EUBAM Rafah, launched in 2005, is to monitor the implementation of the Israeli-Palestinian Agreement on Movement and Access between Gaza and Egypt.[6] Because the Rafah crossing is the only land connection between Palestine and the outside world, it is vital for the inhabitants and the economy of Gaza. EUBAM's main task is to monitor the compliance of Palestinian customs officials with the agreement. In addition, it has a mandate to strengthen the capacity of the Palestinian border police. The European Commission was displeased about the second objective because it regards capacity-building activities of this kind as its turf. Initially, EUBAM was a success, rapidly building its strength to about eighty experts, whose presence allowed the crossing to be opened most of the time. When relations between Israel and the Palestinian Authority soured over the kidnapping of an Israeli soldier by Palestinians, the crossing was opened rarely. After the takeover of Gaza by Hamas in 2007, the crossing was closed. The EU suspended EUBAM, putting it on standby with a significantly downsized staff who wait for the reopening of the border crossing.

With the deployment of its two Palestinian CSDP missions, the EU has stepped up its involvement in the Middle East peace process. More than chief supplier of funds to the Palestinians, it has become a security provider, albeit one with a rather limited role. The limitations have to do with the unwillingness of the United States and Israel to see the less pro-Israeli EU play a greater role in the strategically important region. Also, a more robust EU role in the Middle East is hampered by cross-national differences among EU states regarding policy toward Israel, the Palestinians, and their neighbors, including

Iran and Syria. The dispatch of the small CSDP missions had the support of Washington and, to a lesser degree, of Israel. Cooperation on the ground with the Americans has been good. Both EUPOL COPPS and EUBAM Rafah have contributed to Washington's reevaluation of the CSDP's value to US foreign policy. However, operational cooperation in the region has come at the cost of subordinating EU security sector reform and EU diplomacy more broadly to US policy on the Israeli-Palestinian conflict.

The EU Integrated Rule of Law Mission for Iraq (EUJUST LEX Iraq), July 2005–

Two years after the invasion of Iraq by a US-led coalition of the willing, the EU agreed upon a civilian CSDP mission to assist in reforming the Iraqi security sector. EUJUST LEX Iraq was launched in 2005, and its staff has grown to about seventy. The mission provides training and mentoring to the whole Iraqi criminal justice system. The training courses equip high- and mid-level staff with modern leadership and management skills that are respectful of human rights, facilitate collaboration among the stakeholders of the criminal justice system, and enable the police to run effective crime investigations. For security reasons, EUJUST LEX training was conducted in the EU until 2010, after which the mission extended its pilot in-country training projects to a full-fledged in-country training program. This has enhanced the impact of the mission, not least through improved cooperation and coordination with local authorities. Mission staff have been redeployed from the coordinating office in Brussels to the new office in Bagdad and other Iraqi cities. The mission's primary task is to organize the training, which is provided by individual EU states, both in the EU and in Iraq. A typical training course lasts three weeks. Most of the trainees come from the Iraqi Police Service, with judiciary personnel providing the second largest contingent. The mission also organizes short Work Experience Secondments in EU countries. The secondments provide Iraqis with additional hands-on, on-the-job training.

EUJUST LEX Iraq has encountered a number of management challenges. To begin with, quality control has been a problem. While the mission has developed a general curriculum, training courses differ in content and quality across the EU states organizing them. Second, because the mission is a small contribution to the huge task of rebuilding Iraq along Western lines, its political influence has been meager. Under these conditions, it is not surprising that the mission has had little influence on the selection of trainees and the selection criteria. Third and closely related, the mission has neither the means nor the authority to monitor the reintegration of trained personnel into the Iraqi criminal justice system. By implication, it has been unable to assess the impact of EU-trained staff on the workings of the Iraqi justice system. These problems notwithstanding, EUJUST LEX has raised the skill levels of thousands of Iraqi police, judiciary, and penitentiary personnel, among them a considerable number of women and Kurds.

The main challenge faced by the mission is that it is risibly small compared to the challenges faced by the justice system in Iraq. The problem has its roots in the deployment decision. The primary reason for the EU to dispatch the mission was to mend intra-EU and transatlantic relations, which had been strained to the breaking point by the US-led invasion of Iraq. Since then, the EU has judged the mission more by its symbolic value than by its actual state-building impact. There are a number of reasons for the lack of will among EU states to put together a CSDP operation that would maximize the EU's leverage over the stabilization and reconstruction process in Iraq. First, policy differences over the postwar reconstruction of Iraq remain among member states, including Europeanists and Atlanticists. Second, EU states have a low tolerance threshold when it comes to risking the lives of civilian CSDP personnel. Iraq is a dangerous place in which high-impact terrorist attacks remain frequent. The result of these disagreements and concerns is that the member states cannot muster the political will to give the mission the resources it needs to make a real difference in Iraq's justice sector.

Notes

1. This chapter does not discuss the border assistance mission to Moldova and Ukraine (EUBAM Moldova-Ukraine). Properly speaking, EUBAM Moldova is not a CSDP operation but is run by the European Commission.

2. Proxima 2 was followed by an EU Police Advisory Team of about thirty experts who were deployed from December 2005 to June 2006. The team was a bridging measure, covering the interlude between the end of Proxima 2 and the start of the European Commission police reform project.

3. The EU is officially one of the cochairs of the Geneva talks among Russia, Georgia, the United States, South Ossetia, and Abkhazia. In fact, it

runs the diplomatic talks, which occur periodically in Geneva to deal with the fallout of the war (for more, see Merlingen and Ostrauskaitė 2010).

4. At the end of February 2011, the mandate of the EUSR for the Middle East peace process, like that of some other EUSRs, was not renewed, as had been customary previously. This was due to High Representative Ashton's skepticism toward EUSRs in general. However, pressure by EU states persuaded her to agree to nominate a new EUSR for the Middle East peace process later in 2011. For High Representative Ashton's controversial views on EUSRs, see Chapter 4.

5. Since 2007, Gaza has been ruled by Hamas, and the West Bank by a technocratic government allied with Fatah. In April 2011, reconciliation talks between the two groups led to an agreement to form a joint interim government of both the West Bank and the Gaza Strip. The EU has indicated that it would work with a Palestinian unity government. If the EU were to recognize a future unity government, COPPS would face a new, more benign environment in the areas of politics and security in which to carry out its reforms.

6. Prior to its pullout from Gaza, Israel managed the border crossing.

CHAPTER 10

EU Operations in Africa and Asia

THIS CHAPTER SURVEYS THE ELEVEN OPERATIONS (MILITARY and civilian) that the EU has deployed in Africa and Asia. The chapter follows the same structure as the preceding one, providing for each mission a brief background to the conflict that prompted the CSDP deployment. Moreover, the main reasons for the deployment of the missions, their basic objectives, the obstacles encountered, and their achievements are discussed. A number of points emerge from this survey. As mentioned in the previous chapter, all CSDP operations, including in Africa and Asia, have focused on the stabilization and reconstruction of host countries and have been deployed with their consent. Furthermore, more than two-thirds of all military CSDP operations have been in Africa. Most were initiated by France, which has also been the largest troop contributor. In contrast to the CSDP operations in Europe, military EU operations in Africa were run without recourse to NATO capabilities and assets. All were of relatively small size. The largest EU force numbered less than 4,000 troops. The military CSDP had its baptism by fire in Africa where EU troops had to engage for the first time in firefights to implement their mission. CSDP deployments have centered on the Democratic Republic of Congo, which has hosted three civilian and two military missions. In Afghanistan, a civilian mission was for the first time deployed in a hostile environment. The impact of both civilian and military operations in Africa and Asia has been patchy. They have provided temporary relief to people in distress and carried out small-

151

scale security sector reforms. These activities have saved lives, raised the skill levels of local troops and the local police, and introduced modernizing reforms in the security sector. However, in most cases, they have left the larger structures of violence affecting host countries virtually untouched.

The EU and Africa

Africa has been one of the geographical focuses of EU foreign policy. For decades trade and development aid topped the agenda. Since the end of the Cold War, the EU has deepened interregional cooperation between itself and Africa and has successfully promoted its model of regional integration on the continent. It remains Africa's most important trading partner. In the early 1990s, conflict prevention, conflict resolution, and peace-building in Africa became a growing concern in Brussels (Olsen 2002). Since then the EU's thinking on African security and prosperity has evolved. The 2005 EU Strategy for Africa and the 2007 Joint EU-Africa Strategy have been milestones in this development. The EU has not abandoned its objective of promoting long-term development on the continent, but it has reshuffled its priorities, placing peace and security in Africa at the center of its concerns. On the one hand, it has provided financial assistance to the buildup of common African peace support capabilities. On the other, it has deployed more CSDP missions in Africa than anywhere else.

The EU's growing security involvement in Africa is related to new security threats emanating from the continent and Africa's heightened global geo-economic importance. Secondary normative reasons have facilitated the reorientation of EU foreign policy (Olsen 2009). Weak state structures and corruption in Africa have generated security threats to the EU in the form of human trafficking, organized crime, and terrorism. The east African coastline and the Guinea Gulf region in western Africa have become important transit routes for heroin from Asia and cocaine from Latin America. Failing or failed states may foster piracy, such as that off the coast of Somalia, which has threatened shipping routes vital for European and international trade. As the 2004 attacks on Madrid have shown, northern Africa especially is a potential platform for terrorist attacks on the EU. Also, Africa matters to Europe because of its natural resources. EU prosperity is vulnerable to interruptions of supplies from Africa. For instance, EU energy security depends on access to oil and gas from

Africa. In recent years, the geo-economic importance of the continent has grown considerably. Emerging powers, especially China, have joined Europeans and Americans as important players in what some commentators have called a new scramble for Africa. This is the geopolitical and geo-economic context that has inclined the EU to deploy CSDP operations in Africa.

However, with the exception of the anti-piracy mission Atalanta and the associated EU Training Mission in Uganda, African CSDP operations have not been deployed to tackle direct security threats against the EU. Rather, the proximate cause of the proliferation of missions in Africa has been the policy entrepreneurship of former colonial powers such as France, Belgium, and Portugal, which regard the CSDP as a force multiplier that enables them to pursue their national objectives in Africa more effectively. In the same vein, France and Belgium regard CSDP deployments in Africa as a means to advance their Europeanist agenda of reinforcing the EU's international role vis-à-vis the United States and NATO. Yet without the EU's long-standing commitment to development and peace in Africa, the former colonial powers would not have been able to upload their policy preferences to the EU. The official EU discourse of solidarity with Africa, which has been reinforced by Brussels' commitment to the Responsibility to Protect, has provided an enabling condition for mission deployments on the continent. The discourse has made it difficult for skeptics such as Germany to veto CSDP interventions in Africa that are justified in the name of humanitarianism. Also, it has prompted countries such as Sweden and Ireland, which are committed to the international promotion of human security, to support CSDP peace missions on the continent.

CSDP Peacekeeping and Security Sector Reform in the Democratic Republic of Congo

The Democratic Republic of Congo (DRC), with about sixty million inhabitants, is rich in natural resources and hence of some considerable geo-economic importance. The EU is the main trading partner of this potential powerhouse in Africa, which is a former Belgian colony that gained independence in 1960. After a tumultuous first few years of independence, Mobuto Sese Seko came to power in a putsch in 1965 and presided over the country's descent into armed conflicts. In the wake of the 1994 Rwandan genocide, the Kivu region in the east of the DRC became embroiled in a cross-border conflict. On one side were local Hutus and Hutu refugees from Rwanda, where they had carried out massacres against their Tutsi compatriots. On the other side were local Tutsis and Tutsi government forces from Rwanda. The latter wanted to eliminate the threat posed by the genocidal Hutu militias hiding in the DRC. The Rwandan government accused the Mobutu regime of giving sanctuary to the Rwandan Hutu militias and joined forces with Uganda, Burundi, and Congolese rebel groups led by Laurent Kabila. Together they succeeded in driving Mobuto from power in 1997. However, this did not usher in peace, as soon the former allies were fighting each other. Kabila, the DRC's new strongman, tried to push Rwanda and Uganda out of the DRC, leading in 1998 to a regional conflagration that involved no fewer than nine African countries and numerous armed militias in the DRC. As a result of the fighting between 1998 und 2004, about four million people died. Besides the Kivu region, a particular flashpoint was the resource-rich Ituri province in the northeast of the DRC where the presence of foreign troops, notably from Uganda, aggravated the long-standing conflict between the ethnic groups of the Hema and Lendu.

In 1999, a cease-fire agreement was signed. The UN Organization Mission (MONUC) was dispatched to the DRC to keep the peace, but the Blue Helmets were unable to prevent a resumption of the conflict. Peace had another chance when, in 2001, Kabila's son came to power after his father's assassination. Cajoled by South Africa and Angola and supported by the international community, he and the other parties to the conflict signed a series of peace agreements, and foreign troops left the DRC. The process culminated in an all-Congolese power-sharing agreement at the end of 2002, which stipulated the disarmament and demobilization of all rebel groups, their integration into the armed forces or civil society, the reform of the security sector, the adoption of a new constitution, and democratic elections. MONUC was to assist in and supervise the transition to peace and democracy. Against this backdrop, the EU reinforced its engagement in the DRC. The drivers of the policy were France and Belgium, which have long-standing political and commercial interests in the country. The EUSR for the African Great Lakes region coordinated the growing EU action on the ground.

The EU Military Operation Artemis in the DRC (EUFOR Artemis), June–September 2003.

At the end of 2002, Uganda began to withdraw its forces from Ituri, which led to civil war between Hema and Lendu militias and atrocities against civilians (International Crisis Group 2003). Although MONUC was in charge of protecting Bunia, the capital of the province, the Blue Helmets were overwhelmed by the task. To avoid a humanitarian disaster, the UN Secretary-General asked the international community for temporary reinforcements. Although France agreed in principle to send a force to Bunia, it asked the EU to allow the French-led force to operate under the CSDP label. The British supported the idea, while Germany was skeptical of it. But Paris persisted, and with London in support of the mission and in light of the plea by the UN, Berlin had little choice but to agree to the French-led CSDP operation. Paris saw the mission as an opportunity to polish its reputation in Africa, which had been tarnished by its support for the genocidal Hutu government in Rwanda. Paris also wanted the mission to demonstrate to Europeans and the world at large that the CSDP was alive and kicking (Duke 2008a; Gegout 2005). The acrimonious intra-EU debate in the runup to the US-led invasion of Iraq in 2003 cast doubts on the future of the CSDP. Finally, Paris lobbied for the mission to signal to the United States and NATO that they had no right of first refusal and that the EU was willing and able to launch autonomous CSDP missions that did not rely on NATO capabilities and assets.[1]

EUFOR Artemis was charged, under Chapter 7 of the United Nations Charter, to restore peace and security in Bunia and its surroundings, if necessary by force. Its mandate included the protection of refugee camps, UN and NGO personnel, and the airport, which was crucial for flying in humanitarian assistance. Paris provided the headquarters of EUFOR Artemis, most of the planning staff, and the logistics, as well as most of the boots on the ground. Neutral Sweden was one of the largest troop contributors, deploying about seventy elite soldiers. About 1,100 troops were dispatched to Bunia, while most of the rest of the about 2,000-strong EU force were in Entebbe, Uganda, from which much of the logistics reached Bunia. Twelve EU states contributed personnel, either in theater or to the operations headquarters in Paris. As planned, on 1 September a reinforced MONUC relieved Artemis.

Judged against its UN mandate, the CSDP operation was a success. Life in town returned to a degree of normality while Artemis was there. Tens of thousands of internally displaced persons flocked back. From an EU political-strategic perspective, too, the mission was an achievement. First, it showed for the first time that the EU was capable of planning and running a stand-alone military operation without recourse to NATO. Second, unlike the military operations in the Western Balkans, Artemis was deployed in a semipermissive environment. It repeatedly came under hostile fire, killed local fighters, and used force to compel militias to leave Bunia and its surroundings (Ulriksen et al. 2004; Giegerich 2008). Third, the mission was the first successful instance of cooperation between the EU and the United Nations in military matters. Fourth, it underlined that the geographic scope of the CSDP went beyond Europe. The mission managed to deploy troops to and supply them in a harsh theater of operation about 6,000 kilometers from Europe. On the downside, the operation brought into focus a number of capability gaps. Among other things, the mission was hampered by a lack of strategic transport capacity and limited interoperability among European troops. Moreover, inadequate communications systems made secure long-distance communication difficult (Bagayoko 2004; Faria 2004). More importantly, the operation failed to make a lasting difference. The short and unambitious mandate made it impossible for the operation to make a contribution to sustainable peace in Ituri (International Crisis Group 2003). When the EU troops left after a few months, civil war returned to the area.

The EU Police (EUPOL) Missions in the DRC, April 2005. Initially, EU support for the peace-building process in the DRC was channeled through the European Commission and bilateral aid by the member states. An important component of this assistance was security sector reform targeting the Congolese police, who were ethnically divided, were institutionally fragmented, lacked training and equipment, were corrupt, and were often a source of insecurity for the population rather than a provider of security (International Crisis Group 2006). The main international actor involved in efforts to create a professional, effective, and representative police has been MONUC. One of the EU's first projects was to provide funds to refurbish a police training center and to train and provide equipment to recruits for a new special force. The creation of the Integrated Police Unit was seen as an important project to provide security to government institutions. In 2004, the Council agreed to follow up this European Commission project with a CSDP police mission. The decision reflected the desire of EU states to raise the EU's political profile in the international stabilization and reconstruction of the DRC. Also, the deployment provided an opportunity for the EU to extend the civilian CSDP for the first time beyond Europe. Started in April 2005, EUPOL Kinshasa was mandated to advise local authorities on the launch and management of the Integrated Police Unit. In particular, the mission was asked to make sure that the arms and ammunition given to the force by member states were used according to human rights standards.

Mission planners expected that the EU-trained Integrated Police Unit would offer a model of professionalism for the other police forces in the DRC's capital, Kinshasa.

Made up of just over twenty international police advisers, EUPOL Kinshasa was the first civilian CSDP operation in Africa. Unlike MONUC, which covers the whole country, the EU mission was deployed in the DRC capital. Most of the staff was collocated with the Integrated Police Unit. As in other theaters, the civilian CSDP mission suffered from start-up problems related to logistics and procurement. At the end of 2005, the mandate was enlarged. Additional tasks included supervising the integration of the Integrated Police Unit into the Congolese National Police and promoting broader police reforms. On an operational level, the mission was tasked to advise the local police on how to ensure the general elections of July 2006 proceeded without major security incidents.

Though not free from irregularities, the elections were hailed by the international community as a success. In their wake, the EU decided to reinforce its police mission. Brussels refocused the mandate on strategic issues related to country-wide police reform and the criminal justice system. EUPOL DR Congo, which replaced EUPOL Kinshasa, was launched in July 2007. The mission, which has about sixty internationals, has an ambitious mandate to anchor Congolese law enforcement to Western professional policing standards. Hence, it promotes democratic accountability, human rights norms, and principles of good governance. To achieve these objectives, the mission focuses on strengthening the ethnic integration of the police, community policing, and the interface between law enforcement and the judiciary. In 2008, the deployment zone was extended to the violent eastern part of the DRC, and the remit of the CSDP mission was further extended. Its enlarged brief includes advisory work on violence against women, the protection of children living in environments marked by armed conflicts, and the modernization of the border police and the audit inspectorate, which deals with misconduct, administrative malfunctions, and financial irregularities in the police.

Like other international police aid providers in the DRC, the EUPOL missions have had mixed results. Part of the problem is that the CSDP missions have suffered from mission creep. Over time their mandates have become ever more ambitious, but few new resources were allocated. The result has been a wide gap between expectations (EU and local) and results on the ground. On the plus side, the CSDP missions have upgraded the management of the Congolese police and contributed to improved local policing skills. Also, EUPOL Kinshasa played a role in ensuring the success of the 2006 elections. However, there is little evidence that the EU has succeeded in its aim to transform Congolese law enforcement into a service with human rights at its core. When not monitored by internationals, the police continue to indulge in widespread human rights violations, which have been documented by numerous human rights groups and MONUC reports. For instance, in Bas Congo province at the beginning of 2008, the police carried out an operation against a religious sect whose members had allegedly committed serious crimes. A MONUC fact-finding mission dispatched after the event determined that the police, led by units from the EU-trained Integrated Police Unit and another special force, used live ammunition against unarmed civilians. The latter believed that their "knife-shaped pieces of wood, stones and palm and cola nuts . . . could be magically transformed into explosive grenades." The police operation resulted in at least 100 deaths, and the police "dumped a large number of bodies in a river in an attempt to destroy evidence." Moreover, officers systematically looted and destroyed private property belonging to the sect and its members (Human Rights Watch 2009; United Nations 2008: 4).

The EU Security Sector Reform Mission in the DRC (EUSEC DR Congo), June 2005– .

In addition to the EUPOL missions, the EU dispatched a further CSDP mission to the DRC to deal with military reforms. At the beginning of the new millennium, the Congolese armed forces were ethnically divided, badly trained, irregularly paid, corrupt, and politicized instruments of personal power. They were a major source of insecurity for citizens (International Crisis Group 2006). EUSEC DR Congo was pushed by France and Belgium, while some member states doubted the usefulness of yet another CSDP intervention in the country. However, they were rhetorically entrapped by the EU's publicly stated humanitarian commitment to building sustainable peace in the DRC.

The lead actor in international efforts to assist the DRC in reforming its national armed forces has been the United Nations. Assisting in this task is EUSEC DR Congo, for which the EU authorized sixty military and civilian adviser posts but has difficulties filling. Most of the mission staff is placed with senior Congolese political and military authorities in Kinshasa. Initially the mission did not cover the conflict-ridden eastern DRC, but is now present in the area. For a short period, EUSEC DR Congo was reinforced by US personnel, but its participation was discontinued in 2011. After Kosovo, this was the second time that the United States participated in a CSDP mission. EUSEC's objective is to build effective and disciplined Congolese armed forces that comply with democratic norms, the rule of law, human rights, and principles of good governance. Over time, the EU has incrementally enlarged the mission's brief. CSDP advisers are engaged in improving military training, building up the administrative capacity of the armed forces, enhancing their financial management, and combating sexual violence. For example, one CSDP project separated the chain of payment from the chain of command in order to prevent senior officers from embezzling the pay of privates (Martinelli 2008). Another important project was a census of the armed forces, which identified a considerable number of "ghost soldiers" whose pay was pocketed by corrupt officers (Clément 2009). Last but not least, EUSEC helps interested EU states to identify, organize, and supervise bilateral aid projects to plug the most serious capability shortfalls of the Congolese armed forces. The mission's increasing objectives have widened its funding gap, and staff have struggled to raise money from EU states for mission projects.

Like the EUPOL missions, EUSEC has been hampered by a lack of coherence among the activities of the numerous international donors working on Congolese security sector reform. The slow democratization process and the continuing warfare between government forces and rebel groups have been even greater problems. In its 2007 World Report, Human Rights Watch (2007: 110) claimed that Congolese "soldiers killed, raped, and tortured civilians in the provinces of Katanga, Ituri, and North and South Kivu." Similar allegations were contained in its 2009 and 2010 reports. Clearly, the impact of EUSEC as well as other international actors such as MONUC on good governance in the military has been limited. The CSDP-guided reform of the payment system and other small administrative improvements are not negligible but have not stopped the widespread disregard of human rights by the military. General economic underdevelopment and a lack of resources for the armed forces remain a major problem. Soldiers continue to receive low salaries, which are paid irregularly. Hence, they continue to see the population as an easy source of illicit income (Davis 2009). To change this, something more than the EU's limited security sector reforms are needed.

The EU Military Operation in the DRC (EUFOR DR Congo), June 2006–November 2006.

The United Nations was mandated to ensure a secure environment for the 2006 DRC general elections. Because this was a huge challenge, it asked the EU to help by making "available a deterrent force" against spoilers of the electoral process (United

Nations Security Council 2006). After some hesitation, the EU agreed. Paris and London cajoled a reluctant Germany to take the lead in organizing and commanding the operation, and Berlin had little choice but to acquiesce. This had to do not only with pressure from its partners but with the fact that the EU was publicly committed to and had invested in the Congolese peace process. The elections were crucial to the success of the process. Failure to respond positively to the UN request would have negatively affected the EU's public image. Also, France and other EU states wanted to score a CSDP success in the wake of the public relations disaster of the rejection of the draft European constitution by French and Dutch voters in 2005 (Haine and Giegerich 2006). Germany agreed to lead EUFOR DR Congo but insisted on a limited deployment area; thus the EU troops were concentrated in the capital and not deployed to insecure areas in the east. Also, Berlin insisted on a strict time limit for the operation—four months.

EUFOR DR Congo, acting under a UN Security Council resolution, was tasked to protect civilians in its area of operation, back up MONUC, and secure Kinshasa Airport. Most of the force was based in neighboring Gabon. Of about 2,400 deployed troops, fewer than 1,000 were stationed in Kinshasa, and they carried out day and night patrols to keep the city safe. The battalion-sized force in Gabon acted as a rapidly deployable reserve that could be dispatched to reinforce the troops in Kinshasa when sporadic violence occurred after the first round of the elections (Gegout 2007: 7). EUFOR could also draw on a strategic over-the-horizon reserve of about 1,500 troops in Europe, although this option was not used. The high representative for the CFSP tried to justify the fact that the EU deployed fewer than 1,000 soldiers to the DRC to secure elections in the huge country by saying that the EU wanted to avoid "an unnecessary heavy military presence in Kinshasa" (Solana 2007). A more accurate assessment is that EUFOR was "a 'classic' evacuation operation, ready to take out European citizens in case of trouble" (Biscop 2007: 10). The two main troop contributors were Germany and France, and a German general was in charge of the overall operation, while the force commander on the ground was French. Altogether twenty-one EU countries contributed personnel to EUFOR. Turkey and Switzerland were the only non-EU participants in the operation.

As far as the EU is concerned, the operation was a success. It contributed to the maintenance of public order during the elections in Kinshasa. Moreover, the operation was the first truly multinational EU force outside Europe (Brauss 2007), and Germany and France shared command responsibilities. The national composition of the CSDP troops was considerably less one-sided than in the case of EUFOR Artemis, which was largely a French show. On the downside, the operation faced the same capability shortfalls that three years earlier had troubled EUFOR Artemis (Martinelli 2008; Major 2009).

Concerning the overall CSDP engagement in the DRC, the five missions represent a limited EU investment in the stabilization and reconstruction of the DRC. The big country faces even bigger security challenges. Critics of EUFOR DR Congo argued that it was more about "European form than African substance, comforting rhetoric than relevant action" (Haine and Giegerich 2006). The judgment can be extended to all EU DRC missions. The country continues to be afflicted by conflicts in which neither side complies with even minimal standards of human rights. Troops and police forces trained and advised by the EU have been implicated in atrocities.

The EU Civilian-Military Supporting Action to the African Union Mission in Sudan, July 2005–December 2007

Since Sudan gained independence from British rule in 1956, it has been torn apart by civil wars that have pitted various regions against the central government. Since 2003, the world's attention has been captured by the civil war in Darfur—a region in western Sudan. It has pitted mostly Muslim government forces and allied Arab Janjaweed militias against various black African rebel groups. The US Congress accused the government in Khartoum of perpetrating genocide in Darfur. In 2009, the International Criminal Court issued an arrest warrant for Sudanese president Omar el Bashir, who stands accused of crimes against humanity and war crimes in relation to his government's prosecution of the war in Darfur. Sudan's instability is linked to struggles over the control of resources. The country is rich in oil, with the main oil deposits in South Sudan, which became a sovereign state in July 2011.[2] Darfur also has deposits, which give it considerable geo-economic importance. China imports a considerable amount of Sudanese oil and has invested heavily in the country's oil industry. Geo-economic and human rights concerns combine to ensure that Sudan remains on the West's radar screens. This potent mix also goes a long way toward explaining the CSDP deployments in and around the country.

In 2004, the main parties to the conflict in Darfur signed a humanitarian cease-fire agreement to facilitate the delivery of humanitarian assistance and to prepare the ground for peace. A Ceasefire Commission was set up, and the African Union agreed to send a small monitoring mission (AMIS 1). However, when the security situation worsened, the African Union transformed the observer mission into a sizeable peacekeeping force of a few thousand troops (AMIS 2). The mandate was enlarged to include confidence-building, the protection of civilians, and humanitarian assistance. The EU assisted the African Union in getting its peace support operations in Darfur up and running. The African Peace Facility, managed by the European Commission, and bilateral assistance from member states provided about €500 million (US$708 million) to AMIS (1 and 2) (Council of the European Union 2008c). In 2005, the EU agreed to upgrade its assistance to AMIS 2 through a CSDP operation—the awkwardly named Civilian-Military Supporting Action to AMIS 2.[3]

The CSDP mission consisted of just under fifty police advisers, operational and logistics planners, and military observers. Some were collocated with staff in the African Union headquarters in Ethiopia, while the rest were collocated with AMIS 2 personnel in Sudan. The civilian pillar of the mission focused on police aid and covered, among other things, in-mission training for AMIS 2 police, the development of a unit within the African Union secretariat capable of planning and running police missions, and advice to the AMIS 2 police leadership. In a similar vein, the military pillar focused on providing technical assistance to the African Union troops. Also, it helped organize strategic and in-theater airlift to support the buildup and rotation of African troops deployed in Darfur. The CSDP support for AMIS 2 ended when it was replaced by the African Union/United Nations Hybrid Operation in Darfur (UNAMID), made up of African Union and UN troops.

The EU mission was a unique construct, because it did not conform to the established CSDP mission format. It was coordinated and managed in Brussels by an ad hoc Joint Coordination Team. On the ground, coordination with the African Union was managed by a Coordination Cell in Addis Ababa and the EUSR for Sudan, both authorized to issue instructions to the CSDP personnel. EU military personnel collocated with AMIS 2 were under the latter's operational command rather than that of an EU force commander.

As to the achievements of the CSDP mission, it reinforced the close security partnership between the EU and the African Union. More importantly, it provided capacity-building and operational support to the African troops in Sudan. It is clear that without the mission and the overall EU aid package, the African Union would have achieved even less in Darfur than it did from 2004 to 2007. In line with its limited mandate, AMIS 2 created pockets of stability in Darfur and facilitated the delivery of humanitarian relief. The inability of AMIS 2 to keep the peace in Sudan and to stop mass atrocity crimes is also the greatest failure of the EU mission.

The EU Military Operation in the Republic of Chad and in the Central African Republic (EUFOR Chad/Central African Republic), January 2008–March 2009

The conflict in Darfur has an important regional dimension. The Chadian government has supported the rebels in Darfur. Khartoum has supported insurgencies against the government in N'djamena. Moreover, many Darfuris displaced by the civil war have ended up in Chad and the Central African Republic (CAR), both former French colonies, which retain close political and economic relations with the former mother country. Both countries are underdeveloped, plagued by internal instability, and run by regimes with shaky democratic credentials. Because Chad is rich in oil, US oil companies have an important presence in the country, and China has recently stepped up its engagement in the country's oil industry.

In 2007, newly elected French president Sarkozy injected new momentum into EU policy in the region by proposing to deploy a military CSDP operation to Chad and CAR. Given the political obstacles to CSDP intervention in Darfur, Paris saw an operation in Sudan's neighbors as a second-best solution that would demonstrate that the EU could be a force for good in a bad neighborhood. EU governments skeptical of the initiative thought that Paris's real objective was to use the EU as a cover for its military support for its authoritarian client regime in Chad. Yet with British support, Paris was able to persuade the skeptics to back the humanitarian operation, although the skeptics insisted that the EU troops adhere to strict political neutrality among government forces and insurgents in Chad.

EUFOR Chad/CAR was authorized by the UN Security Council. Its time-limited mandate was to protect internally displaced persons and Sudanese refugees, to secure humanitarian aid deliveries to them, and to safeguard UN personnel and facilities. The United Nations also decided to dispatch a small mission of its own, the UN Mission in the Central African Republic and Chad (MINURCAT). Its tasks included the promotion of the rule of law, law enforcement, and human rights through capacity-building measures. At the beginning of 2009, the United Nations expanded MINURCAT's mandate to include military peacekeeping. When EUFOR Chad/CAR's mandate expired, the Blue Helmets took over from the EU troops.

EUFOR Chad/CAR had about 3,700 troops in theater. The largest troop contributors were France with 1,700 soldiers, and Ireland and Poland with 400 soldiers each, while neutral Austria deployed 160 troops. Overall, twenty-three EU states participated in the operation, which was headquartered in Paris and run by an Irish general, while the troops on the ground were commanded by a French general. Most of the EUFOR soldiers were stationed in Chad, while a contingent of around 200 troops was tasked to protect refugees in the CAR. The operation in Chad and the CAR was a tough military assignment for the EU. Although the area of operation only covered a small part of the two countries, it was vast. At around 280,000 square kilometers, it was about the size of Italy. The terrain was austere, the climate was forbidding, and the deployment area lacked even the most basic infrastructure. To implement its mandate, the force carried out short-, medium- and long-term patrols to deter attacks on civilians and international aid workers. Also, the patrols aimed at reassuring the 500,000 refugees and internally displaced persons in the area of operation that the EU soldiers were there to protect them. A rapid intervention capability ensured that in case of trouble EUFOR could respond effectively.

Arguably, the main weakness of the EU intervention was that it tackled only the symptoms of insecurity in the region. It did not address its causes, namely the civil war in western Sudan and the political instability of the regimes in Chad and the CAR. The fragility of the Chadian government was underlined by a rebel assault on the capital just before the EU troops were scheduled to disembark. As a result, the deployment had to be halted for a number of days while the Chadian government repelled the insurgents. As to Darfur, the process of pacification and peace-building should have been well under way in 2008. However, the conflict continued unabated despite peace negotiations and numerous cease-fires. To make matters worse, UNAMID experienced severe problems in its buildup phase throughout 2008. The upshot was that instability in Darfur spilled over into EUFOR's area of operation. The fact that the mission was small did not help. Outside the area patrolled by the Europeans, violence and human rights violations continued (Amnesty International 2009; Oxfam 2009). This said, in their area of operation, the Europeans did make a difference. Among other things, the improved security environment prompted about 10,000 internally displaced people to return to their villages (General Secretariat of the Council of the EU 2009).

As to operational challenges, mission buildup was delayed by the EU's lack of strategic and tactical airlift. As the operation commander put it, "for a while we were a mission without means" (Nash 2008: 18). The problem was aggravated by a lack of political will among the member states. Even after five Force Generation Conferences, the EU fell short of its target and had to reduce the planned number of 4,000 troops by around 300 (Ehrhart 2008). Toward the end of the mission, tactical in-theater airlift was improved with the help of Russia, which deployed four helicopters and about 100 personnel to EUFOR.

The EU Security Sector Reform Mission in Guinea-Bissau (SSR Guinea-Bissau), February 2008–September 2010

Guinea-Bissau is one of the poorest countries in the world. Throughout the 1980s and early 1990s, the former Portuguese colony was run by a dictator. Since democratic elections in the first half of the 1990s, the country has been politically unstable, and the armed forces have been a major troublemaker. In the new millennium, the government initiated plans to overhaul the security sector, with support provided by the United Nations, Britain, and the European Commission. Portugal especially was eager to see a reinforcement of the EU's engagement in the country and proposed to deploy a civilian CSDP mission. Because of Guinea-Bissau's importance to Europe, the EU agreed in early 2007 to the deployment. Due to its grinding poverty and the weak state institutions, Guinea-Bissau has evolved into a major transit route for cocaine from South America to Europe. The drug trade in Guinea-Bissau is greater than the country's entire national income (United Nations Office on Drugs and Crime 2007).

EU SSR Guinea-Bissau was a small mission composed of about twenty international staff. The overstretched military and civilian advisers were tasked to support local authorities in implementing the national security sector reform strategy. They assisted in planning and managing the downsizing and restructuring of the badly trained and undisciplined armed forces, focusing on capacity-building (police and military). The mission identified skills and equipment gaps and solicited and coordinated international aid projects aimed at addressing them. An important component of the capacity-building work was the mainstreaming of counternarcotics into daily police work and the improvement of criminal investigations. Also, mission advisers worked with local justice system personnel on upgrading the interface between the police and prosecutors.

On paper, security sector reform in Guinea-Bissau made considerable progress while the CSDP mission was there. Numerous new laws and regulations were drafted and passed. However, in practice, the situation was not good. Practical improvements were impeded by the high level of political instability in the country. In 2008, two failed coups were carried out by plotters from within the armed forces. In 2009, the president was killed by mutinous troops. In 2010, there was yet another military coup attempt. Also, powerful figures in the army oppose security sector reform because it would diminish their institution's political influence and eliminate the impunity they have enjoyed (Observatoire de l'Afrique 2008). Senior officers are thought to be involved in the lucrative drug trade (BBC News 2010). Entrenched interests thus resist meaningful security sector reform. In light of these obstacles to serious security sector reform, the EU had little choice but to discontinue its CSDP mission. If the mission had been considerably larger, given more resources, and backed up forcefully by diplomatic pressure from the African Union and the EU, it might have had a chance to succeed. This would have involved rebuilding the armed forces from scratch. Without such a root-and-branch reform, Guinea-Bissau is likely to remain a failed state.

The EU Naval Operation Somalia (NAVFOR ATALANTA), December 2008–

Since the 1990s, Somalia has experienced civil strife, and external interventions have failed to pacify the country. The constant fighting has left Somalia a failed state and dependent on international aid. In the absence of an authoritative central government, Somali pirates have flourished, preying on ships along the 3,000-kilometer-long coast of Somalia (Middleton 2008),[4] which has constituted a geo-economic problem of global importance. The Gulf of Aden is a crucial international shipping corridor through which about 20 percent of global trade passes (European Union Naval Force 2010), making it a strategic choke point of the global economic system. The Somali pirates have hijacked commercial ships and threatened vessels of the United Nations World Food Programme, which carry humanitarian deliveries to Somalia. Since 2008, international anti-piracy efforts have mushroomed in the region. The United States has dispatched warships to carry out anti-piracy patrols, as have NATO and the EU. Other countries with commercial interests in the area such as Russia and China have also deployed warships.

In September 2008, the EU decided to establish the EU Naval Coordination Cell (EU NAVCO), which was mandated to support surveillance and protection activities undertaken by member states off the Somali coast. In addition, it served as an informational clearing house and coordinating agency, linking EU navies, shipping companies, and international organizations with stakes in the region, such as the UN World Food Programme. In December 2008, the EU launched its first-ever CSDP naval operation: NAVFOR Atalanta, tasked to patrol the Somali coast with a view to deterring, preventing, and repressing acts of piracy and armed robbery.[5] It escorts UN vessels, protects merchant ships, and monitors fishing activities. In the multilateral coordination of the heavy presence of military vessels in the region, it has established itself as a linchpin. Commanded from a British operational headquarters, the operation, which has around ten ships as well as surveillance planes and helicopters, is authorized to use force in pursuit of its mandate.

Among all military CSDP operations, Atalanta is the one that most clearly reflects EU security concerns. Because 95 percent of EU sea-based trade passes through the Gulf of Aden, the threat posed by piracy in the gulf to EU economic security played a central role in its deployment. Atalanta is a response to "the strategic threat to the Union's commercial sea-lanes" (Howorth 2009: 16; Helly 2009). Humanitarian concerns played a secondary role in the deployment decision. In the same year as Atalanta was launched, the EU refused to heed calls by the UN Secretary-General and numerous nongovernmental actors who called on the EU to intervene militarily in eastern DRC to alleviate the grave humanitarian situation there.

The naval deployments of the EU and other concerned countries and organizations have succeeded in containing the threat posed by piracy to humanitarian and merchant vessels. However, piracy has not been eliminated and retains its disruptive potential. Because naval efforts only tackle the symptoms of the security problem, the international community has moved to tackle the root cause—state failure. It has reinforced its efforts to strengthen the Somali government—the Transitional Federal Government, which struggles against Islamic insurgents, some of whom are accused by the West of having links with Al-Qaida. The government's hold on the country is patchy, and its survival depends on funding by Western powers and the several thousand African Union peacekeepers deployed to Somalia. The troops are partly financed by the EU, which also provides political and economic development aid and technical assistance. To strengthen the capability of the central government to battle the insurgents, the EU, which is Somalia's largest donor, launched its seventh military CSDP operation.

The EU Training Mission Somalia (EUTM Somalia), April 2010–

In 2010, the EU launched the 150-strong military training mission EUTM Somalia.[6] It was given a mandate until July 2011 to train 2,000 Somali recruits, though at the time of writing discussions are under way in the EU to extend the mission, albeit with a modified mandate. For security and logistical reasons, the training was carried out in Uganda. Kampala is the main troop contributor to the African Union mission in Somalia and is itself engaged in training Somali government forces. The military CSDP mission cooperated closely with the Ugandan training mission. While EU training covered topics such as human rights and the protection of civilians, the stress was on combat skills, including urban combat. EUTM Somalia established close working relations with US and African Union forces in Somalia. The latter mentored the newly trained soldiers once they were back in Somalia. The United States transported recruits to their training in Uganda and paid 50 percent of their salaries once their training was completed (European Security Review 2010). Regular pay is important to ensure the soldiers do not defect. Such defections, often to the enemy, severely undermined earlier efforts by Ethiopia to strengthen the Somali central government by training Somali soldiers and police officers.[7] The EU and the United States wanted to avoid their training mission experiencing a similar fate. The US contribution to the EUTM is yet another sign of the growing cooperation between the United States and the CSDP.

In terms of impact, the EUTM was a small contribution to Somalia's big problems. However, the EU mission was only one of several international training missions designed to build up Somali security forces—soldiers and police officers. Besides bilateral training arrangements such as that between France and the Somali government, the African Union and the United Nations are key players in this policy domain. Yet it remains to be seen whether their interventions can make a difference. Skeptics call for a forceful return of

Western troops to the country, from which they were ejected in 2005, when the UN peacekeeping mission and its Western backers came under heavy fire from local insurgents.

The EU and Asia

EU relations with Asia have never been as close as those with Africa. In the late 1970s and early 1980s, the economic success first of Japan and then of the Asian tigers alerted Europe to the importance of the region (Filippini 2007; Wiessala 2002). Since then, commercial inter-actions have topped Europe-Asia relations, accompanied by the well-honed EU foreign policy of promoting economic development, democracy, the rule of law, and human rights. To date, the EU's security role in the region is weak. Whereas the EU is a member of the ASEAN Regional Forum, the only multinational, cooperative security forum in Asia, Brussels's practical contribution to security in the region is minimal. So are its security relations with regional military powers such as China. This said, the EU has supported preventive diplomacy (for instance in North Korea) and peace-building (for instance in East Timor). Its CSDP operations in the region have raised its political profile but not its reputation as a military actor. Many countries in the region do not regard the EU as a military power, and the United States remains the principal external security actor in the area.

The Aceh Monitoring Mission (AMM), September 2005–December 2006

For about thirty years, the northwest region of the Indonesian island of Sumatra—Aceh—was ravaged by civil war (Braud and Grevi 2005). The Free Aceh Movement (GAM) fought the central govern-ment because it wanted independence for the territory. Although numerous peace talks failed, the devastation visited upon Aceh by the 2004 tsunami opened a window of opportunity for a new peace round, because Indonesia needed international support to deal with the consequences. With the limelight on Aceh and nudged by the international community, the parties to the conflict resumed peace talks. The Crisis Management Initiative—the NGO run by the former Finnish president Martti Ahtisaari—facilitated the negotiations. On 15 August 2005, the parties agreed to a memorandum of understand-ing. In the peace deal, GAM gave up its demand for independence in favor of greater autonomy for Aceh and agreed to demobilize its 3,000 troops and to decommission its weapons. In turn, the government granted far-reaching autonomy and codecision rights to the region. Jakarta promised amnesty to former rebels; agreed to the reintegration of GAM fighters into civil society, the police, and the armed forces; and pledged to withdraw its counterinsurgency forces (military and police) from the region. To oversee and guide the implementation of the peace deal, the EU and the Association of Southeast Asian Nations (ASEAN) were asked to establish the AMM, but some EU states voiced concerns. In view of Aceh's previous record of unsuccessful peace initiatives, they feared that such a mission might end in failure. Yet the proponents of the AMM won the day, arguing that a CSDP deployment in Asia would showcase the EU's global security vocation at relatively low cost.

The AMM was the first CSDP mission run in cooperation with another international organization. It had a staff of nearly 240, of whom just under 130 were EU nationals. Given the EU's crisis management experience, ASEAN did not object to Brussels taking the lead in organizing and running the mission. The mandate went beyond monitoring activities as traditionally understood. The AMM was authorized to "rule on disputed amnesty cases" and to "investigate and rule on complaints and alleged violations" of the peace accord (Council of the European Union 2005: 14).[8] Its main security-related tasks were to provide a safe environment for and to monitor the demobilization of GAM fighters, to document the decommissioning of their weapons, and to check if excess Indonesian military and police forces withdrew from the region. In addition, the mission was asked to monitor the human rights situation, the reintegration of GAM members into civil society, and the elaboration of laws aimed at ensuring the transition of Aceh toward an autonomous and democratically governed region in Indonesia.

The main operational challenge for the AMM was the tight deployment schedule. The decommissioning of weapons was scheduled to begin on 15 September 2005—that is, within a month of the signing of the memorandum of understanding. To meet the deadline, CSDP rules were circumvented. On the day of the signing, the AMM–Initial Monitoring Presence (AMM-IMP) was set up. Legally, it was not an EU mission because it was funded not from the EU budget but by member states and non-EU states. Individual states also provided contributions in kind. The AMM-IMP procured equipment, rented accommodations and offices, and put in place the administrative structure and logistics of the mission. This preparatory work made it possible for the AMM to be fully operational on 15 September.

The demilitarization of Aceh proceeded smoothly, and the AMM played an important role in this success story. It arbitrated cases of disagreements among the two parties to the peace deal. More generally, the mission made a difference by engaging in "prevention through monitoring." Any attempt by one of the parties to retreat from its commitments made under the memorandum of understanding would have been witnessed by the AMM. Neither the former rebels nor the Indonesian government wanted to be named and shamed and possibly punished by the international community at a time when Aceh was still suffering from the aftermath of the tsunami.

The AMM squarely focused on its security-related tasks. By and large, it stayed away from its secondary mandate objectives—monitoring human rights and the legislative process. A number of factors explain this choice: the mission had few staff, its mandate was short, it lacked sticks and carrots, and it potentially could get sucked into politicking among local forces, as has happened in other theaters of operation such as Bosnia. Some observers criticized the mission for its neglect of transitional justice issues (Järvinen 2007). However, arguably, the CSDP is not the right vehicle to address such issues. This is the strength of the European Commission. Its follow-up capacity-building projects in Aceh have emphasized human rights.

The EU Police Mission in Afghanistan (EUPOL Afghanistan), June 2007–

In response to the terrorist attacks of September 11, Washington launched a war against the Taliban in Afghanistan, who provided a safe haven for Osama bin Laden and his followers. After the Taliban were driven from power, the multinational International Security Assistance Force was deployed to the country to stabilize and secure Afghanistan under a UN mandate. In 2003, when NATO took over command of the force, the West initially had high hopes for a quick success in building sustainable peace in Afghanistan, but these expectations turned out to be misplaced.

Virtually all EU states believe that the United States and NATO cannot afford to fail in Afghanistan because of the damage this would cause to the West's reputation. Moreover, failure would encourage further terrorist attacks and undermine the West's international leadership. Yet the launch of the civilian mission EUPOL Afghanistan in

2007 was not a strategic decision. It was not rooted in a coolheaded assessment of EU and Western interests at stake in Afghanistan and the means needed to defend them but was a response to demands from both Washington and Berlin to which the EU felt it could not say no. As the peace-building project ran into ever more problems, the Americans stepped up pressure on the Europeans to show greater solidarity with them and to contribute more to secure Afghanistan for the West. The Europeans felt obliged to assist their main ally in the difficult pacification of Afghanistan. Germany's demands arose out of its small police training program in Afghanistan, which it had launched in 2002 to show its solidarity with the United States after the September 11 attacks and to promote good governance in Afghanistan. Yet it soon became clear that the forty or so German trainers were insufficient to push forward the Westernization of the local police (Gross 2009b). Being eager to share the financial burden of an expanded police intervention with its EU partners and to deflect growing domestic criticism of its involvement in the faraway country, Berlin pushed for integrating the German police program into a CSDP training mission. Fellow EU governments were not in a position to reject the request of one of the main financial underwriters of the CSDP.

Initially, Brussels intended to dispatch about 160 European police officers to Afghanistan (EU Military Staff 2007: 12). Within a year, the mission was authorized to increase its international staff to about 400, including around 270 police officers, although it has never reached the authorized strength. Cooperation with NATO has been challenging, primarily because of different strategic priorities. The alliance leads a considerably larger push to reform and modernize Afghanistan's security sector, including the police. The NATO Training Mission–Afghanistan (NTM-A) emphasizes the capacity of the Afghan National Police to maintain public security, including through the use of force. The goal is to enhance its operational capabilities and survivability in the battle against the Taliban. EUPOL's focus is different, emphasizing intelligence-led policing, criminal investigations, anticorruption measures, and the police-prosecutor interface. For instance, mission legal advisers have worked with the interior ministry on drafting antiterrorism laws and an anticorruption strategy. Also, EUPOL develops and delivers train-the-trainer courses, which cover subjects such as basic policing skills, policing and human rights, and criminal investigations. Last but not least, EUPOL works with the European Commission, EU, and non-EU states to identify, facilitate, coordinate, and implement police aid projects. The Commission's support to Afghanistan includes considerable police-related funding and contributions to the Law and Order Trust Fund for Afghanistan, which pays for running the Afghan National Police (General Secretariat of the Council of the EU 2010). EUPOL staff outside Kabul depend for their security on NATO and are colocated with the Provincial Reconstruction Teams of the International Security Assistance Force. This has led to tensions between the reconstruction teams and CSDP personnel, as both have their own distinct operational priorities, which occasionally come into conflict because CSDP personnel are dependent on the willingness and capacity of the teams to protect them whenever they venture outside their compounds.

EUPOL Afghanistan is a real test for the EU, and it is not doing well. Beginning with external challenges, EUPOL operates in a hostile environment and is the first civilian CSDP mission to do so. In 2006, the Afghanistan Compact was agreed to by the government in Kabul and the Western-led international community. It promised that "all illegal armed groups [would] be disbanded by end-2007 in all provinces" (Building on Success: The London Conference on Afghanistan 2006: 6). When the EU mission deployed, this optimism about Afghanistan's future had faded away. Since then, the country has remained at risk of becoming a failed state. The international peace support operation overlaps with war fighting. The endemic insecurity hampers EUPOL activities and impact and constrains the movement of its unarmed staff. As to the Afghan police, it remains woefully undertrained and underequipped. Police corruption and political interference in operational policing decisions are common. The fact that numerous international actors are involved in security sector reform does not help, because they often work with different policing and legal standards and pursue conflicting objectives (International Crisis Group 2007; Peral 2009). EUPOL has sought to bring some order into these efforts by taking the lead in the International Police Coordination Board, which brings together international police reformers, including the NTM-A and Afghan stakeholders, but coordination has proved tricky. Not all international police aid donors are keen on being coordinated by the EU.

As to homemade challenges, the mission has had to contend with a number of issues. Full operational capability was delayed by the challenge of putting in place an adequate security dispositive for mission staff. Also, the mission struggled for a considerable period of time with management problems, including frequent leadership changes and internal reorganizations. Given the scale of the public security problems and the size of the country, the mission's autho-

rized personnel strength is clearly inadequate.[9] Also, it is dispropor-
tionately small compared to the much larger CSDP mission in the
much smaller Kosovo, which, in addition, enjoys relative peace. The
small size of EUPOL Afghanistan is aggravated by the persistent difficulties of filling the authorized posts, especially operational police
officers. As the EU itself acknowledges in internal discussions, these
factors limit mission impact and credibility (Dempsey 2009).

EUPOL Afghanistan underlines the persistent problem of civilian
CSDP missions in recruiting sufficient personnel. More importantly,
it underlines the inability of EU states to agree on common policies
on key foreign policy issues. The EU lacks a coherent strategy on
Afghanistan. Internal policy differences prevent the EU from making
more strenuous efforts to mobilize its available resources to make a
real difference on the ground. And when additional resources are
mobilized, they do not benefit EUPOL. In 2009, Europeans decided
to upgrade their involvement in police reforms in Afghanistan and
dispatched elements of the armed European Gendarmerie Force to
beef up the NATO-led police training. The EU believes that its small
CSDP mission in Afghanistan raises its profile as an international
security provider. The danger is that third countries look at what the
EU does there and conclude that the CSDP remains a paper tiger.

Notes

1. The right of first refusal refers to the political view, pushed in particular by the United States, that the EU could only launch CSDP missions after
NATO had been offered the opportunity to undertake the missions but had
declined in favor of the EU. The EU launched EUFOR Artemis without prior
consultation with the US.

2. South Sudan decided overwhelmingly to secede from Sudan in a ref-
erendum in January 2011, and the Sudanese government in Khartoum
accepted the decision. South Sudan accounts for about 75 percent of Sudan's
oil production, which is pumped through a pipeline to northern Sudan, where
it is shipped to buyers around the world.

3. In April 2007, Brussels amended the mandate of its Civilian-Military
Supporting Action to AMIS 2 to task the EU mission to support the start-up
of the African Union's peacekeeping operation in Somalia, AMISOM.

4. Piracy partly emerged out of a self-help movement by Somali fisher-
men who tried to extract "license fees" from the European and international
fleets that fished illegally in the country's territorial waters. Some coastal
communities in Somalia still see the pirates as heroes in defending against
poaching by foreign fishing vessels. Also, there have been accusations that
EU countries dump toxic waste off the Somali coast (Pop 2008).

5. The functions of EU NAVCO were incorporated into Atalanta.

6. In a deviation from CSDP standard operating procedures, the commanding officer of EUTM Somalia is double-hatted as operation and force commander.

7. In 2006, Ethiopia invaded Somalia with the (tacit) political support of the United States, the United Nations, and the African Union. Ethiopia backed the pro-Western government and wanted to defeat the Islamic forces that had gained control over much of Somalia. In 2009, Ethiopian troops left the country without having succeeded in defeating the rebels.

8. The head of mission had the power to make binding decisions to resolve disputes. If a dispute persisted, the memorandum of understanding designated Ahtisaari as the final arbiter. An AMM legal expert reviewed about 100 disputed amnesty cases, and all his recommendations were accepted by the parties (Kirwan 2008).

9. When the EU began to consider dispatching a civilian CSDP mission to the country, the EUSR for Afghanistan made the case for a 2,000-strong deployment.

CHAPTER 11

Evaluating CSDP Operations

BY 2011, THE EU HAD DISPATCHED ABOUT 70,000 SOLDIERS and civilian personnel in more than twenty operations. All have been coalitions of the able and willing drawn from among EU states and third countries. The deployments show that the EU has specialized in stabilization and reconstruction operations (military and civilian). Civilian operations have carried out security sector reforms and monitored cease-fire and peace accords, while military operations have carried out postconflict stabilization tasks, notably peacekeeping. All operations were conducted with the consent of the host nations. The EU has not done forced-entry operations and has not fought any wars (conventional or unconventional). Also, the balance between military and civilian deployments is skewed. There have only been seven military operations, which is surprising because the CSDP was conceived to give the EU military firepower. Going beyond these general observations, this chapter asks how well CSDP operations (military and civilian) have worked, what differences they have made, and why they have not done better. CSDP missions have a mixed balance sheet, and the chapter explains why this is so. Measuring success in politics is not straightforward and depends on the choice of measuring rod. In this chapter, a series of evaluation criteria are used to offer a nuanced judgment of the CSDP record.

Evaluating Mission Success

One of the most commonly used yardsticks to evaluate CSDP operations is how well they have carried out their mandates. This measuring rod directs attention to mission design and management, including the provision of sufficient funds and personnel. The record shows that some of the issues, particularly civil-military coordination, regularly flagged by the EU itself and by policy analysts are less important than generally assumed. Insufficient cooperation between military and civilian missions has not been a major obstacle standing in the way of effective mandate implementation. The lack of civil-military integration in the planning and initial conduct of EUFOR Althea and the EUPM, and the dysfunctional policy overlaps this failure generated, were exceptional. This said, civil-military coordination is an important issue in any nation-building intervention, notably when carried out in hostile environments. As the EU intends to involve itself more firmly in such interventions in the future, including through the concurrent use of Battle Groups and civilian missions, the need for tight civil-military cooperation will grow. Also, civilian operations would clearly benefit from better civil-military cooperation in capability development in areas such as transportation, communications, security, and logistics.

A number of severe hiccups in mission start-up and in the implementation phase have affected mandate implementation. Initially, civilian missions were hampered by their narrow mandates, which ignored functional linkages in the security sector. The functional interdependence between the various components of the security sector, such as policing and prosecution, requires a holistic approach to reforms. The narrow focus of the first generation of civilian CSDP missions reflected the decision by the EU to build up the civilian CSDP around discrete priority areas such as law enforcement and the rule of law. Second-generation missions in Iraq, Afghanistan, and Kosovo no longer suffer from this problem but have benefited from the EU's turn to multifunctional mission designs.

Among the most challenging or simply most annoying issues for civilian CSDP missions have been cumbersome funding procedures and difficulties in recruiting and retaining qualified personnel. The costs of civilian missions are funded from the EU budget, which is managed by the European Commission. Commission red tape has caused many delays in the procurement of basic mission equipment such as computers, telephones, and armored cars. Also, missions from Kosovo to the DRC and Afghanistan have struggled to reach and maintain their authorized personnel strength. In the absence of effective national recruitment mechanisms, including incentive packages, there are simply not enough volunteers for the largest and toughest missions. Military operations do not have this problem because soldiers go where they are ordered. However, military operations have suffered from a lack of strategic and tactical airlift, which has made rapid interventions, rotations in and out of theater, and logistics challenging. Both civilian and military missions have been affected by bureaucratic infighting among different branches of EU foreign policy and by related difficulties in coordinating action on the ground among different members of the EU family.[1] Institutional politicking and turfing have prevented the EU from making the most of its comprehensive toolbox for tackling international security problems.

These shortcomings and difficulties have degraded mandate implementation. They have contributed to the fact that missions have failed to achieve all their objectives and that some objectives have been accomplished only with considerable delay. Yet such problems are not unusual but are familiar to any international security provider. They do not invalidate the judgment that CSDP missions have, by and large, been reasonably efficient and effective in accomplishing their mandates. This is true even of the CSDP police mission in Afghanistan, which diligently carries out its mandate to "support the reform process towards a trusted and efficient police service." Measured in terms of how well operations have fulfilled their mandates, the CSDP must be judged a qualified success. For critics of the CSDP, this very success is part of the problem. They argue that easy or vaguely formulated mission mandates exclude the possibility of failure. The price for success on this count is a CSDP that is irrelevant to most contemporary security problems.

Another evaluation criterion is whether CSDP operations have enhanced the EU's visibility in international security affairs. The answer is yes. From eastern and southeastern Europe to Africa and Asia, the EU has planted the CSDP flag, and local governments have taken note. While the international assessment of CSDP operations may not in each case be positive, international demand for them has risen considerably. Both troubled countries themselves and the international community have asked the EU to deploy its forces and civilian personnel to deal with trouble spots. Especially satisfying for the EU, Washington has shown its appreciation of the CSDP by supporting or advocating EU deployments in the Western Balkans, the Middle East, and Afghanistan. Overall, there has been more international demand for CSDP operations than the EU has been willing to meet.

A closely related yardstick measures the geopolitical impact of CSDP operations. On this count, success has been limited. For instance, in the Western Balkans and Georgia, CSDP operations have strengthened the credibility and political influence of the EU and have given it additional diplomatic leverage in relations with the concerned governments. This said, the EU's influence in world politics is mostly shaped by non-CSDP actions such as the European Neighbourhood Policy and trade and development policies. The geopolitical impact of CSDP operations is often limited by the fact that it is a common rather than single policy. National foreign policies coexist with the CSDP, and when the former diverge they inevitably undermine the latter. This has obviously been the case in Afghanistan and Iraq but also in less prominent missions in post-Soviet space and Africa. On geopolitical matters, it is the United States that continues to be the preferred interlocutor of policymakers in places such as Georgia, Afghanistan, and Palestine, where the EU planted its CSDP flag. In Africa, CSDP deployments have not prevented China from enhancing its commercial and political presence and influence in geo-economically important countries such as the DRC and Chad. For Washington, NATO and not the EU remains the privileged interlocutor in international security matters. Also, the CSDP has had little impact on Russia's attitudes toward the EU. Critics use these facts to argue that it is incumbent upon the EU to use the CSDP more robustly to defend and promote its interests and values abroad. If it fails to get the CSDP right, it will lose out in the emerging strategic environment of a more competitive international system (Howorth 2009).

Moving away from EU-centric yardsticks for evaluating CSDP operations, more demanding yardsticks measure what difference the CSDP operations have made in the world. Their ability to make a difference has been varied and limited, though not negligible.

To begin with, CSDP troops have successfully kept the peace in a number of postconflict societies and protected vulnerable population groups. CSDP monitors have facilitated the implementation of ceasefire agreements and peace deals, while CSDP police officers have made law enforcement more effective and democratic. CSDP judges and prosecutors have strengthened the rule of law, and CSDP penitentiary experts have made prisons more humane. In carrying out these tasks, CSDP missions have prevented conflicts, promoted stability, and contributed to good governance. Furthermore, CSDP operations, especially those in the Western Balkans, have undoubtedly strengthened EU internal security. Through their security sector reforms, the missions have combated organized crime in their host countries and the associated threats to the EU, such as drug trafficking, weapons smuggling, and illegal migration.

On the downside, the CSDP operations' success in making a difference in the world does not reflect a focus on interventions concerned with achieving maximum impact on stability, peace, and human security. As the former head of the EDA put it, "The issue with [the CSDP] operational record as a whole is its lack of ambition" (Witney 2008: 41). For the most part, the EU has avoided sending its troops into harm's way. Most operations have operated in permissive or semipermissive environments. The EU has not stopped harm when it could have done so for fear of casualties among its troops and civilian personnel. It has refused to authorize robust peacemaking operations to stop brutal civil strife, even with the blessing of the United Nations, because it did not want to allocate the necessary funds. Many missions have been small, drawing on an EU staff of less than 100, although some had only 10 to 30 EU staff. The largest military mission has been EUFOR Althea, which initially had 7,000 troops, while the largest civilian mission has been EULEX Kosovo, which has an authorized strength of nearly 2,000 internationals. When judged against the security challenges on the ground, most missions have been underresourced. However, their symbolic impact has been at least as important as their practical impact, because they have boosted the collective identity and self-confidence of the EU. The limitations in size, resources, and real-world impact of CSDP operations have prompted some analysts to argue that the CSDP has "come to serve as an alibi for a tendency to avoid broader international security responsibilities" (Menon 2009: 228). Clearly, CSDP missions have not made as much difference in the world as one would expect, given the EU's capabilities and its identity and global vision as a force for good. Hence, those who support this vision challenge the EU to do more to live up to its ideals (Glasius and Kaldor 2006).

Finally, the impact of CSDP operations can also be analyzed by looking at one of the most salient contemporary international security issues—international terrorism. Such an analysis shows that combating global terrorism is not one of the strengths of CSDP missions (Keohane 2008; Shepherd 2006). In this area, they are bit players. This fact reflects general shortcomings of EU security policy. EU states often find it hard to cooperate because they have divergent threat perceptions and national interests. Furthermore, many states are reluctant to allocate more national resources to give the CSDP a greater role in counterterrorism. Critics who focus on what they consider the EU's irresponsible softness on terrorism overlook many EU governments' genuine conviction that the best way to fight the phenomenon is not through military force (Delpech 2002). For Western European states, this conviction is rooted in the experience of Euro-terrorism, which had its heyday in the 1970s and 1980s.[2] Europeans framed their mostly homegrown terrorism as an instance of organized crime. Hence, they dealt with it by means of the police and courts, and the predominance of the justice model of fighting terrorism persisted after September 11. The high representative for the CFSP, Solana, expressed the EU's approach thus: "I firmly believe that the military option alone cannot defeat terror. Judicial, police, and intelligence cooperation should be the focal point for action. This does not mean that we are not working on how [the CSDP] can offer a meaningful contribution. But [the CSDP] is not at the core of our efforts" (Solana 2004a).

The EU has identified four counterterrorism roles for the CSDP (Council of the European Union 2004). First, CSDP missions may contribute to the prevention of terrorism in their theaters of operation through noncombat operations such as the gathering of tactical intelligence about terrorist activities. Second, CSDP operations may help protect critical civilian infrastructures in their host countries against terrorist plots. Third, CSDP operations may carry out consequence management, that is, carry out reactive measures to mitigate or ameliorate the destructive effects of terrorist attacks.[3] Finally, CSDP missions may support third countries in their fight against terrorism. Much of what can be counted as, admittedly, indirect CSDP counterterrorism falls under this last category. CSDP stabilization and reconstruction missions have improved the effectiveness of local armed forces, law enforcement, and border security. Effective security services make it harder for terrorists to get away with their actions and to use the country as a safe haven. Moreover, CSDP missions have improved the governance of local security sectors. Accountable security governance reduces the likelihood of violent radicalization and terrorist recruitment among citizens. It also makes it less likely that local security sector personnel go rogue by becoming involved in terrorist acts.

The EU can justifiably claim that its CSDP missions have been part of international efforts to combat global terrorism. Yet in crucial theaters of confrontation between terrorism and its opponents, such as in Afghanistan and Iraq, CSDP operations have lacked the resources to bring about substantial reforms of the local security sectors. The risibly low personnel strength of EUPOL Afghanistan is a worst case and has condemned the mission to a marginal role in the stabilization and reconstruction of policing in Afghanistan. The even smaller EUJUST LEX Iraq is hardly more impressive. On the issue of combating international terrorism, the CSDP falls short not only of the expectations of its critics but of its own aspirations.

In conclusion, CSDP operations have a mixed record. They have improved the "actorness" of the EU in security affairs, that is, its "capacity to behave actively and deliberately in relation to other actors in the international system" (Sjöstedt 1977: 16). Mission impact on international crises has been real but limited. The EU could have used the CSDP more forcefully to make a difference in world politics and shown a greater willingness to share the burden of global security management with the United States. Observers have criticized the EU for the gap between its aspirations and potential power and the modest operational record of the CSDP (Hill 1993; Toje 2008). This discrepancy, in turn, explains why CSDP missions have done little to change the EU's relations with major security providers and rivals. While taking note of the CSDP, they have realized that for the time being it remains an underresourced capability for the projection of limited power. The danger for the EU is that, if the limitations of its CSDP missions persist, they will do it more damage than good in the long run. Indeed, some observers claim that this is already happening. "By choosing marginal activities, the EU has actually increased skepticism about its seriousness of purpose rather than built a foundation for more complex and demanding undertakings" (Schake 2006: 105).

Explaining the Limited Record of CSDP Missions

What explains the limited record of CSDP missions? There are two main reasons why CSDP operations have not achieved more. One is related to political will, the other to capabilities and manpower. Both are closely related. Beginning with capabilities and manpower, the EU's record of building up its military capabilities is respectable but limited (see Chapter 6). For the time being, many armed conflicts around the world remain too demanding for CSDP expeditionary forces to make a difference. The civilian CSDP has been hampered by national administrative systems, which have been ill prepared for meeting the personnel requirements of CSDP deployments. As Swedish foreign minister Carl Bildt (2008) put it, "While we have standing military units ready to go—notably the two EU Battle Groups ready to deploy within 10 days—we don't have policemen, judges, lawyers or different instructors ready in the same way."

Yet the capability and manpower arguments have their limits. The key problem of the CSDP lies somewhere else. Shortfalls notwithstanding, EU states together have powerful civilian and military means of intervention. Although the EU has Battle Groups on standby for robust interventions, they have not been deployed. Also, it is not for a lack of manpower that the EU has not fielded a stronger police mission in Afghanistan. The biggest challenge faced by the CSDP is the lack of sufficient political will to make the most of existing CSDP capabilities and available human resources. A multidimensional problem (Keukeleire and MacNaughtan 2008: 140–141), the issue of political will refers to divergent national interests on specific policy issues such as a particular CSDP deployment. More broadly, it refers to different national worldviews and conceptions of the CSDP's role. For instance, some EU states want the EU to be primarily a civilian foreign policy actor, while others are reluctant to act forcefully without the United States. Certain states do not want to bear the costs in blood and money of mounting robust CSDP missions (for more on these divergent views, see Chapter 7).

The problem of political will is less acute in the case of civilian missions than in the case of military missions. Civilian deployments frequently rise above the lowest common denominator of member governments, not because EU states share an actionable strategic vision of the role of civilian CSDP operations in the world but because even small states are able to upload their preferences to the CSDP. Often backed by EU officials, they manage to persuade other capitals to back their pet CSDP projects. Fellow EU states let themselves be persuaded because the proposed missions tend to be cheap and unlikely to result in casualties. The successful uploading of national preferences to the CSDP has given the civilian CSDP an activist profile, and the considerable number of civilian deployments is a sign of the CSDP's success. Yet the role of policy entrepreneurs in shaping civilian deployment decisions has a downside, because the ensuing deployment pattern makes little sense in strategic terms and reflects a proliferation of mostly small missions that struggle to make a difference on the ground.

When it comes to military EU operations, the political will problem is severe. Because decisions remain closely tied to the lowest common denominator of states, military deployments have been few and, with the exception of EUFOR Althea, unreasonably short and lacking in ambition. Just like civilian deployments, they have not amounted to the strategic positioning of the EU on the international stage. Policy entrepreneurship and uploading have influenced military deployment decisions, notably in Africa, but their impact has been less powerful than in the civilian CSDP. The political constraints holding EU military deployments in check are powerful. Military operations tend to be politically more salient and controversial within and between EU states than civilian ones. To begin with, they raise politically hard questions about the division of labor between the EU and NATO. Atlanticist EU governments (more pro-US) and Europeanist EU governments (less pro-US) are likely to provide contradictory answers to these questions. Also, military EU operations are more expensive than civilian ones and tend to be larger than civilian missions, and participating governments have to pick up most of the costs of deploying and running them. This limits the enthusiasm of countries such as Germany for EU military deployments. They see their own armed forces and the military CSDP as an easy source of budget savings. By cutting back on their armed forces and limiting funding for the military CSDP, they save money.

The main political obstacle standing in the way of more robust military CSDP deployments is that for each proposed operation there are EU governments reluctant to send their soldiers to die for its objectives. This points to a dilemma between effectiveness and the consensus principle. If consensus among EU states remains a requirement for military missions, then deployments will continue to be unimpressive. Asle Toje calls this phenomenon the consensus-expectations gap. The "lack of decisionmaking procedures capable of overcoming dissent [opens] a gap between what the member-states are expected to agree on and what they are actually able to consent to" (Giegerich 2008; Toje 2008: 122). The argument leads to the conclusion that unless the EU changes the procedures it uses to decide military operations, it will be condemned to remain a military player of limited importance. One solution that has been proposed to plug the consensus-expectations gap is the creation of directorates made up of a few like-minded countries that are ready and able to exercise leadership on CSDP issues (Giegerich and Gross 2006; Keukeleire 2001). While not as elegant as the alternative of extending majority voting to CSDP deployment decisions, the idea has the advantage of being more realistic. Directorates would make the EU more like NATO, in which political-military decisionmaking benefits from the existence of a military and diplomatic leader, which is powerful enough to organize collective NATO action. CSDP directorates would be the equivalent of US leadership in NATO. Membership scenarios for CSDP directorates range from variable, issue-specific leadership coalitions to institutionalized small-group leadership centered on the Big Two—Britain and France—or the Big Three, which includes Germany.

The Lisbon Treaty provides a partial solution to the vexing consensus-expectations gap in the form of a provision for permanent

structured cooperation. The notion of permanent structured cooperation is not identical to the concept of directorate. However, they share
the idea of a pioneer group of countries leading the way in military
cooperation. Permanent structured cooperation allows the militarily
more capable member states to press ahead with deeper military integration. The provision can be used to promote closer cooperation in
EU capability development and the qualitative improvement of
forces. While permanent structured cooperation formally does not
apply to deployments, "one may reasonably expect those who participate [in permanent structured cooperation] to show more willingness
to participate in operations" (Biscop 2008: 12).

The accomplishments of the CSDP are real but so are its limitations. The overall record of CSDP missions is characterized by incompleteness, unevenness, and partial frustration. This is not unique to the
CSDP. Indeed, this is precisely how Philippe Schmitter (1970, 2004)
has characterized EU integration. Schmitter argues that interaction
between incompleteness, unevenness, and partial frustration has pro-
pelled European integration forward. There is considerable evidence
that such a dialectic is also at work in the CSDP. There have been slow
but steady improvements in the planning, command, and control of
CSDP missions. Capability gaps are being tackled, and a common
strategic culture is being forged by the EU's PSC. The EU has shown a
persistent readiness to deploy missions, albeit so far in a haphazard way.
The Lisbon Treaty continues to improve coordination between the
CFSP and supranational foreign policy, enabling CSDP missions to benefit from closer cooperation with EU embassies on the ground. Last but
not least, permanent structured cooperation provides a means for the EU
to limit the negative impact of the political will problem and to send
more robust missions into harm's way to promote peace and security.

Notes

1. Some of these problems are alleviated though not eliminated by the
Lisbon Treaty. Improvements are to be expected when it comes to interinstitutional bureaucratic politics, insufficient coordination on the ground, and
the cumbersome procurement procedures. The former two problems are alleviated by the creation of the EU diplomatic service, while the latter problem
is alleviated by the creation of new rapid financing mechanisms stipulated by
the Lisbon Treaty.

2. The most notorious terror groups of the time were the ethnonationalist
group Basque Homeland and Freedom (Euskadi Ta Askatasuna, or ETA), the
West German Red Army Faction (Rote Armee Fraktion, or RAF), the Italian

Red Brigade (Brigate Rosse), the French Direct Action (Action Directe), and the Irish Republican Army (IRA).

3. While CSDP missions can only be used outside the EU, CSDP structures and capabilities may be used to protect citizens and institutions in the EU against terrorist attacks and to deal with the consequences of such attacks. To this end, the EUMS maintains a "database of military assets and capabilities relevant to the protection of civilian populations against the effects of terrorist attacks" (European Commission 2003).

PART 3

Partnerships and Rivalries

CHAPTER 12

Transatlantic Relations

THIS CHAPTER ANALYZES HOW THE EU QUEST FOR A GREATER role in international security affairs has affected transatlantic relations and NATO. When the CSDP was launched in 1999, the United States was seriously concerned about its implications for relations among the allies. It laid down a number of lines in the sand that the EU was not supposed to cross and tried to "bind" the CSDP to NATO. September 11 distracted the United States from the CSDP problem and ushered in a period when Washington's attitudes toward the CSDP were characterized by benign neglect. The transatlantic crisis over the invasion of Iraq shattered Washington's benign neglect of the CSDP, which got mixed up in the fallout from the conflict. Countries that opposed the US-led invasion of Iraq used the transatlantic crisis to argue for making the CSDP more autonomous from US-led NATO. Washington saw this initiative as a grave challenge to the transatlantic relationship. Yet pragmatism prevailed. Since the second term of the George W. Bush administration, foreign and security policy coordination among the transatlantic allies has been good. Washington realized that its earlier fears of the EU becoming a military peer competitor were exaggerated. Also, it needed CSDP help in the nation-building efforts that followed its military campaigns in Afghanistan and Iraq. Since then Washington has supported new CSDP deployments, and EU-NATO cooperation has improved, though important stumbling blocks remain. More by chance than design, a new division of labor in international security affairs has emerged between the United States and the EU. The former specializes in hard security, the latter in soft security, but both have made strides in closing their respective capability gaps. Yet US support for the CSDP, now and for the foreseeable future, remains conditional on the EU accepting US leadership in transatlantic and global security.

The Transformation of Post–Cold War European Security: NATO and the EU

During the Cold War, the EU had to accept a subordinate role in European and global security affairs. Europe was divided between two hostile blocs—the West led by the United States and the East led by the Soviet Union. Both blocs were armed to the teeth. Through NATO, the United States organized the West's defense and extended security guarantees to its European allies. Washington was the EU's undisputed leader in international security affairs, though this did not prevent numerous intra-alliance disputes. Western Europeans were strategic followers, despite occasional efforts by some governments to carve out a more independent role for themselves and the EU in international affairs.[1] The EU developed an embryonic common foreign policy but did not touch military security. However, the end of the Cold War at the end of the 1980s fundamentally changed the security situation in Europe. When the Communist East Bloc collapsed, Western Europe no longer faced any state-based threats from the East. Instead, political and economic instability and interethnic conflicts in eastern and southeastern Europe posed new nontraditional security threats to the EU, including trafficking in radioactive material from the former Soviet Union, drug trafficking, illegal migration, and the spillover of regional conflicts into the EU. The new geopolitical situation in Europe put pressure on NATO and the EU to adjust and created opportunities for them to redefine their security roles. The resulting changes in European security policies and institutions were gradual and partial adaptations rather than revolutions.

The collapse of the Soviet Union has left the United States as the principal global power. At first hesitantly, it began to extend its security influence into the former Communist East Bloc and the Western Balkans. US-dominated NATO has been a key vehicle in this ongoing process, with the United States leading the drive to reform the "coldest of Cold War organisations" (Forster 2006: 3). The alliance was rebranded as a security management organization that provides security not just to alliance members but to all European states. In 1994, the Partnership for Peace program was established. It is open to any European and post-Soviet state that is not a member of NATO. The partnership provides assistance to governments interested in carrying out defense reforms and in modernizing their armed forces along NATO standards. In 1997, NATO invited the Czech Republic, Hungary, and Poland to begin accession talks. This set in motion a process of eastward enlargement, which has seen NATO swell to twenty-eight members by 2011. Last but not least, the alliance launched out-of-area peacekeeping and peacemaking operations. In 1991, participating states agreed to restructure their armed forces so as to make the alliance fit for both territorial defense and out-of-area operations (North Atlantic Council 1991). Already in the next year, NATO launched an operation in the Adriatic Sea in support of the UN embargo against rump Yugoslavia. Over the following years, it stepped up its military involvement in the Western Balkans. September 11 added new urgency to the transformation of NATO from a place-bound collective defense alliance into an organization capable of both territorial defense and foreign interventions for the purpose of global security management.

The EU, too, has expanded geographically and functionally in the wake of the Cold War. It has extended its economic, political, and security influence into its eastern neighborhood. In the process of enlargement negotiations with its former enemies, it has transformed them into stable liberal democracies. In 2004, eight former Communist countries and newly independent Soviet states joined the EU. Three years later, two more former Communist states followed. Eighteen years after the Berlin Wall separating East from West Germany came crashing down, the EU had expanded its liberal zone of peace deep into the East. Moreover, the eastern enlargement process is still ongoing. All the newly independent states of the former Communist Yugoslavia are scheduled to join the EU. In another major departure from the days of the Cold War, the EU added security and defense to the policy fields in which its members cooperate. Initially, this was done against the backdrop of US calls for a fairer sharing of the costs of transatlantic security, the spread of ethnic conflicts in Europe, and German reunification. The growing importance of stabilization and reconstruction operations across the world, associated with the growth of security interdependence, has provided a further impetus for the development of the CSDP. Unlike the EU's eastern enlargement, its quest for a greater role in international security has been a controversial issue in transatlantic relations. Moreover, it has been bound up with the transformation of NATO.

The Quest for a European Security
and Defense Identity

The end of the Cold War gave rise to divergent views within the transatlantic community of the future of European security. The main divisions were between Washington and Paris. The other states of the transatlantic order sided with either the United States (the Atlanticists) or with France (the Europeanists) or sought to carve out a middle position (for a discussion of Atlanticism, Europeanism and Euroatlanticism, see Chapter 7). Paris saw the end of the Cold War as an opportunity to realize its long-standing goal of a greater European security role at US expense and pursued a two-pronged strategy. On the one hand, it sought to weaken NATO. On the other, it pushed for the transformation of the EU into a military power. The United States, however, wanted to retain its preeminence in European security and opposed French moves to weaken NATO. Also, it sought to channel the EU quest for a greater role in international security into a direction that would not undermine its own security role.

The first element of France's two-pronged strategy was to insist that NATO retain its narrow focus on collective defense as laid down in article 5 of the North Atlantic Treaty. Given the declining importance of territorial defense in Europe after the collapse of the Soviet Union, the French demand was paramount to limiting NATO's role in European and global security. Moreover, Paris made the case for transforming NATO from a militarily integrated, US-led organization into a more traditional alliance, in which participating states retain their military autonomy. French officials and defense experts proposed that NATO rethink its integrated military commands. Since the time of President de Gaulle, Paris had criticized the United States for imposing an integrated command structure on the alliance that largely escaped supervision by the civilian North Atlantic Council. The French argument was that this command structure was a central means through which Washington maintained its preeminence in European security (Bozo 2001; Cogan 2001). In the view from Paris, the linchpin of this structure of control was the supreme allied commander Europe, who is always an American. Paris wanted to do away with this military structure in favor of command arrangements that emphasize arm's-length military relations among coequal states.

The second element of France's two-pronged strategy to create a new European security architecture was to give the EU an independent security and defense role, which would enable the EU to better defend and promote its interests and values abroad and to pacify and stabilize its neighborhood. Also, close EU security cooperation would bind the reunified Germany more tightly to its European partners and defuse the danger that the growth of power associated with reunification would destabilize European politics. Paris joined forces with a willing, albeit more cautious Germany in the run-up to and during the intergovernmental conference negotiating the 1992 Maastricht Treaty. Together they made the case to their EU partners for empowering the EU to pursue "a genuine security policy, which should lead ultimately to a common defense."[2] Moreover, they announced they would establish a Franco-German Eurocorps, which would be open for membership to other EU nations. The proposal was seen by some observers as a move to create the nucleus of a multinational European army, while French plans to weaken NATO and build up Europe as an independent security actor raised alarm bells in the United States.

Washington was in favor of the Europeans doing more to reduce the strain on US manpower and financial resources that came with being Europe's main security provider. With the end of the Cold War, US policymakers clamored for a new transatlantic deal that would see Europeans shoulder more of the responsibility for their security. However, Washington was not willing to play second fiddle to its allies in security matters on the continent and wanted NATO to retain its preeminence in any new European security architecture. To square its own objectives with the EU's aspiration for a greater role in European security and defense, Washington backed the creation of a European Security and Defence Identity. At the same time, it sought to contain this identity within NATO and to make sure it would not amount to a unified EU bloc that would undermine its leadership of the alliance. Secretary of State James Baker and other US foreign policy officials set out to make sure the EU negotiations on the Maastricht Treaty stuck to the concept of the European Security and Defence Identity *within* a US-led NATO. They pointed out to their European allies that Washington would be hostile to any steps that minimized its role in Europe.[3] More precisely, they made two things clear to their European counterparts. First, the United States fully supported a European defense role as long as it remained embedded within NATO. Second, the United States would not tolerate "the *presumption* of a separate European viewpoint" in European security matters (Brenner 1998: 27, emphasis in original; also Laurent 2001; Sloan 2000). As to NATO, after some initial hesitation, Washington realized that the best strategy to keep the alliance in business was to expand its membership and to give it the capacity for foreign interventions. Only by transforming NATO into a pan-European and possibly global security organization would the alliance remain relevant to the security concerns of its member states and receive adequate resources from them.

The result of the tug-of-war between Washington and Paris and their respective Atlanticist and Europeanist visions of European security was a deal slanted in favor of Atlanticism. Washington backed the creation of the CFSP by the Maastricht Treaty, while the Europeans pledged not to do anything that would undermine NATO's role as Europe's premier security organization. In practical terms this pledge meant that the Maastricht Treaty did not endow the EU with independent military capabilities but contracted EU military tasks out to the WEU—the sleepy defense organization dating back to the 1950s (see Chapter 3). The WEU was to be the embodiment of the European Security and Defence Identity. According to (a declaration attached to) the Maastricht Treaty, the WEU was to be both the EU's defense arm and NATO's reinforced European pillar. The United States found this setup acceptable because the WEU had always been subordinate to the alliance. Moreover, it did not have the capabilities to plan operations and to command and control them in the field but would have to rely on NATO. As to Paris, it reconciled itself to the idea that, for the time being, no credible EU alternative to US-dominated NATO existed. This reassessment was facilitated by Europe's powerlessness in the face of the bloody war in Bosnia (Gnesotto 1997; Grant 1997). Paris realized that a stronger European defense role had to be constructed with rather than against the United States. As one French commentator put it, Paris acknowledged that "in order to be more European tomorrow it [was] necessary to be more Atlanticist today" (Jean-Claude Casanova, cited in Grant 1997: 59). Hence, Paris sought a rapprochement with NATO and gave up its opposition to NATO's task expansion. In order to have input into the planning of a NATO-led peace support operation in Bosnia, Paris participated again in some of the work of NATO's Military Committee, from which it had withdrawn in 1966. When the force was deployed in Bosnia in 1995, French troops served in it.

To ready the WEU for its new role as the EU's security arm, the participants of the defense organization designated some of their national troops as "forces answerable" to the WEU, that is, as forces that were ready to be deployed in a WEU operation carried out on behalf of the EU. A WEU planning cell, comprising about forty officers, was set up to prepare contingency plans for the deployment of

WEU troops in EU missions. But these measures did not make a European defense capability. For this, the Europeans needed NATO's help. The alliance agreed and began to elaborate an interface between the two security organizations, which would enable the WEU to get access to NATO capabilities and assets for EU operations.[4] NATO adapted the concept of combined joint task forces, which had been conceived of as a means to enable the alliance to adjust its territorially based command structure to the post–Cold War strategic environment. Combined joint task forces provide the alliance with the capacity to deploy ad hoc headquarters for multinational (combined) and multiservice (joint) formations. They allow "coalitions of the willing" to draw on NATO command and control capabilities to implement out-of-area operations. Back in the 1990s, combined task forces offered NATO a means to give the WEU separable but not separate alliance headquarters. In 1994, NATO declared that the alliance would "make collective assets of the Alliance available . . . for WEU operations undertaken by the European Allies in pursuit of their Common Foreign and Security Policy" (North Atlantic Council 1994). NATO thus promised to give Europeans the means to take on more responsibility for maintaining European security while reaffirming that the alliance remained the main forum for consultation and policy coordination among the allies (Hunter 2002; Sloan 2005). The NATO Summit in Berlin in 1996 declared "the completion of the CJTF concept," thus officially launching the NATO-WEU cooperation. Because WEU access to NATO capabilities and assets had to be approved by the alliance, the NATO-WEU arrangement gave Washington the power to veto any EU operation it did not like. As far as the EU states were concerned, the arrangement seemed a quick fix to implement the "S" in CFSP (Laurent 2001). Yet this expectation remained wishful thinking.

The institutional triangle among the EU, NATO, and the WEU did not galvanize EU states into building up their collective military power to support their declaratory foreign policy. Nor did it advance the development of a common strategic view that could guide CFSP deployment decisions. The debacle of European foreign policy during the violent breakup of Yugoslavia showed that the Maastricht Treaty had done little to undo the legacy of decades of Western European security dependence on the United States. In the absence of US leadership, the EU powers had no appetite for taking on military peace enforcement and peace-building tasks in the former Yugoslavia or elsewhere. The new CFSP notwithstanding, the EU behaved not like the responsible great power it wished to be but like a small power. It proved incapable of forceful action when regional conflicts erupted in its neighborhoods in the Western Balkans, Eastern Europe, and Africa. Also, institutional hurdles stood in the way of a more muscular EU security policy. The mechanics of the interface between NATO and the WEU were Byzantine: forty-five distinct procedural steps were needed to grant the WEU access to alliance assets in order to enable it to carry out military EU operations (Missiroli 2002: endnote 10). Furthermore, the WEU had closer institutional links with NATO than with the EU. The EU Council of Ministers did little to involve the WEU secretary-general in its work on security issues, and the same situation prevailed at the level of diplomats and experts.[5] Social distance rather than close cooperation in military affairs characterized the relationship between the EU and the WEU.

The Creation of the CSDP: US Ambiguous Reaction

Toward the end of 1998, with the credibility of the CFSP at a low, France and Britain agreed to work toward making the EU a military power in its own right. This was the beginning of the CSDP (for the strategic thinking behind the initiative, see Chapter 7). To "sell" the initiative to Washington, Paris and London emphasized that a key goal was to contribute to "the vitality of a modernised Atlantic Alliance" (Franco-British Summit 1998). But the Americans were still alarmed. On the face of it, the initiative seemed to challenge NATO and hence US supremacy in European security.

The US response to the Franco-British initiative, and the subsequent flurry of European diplomatic activity to implement it, were characterized by ambiguity. On the one hand, Washington saw in the CSDP a new opportunity to devolve some of the burden for securing Europe to its European allies. On the other hand, it feared that the new initiative might break its strategic preeminence on the continent. After all, "[c]onditions that are enabling of concerted policies by EU member states are equally conditions that permit the EU to chart a course that may diverge from that of the US" (Brenner 2003: 194).

In Washington's view, it had allowed a European security identity to evolve within NATO at the beginning of the 1990s only to see it grow out of it at the end of the decade. Washington was concerned that in the new millennium the CSDP might grow away from NATO.[6] Yet it also realized that this time the Europeans were serious about developing their own military security policy. Washington thus engaged in damage control. To avoid a hollowing out of NATO and its own he-gemony in European security affairs, the United States drew a number of lines in the sand that the EU was expected not to cross. More con-structively, it tried to tie the CSDP closely to NATO and hence itself. Beginning with the US "binding strategy," Washington consented to extend to the EU access to alliance capabilities and assets along the lines of the previous arrangement with the WEU. This was not an act of philanthropy but calculated self-interest. Granting the EU access to common NATO capabilities and assets was good for devolving European security responsibilities to Europeans. At the same time, Washington hoped that such an arrangement between NATO and the EU would "prevent the creation of an EU counterpart to Supreme Headquarters Allied Powers Europe (SHAPE) and a separate 'EU' army" (United States Department of Defense 2002: chapter 2). Without independent headquarters, the CSDP would not be able to evolve into a rival to NATO. In addition, the United States tried to ensure NATO influence over the CSDP through indirect means, pushing for close interinstitutional cooperation at political and expert levels on defense issues. This would allow the seasoned NATO personnel to shape the organizational setup and capability development of the fledgling CSDP. Also, Washington argued that the EU should draw on SHAPE even when it launched autonomous military operations (Andréani et al. 2001: 27).

As to the lines in the sand, Washington forcefully reminded its European allies that it expected the CSDP to be "consistent with NATO requirements and responsibilities" (Cohen 2000). This was famously expressed by Madeleine Albright in her response to the Franco-British CSDP initiative. She stipulated the three Ds, or better, the three Don'ts that should guide the construction of the CSDP: no diminution of NATO (or no decoupling of the CSDP from NATO), no discrimination against non-EU NATO members, and no duplication of NATO capabilities and assets. Albright was without doubt aware of the fact that, if applied strictly, these conditions would make an autonomous CSDP impossible. For instance, it would force the EU to allow non-EU European NATO members to participate as equals in the political and operational control of all military CSDP operations so as to avoid discrimination. Full compliance with the nonduplica-tion rule would mean that the EU could not acquire planning, intelli-gence, and other essential capabilities and assets. This would keep it dependent on NATO for mounting any serious military operation. In addition to laying down the three Don'ts, Washington sought to give

NATO a right of oversight over CSDP operations, calling for an alliance "right of first refusal." This would allow the EU to take military action "only after NATO had been offered the opportunity to undertake that mission but had referred it to the EU for action" (US Senate resolution, cited in Missiroli 2002: 14).

Practical Challenges in Forging the EU-NATO Strategic Partnership

In December 1999, the CSDP was launched. To make the new policy a success, the EU had to tackle many issues. In particular, it had to build the organizational infrastructure to run the CSDP and to pool and develop the national capabilities required to implement it. Moreover, these tasks required close coordination with NATO, from which the EU wanted to learn and borrow capabilities and assests and with which it wanted to coordinate its capability development and develop a strategic dialogue. In short, the EU wanted a strategic partnership with NATO. Until the creation of the CSDP, no such relationship existed. The EU was a civilian organization that had little interaction with NATO. The creation of the CSDP did away with the institutional triangle EU-NATO-WEU. The EU swallowed the latter, taking over most of its functions. With the middleman WEU gone, the EU and NATO had to forge their own strategic partnership. This required work on four fronts.

First, the EU had to equip itself with internal security standards that met NATO requirements in order to receive restricted military information from the alliance. This was a prerequisite for starting negotiations on the mechanics of the EU-NATO military interface. Despite opposition from within the EU, the two organizations signed an Interim Security Agreement in July 2000.[7] Second, the capability development processes of both institutions needed to be coordinated in order to avoid unnecessary duplication, which was complicated by French concerns. Paris worried about undue NATO influence on the CSDP through the back door of institutionalized military-to-military cooperation. An accord was finally reached, which allowed NATO experts to join their EU counterparts in elaborating the capabilities needed to establish the EU RRF. A third agenda item was the establishment of cooperation structures at both expert and political levels. This involved institutionalizing regular meetings and establishing procedures for consultations between the two institutions. Moreover, measures had to be agreed to to ensure there would be no EU discrimination against non-EU European NATO members in CSDP operations drawing on NATO capabilities and assets. Finally, the mechanics of EU access to NATO capabilities and assets had to be worked out, and procedures established for allowing NATO to monitor the EU's use of NATO's capabilities and assets and, if necessary, to recall them. On each of these four issues EU-NATO working groups were set up to hammer out solutions.

The main hurdle on the road to an EU-NATO strategic partnership was EU access to NATO capabilities and assets. Transferring the borrowing privileges from the WEU to the EU required lengthy negotiations. The principal stumbling block in the negotiations was Turkey—a member of NATO but not of the EU. Ankara insisted that the EU grant it a measure of influence over any EU military operation. The EU was unwilling to give Turkey a say in EU-only operations that did not draw on NATO, while Ankara was unwilling to budge and blocked progress in the EU-NATO negotiations. Turkish decisionmakers were concerned about Greece, its traditional rival and a card-carrying member of the EU, instigating an EU military operation in the Aegean Sea that might harm Turkish interests and wanted to be in a position to prevent this. At the end of 2002, the United States and Britain took the lead in international mediation and brokered a deal that was accepted by all sides.

First, the EU pledged that "under no circumstances, nor in any crisis, [would the CSDP] be used against an Ally" (European Council 2002: 17). Second, it agreed to take account of the interests and concerns of non-EU European NATO allies in considering any military operation. This would involve intensive consultations with them, beginning at the early stage of a crisis. Finally, concerning autonomous EU operations in the geographic proximity of a non-EU European NATO state, the EU made the following concession: it committed itself to giving special consideration to any request by the concerned state to be allowed to take part in such operations. These elements of the compromise met Ankara's security concerns.[8] Conversely, Turkey had to accept the decisionmaking autonomy of the EU. Neither Ankara nor any other non-EU NATO capital has a seat at the table when the EU states decide on whether or not to launch a CSDP operation. Moreover, like any other non-EU country, Turkey can only participate in EU-only operations if it is invited by the EU. Conversely, in EU operations drawing on NATO capabilities and assets, non-EU European NATO states have the right to participate (Dietrich 2006: 384–385; European Council 2002; Missiroli 2002).

In December 2002, the two organizations celebrated their new strategic partnership. At the heart of the relationship is what is common-ly known as the Berlin-Plus agreement, which is shorthand for a pack-age of agreements between the EU and NATO.[9] The Berlin-Plus agree-ment is not legally binding, but rather a gentlemen's agreement (Gosalbo Bono 2006; Haine 2003). The centerpiece of the Berlin-Plus package is assured EU access to NATO planning capabilities. Moreover, additional NATO assets such as deployable headquarters and communi-cation systems are presumed to be available for EU missions. NATO's interests are safeguarded by procedures that enable it to monitor and recall capabilities and assets on loan to the EU. It is important to note that "assured access" does not mean automatic access. NATO can refuse an EU request if its planning capabilities are needed for an operation under article 5 of the North Atlantic Treaty (Reichard 2006: 283).

The Berlin-Plus agreement symbolizes that in military matters the EU and NATO are interlocking institutions. However, the practi-cal military relevance of Berlin-Plus, though clearly not negligible, is limited. What Philip Gordon said of the military relationship between NATO and the WEU also applies to the NATO-EU hookup. "The very capabilities the Europeans need but do not have, NATO does not 'have' either" (Gordon 1997: 264). Gordon referred to assets required for demanding and faraway operations, such as strategic lift, air-refueling capabilities, and satellite intelligence systems.[10] The limited relevance of Berlin-Plus is underlined by the fact that from a total of seven mili-tary CSDP operations so far, only two have had recourse to NATO assets. Moreover, these two military operations—one in Macedonia, the other in Bosnia—were follow-up missions to NATO peacekeeping forces, which made them easy candidates for Berlin-Plus operations, because they simply drew on the capabilities and assets that NATO had itself put in place for its own operations.

Washington's Benign Neglect of the CSDP

In the wake of the Berlin-Plus agreement, the EU crossed many of the lines in the sand that had been drawn by Washington, yet the United States did not seem to care much. "No duplication of capabilities and assets" gave way to "no unnecessary duplication." EU-level capabili-ties to plan, command, and control military operations were put in place. NATO's right of first refusal was shown to be nonexistent in 2003 when a French-led EU military operation was deployed to the

DRC without prior consultation with Washington. Non-EU European alliance members such as Turkey were not granted the same rights as member states in autonomous EU operations.

In general, Washington adopted an attitude of benign neglect toward these developments. A number of factors contributed to this change in perception and policy. The terrorist attacks of September 11 accelerated and reinforced the shift in US strategic priorities away from Europe, which had been under way since the end of the Cold War. Clearly, the CSDP was not uppermost in the minds of US policymakers after the Al-Qaida attacks. Also, Europe's solidarity with the United States in the aftermath of the tragedy soothed Washington's concerns. "We are all Americans"—*nous sommes tous Américains*—editorialized the French newspaper *Le Monde* in its edition of 13 September. Washington had no reason to doubt the sincerity of European support. In response to the September 11 attacks, NATO invoked its collective defense clause for the first time in its history and took concrete, albeit small-scale measures to beef up US defenses. As Washington prepared to launch its war on terrorism in Afghanistan, NATO allies backfilled the gaps opened up by US deployments. The alliance dispatched five AWACS airplanes from its base in Germany to the United States to assist in the patrol of its airspace and deployed a naval force to secure the shipping lanes of the eastern Mediterranean. Also, US policymakers realized that the CSDP did not prevent them from gathering individual EU countries together under their leadership for the purpose of waging their wars of choice. The CSDP had no discernable impact on Washington's ability to attract sizeable European contributions to its military campaigns in Afghanistan and in Iraq. However, many in Washington were dismayed to see that some European governments were ready to disassociate themselves from their US ally on the issue of war against Iraq. The fact that these dissenters started talking up the value of the CSDP as a means to further the EU's strategic independence from the United States did not help. The transatlantic row over the invasion of Iraq severely tested the willingness of the US administration to accommodate the CSDP.

Caught in the Middle: The CSDP and the Iraq Controversy

The transatlantic crisis brought about by the invasion of Iraq nearly rang the death knell for the CSDP. It split the EU in half as supporters and opponents of US policy publicly fell out with each other. On one side was the antiwar camp, which US Secretary of Defense Donald Rumsfeld dismissively called "old Europe." It confronted "new Europe," which was eager to show its support for US policy. Both camps blatantly disregarded the EU (Nice) Treaty obligation to "refrain from any action which is contrary to the interests of the Union or likely to impair its effectiveness as a cohesive force in international relations" (Official Journal of the European Union 2006: 15). Instead, they engaged in "op-ed diplomacy"—the exchange of mutual recriminations in open letters and press conferences (Missiroli 2004/5). The crisis threatened to do lasting damage to transatlantic relations and the EU. The antiwar camp saw Washington's pressure to fall into line with US policy as a call not for burden-sharing but for identity subservience.[11] Their disillusionment with the United States went deep. For instance, Belgian prime minister Guy Verhofstadt wrote a personal letter to President Jacques Chirac of France and Prime Minister Blair of Britain, criticizing Washington for reducing NATO to "a prop to build coalitions for its war against terrorism." He went on to say that the CSDP should be developed into a military alliance completely independent of NATO (cited in Van Staden 2005: 77). Conversely, Washington regarded the antiwar camp as comprising unreliable and ungrateful allies. What is more, for some in the United States it looked as if Paris and Berlin tried to reconfigure Europe into a counterweight to the United States. To prevent agreement on a UN resolution authorizing the use of force against Iraq, France and Germany cooperated with Russia, while the French government eloquently talked about the desirability of ending global US diplomatic-strategic dominance. France and Germany, supported by Belgium, opposed the US request to start NATO planning for Turkey's defense in case Saddam Hussein attacked Turkey in retaliation for an attack by the US-led coalition on Iraq (Gallis 2003).[12]

Last but not least, a few weeks after the campaign against Iraq had begun, the leaders of France, Germany, Belgium, and Luxembourg met for a summit.[13] They discussed the further development of the CSDP, notably its emancipation from NATO dependency and US oversight. The gathering in Brussels ended with a call for the creation of independent EU military headquarters. Against the background of already tense transatlantic relations, Washington interpreted the chocolate summit, as it was called by its detractors, as a challenge to its political and military leadership in Europe. The US ambassador to NATO, Nicholas Burns, called it the "most serious threat to the future of NATO" (cited in Posen 2006: 183). As both intra-European and transatlantic relations experienced a deep crisis, the CSDP seemed to be one of the main victims. Yet, in the following years, transatlantic relations recovered as both Americans and Europeans reassessed their shared interests.

The CSDP and NATO:
Between Pragmatism and Turf Battles

With the creation of the CSDP, the EU stepped on alliance turf and became a security provider. Inevitably, the CSDP has limited NATO's primacy in European security policy and competed for policy space. Yet turf battles have always been constrained by the shared strategic interests of the two security institutions and the fact that twenty-one states are members of both. Operational cooperation between NATO and CSDP personnel in theater has generally been good. Since about 2007, EU-NATO relations have improved. However, political and institutional challenges persist, notably when it comes to strategic cooperation and coordinated defense planning.

NATO remains the most powerful multilateral security provider in the world and is the linchpin of European defense. Shortcomings notwithstanding, it has demonstrated its utility as a force multiplier for the United States in Afghanistan. At the same time, the CSDP has made the EU a serious security player by enhancing the EU's role as a diplomatic-strategic actor in its neighborhood and farther afield. Although the EU (still) lags far behind NATO in terms of raw military power and as a community of military action, it has taken steps to narrow the gap. Conversely, NATO has encountered new challenges in the new millennium, including disagreements about the practical emphasis to be placed on the alliance's different military functions, especially territorial defense and out-of-area operations, the joint funding of non–article 5 operations, and the differential willingness of members to dispatch their soldiers to fight and die for the alliance.[14] The biggest challenge came on the heels of September 11 when NATO was relegated to a minor role in the US-led global war on terror (see, for example, Asmus 2006; Serfaty 2004). This was not its fault. The United States did not want to be boxed in by war by committee but chose to wage the war in Afghanistan with the help of a coalition of the willing rather than through NATO. Once the war was won, it asked the alliance to help in securing the peace. In the case of Iraq, the situation was somewhat different. Even if it wanted to, Washington would not have been able to rely on NATO, because the Iraq war was too controversial. Hence, the United States once again waged war with the help of a coalition of the willing. When transatlantic relations recovered, NATO organized a small mission to help reconstruct Iraq. In short, in the wake of September 11, the alliance seemed, as NATO secretary-general George Robertson put it, to be little more than the US "spare wheel" (cited in Serfaty 2004: 80). Yet this was and remains an incomplete view.

NATO and the EU share important strategic interests in Europe and elsewhere. Moreover, to succeed in their foreign interventions, they need each other, at least in operations that rely on a combination of war-making and nation-building (Dobbins 2006). This explains why diplomatic and operational cooperation has been good, despite occasional hiccups. In Macedonia, the two organizations coordinated their diplomatic activities to bring ethnic clashes to an end in 2001. The transitions from NATO-led peacekeeping forces to EU-led troops in Macedonia (2003) and Bosnia (2004) occurred without any major problems. In Kosovo in 2008, US personnel were for the first time integrated into a CSDP mission. In Afghanistan, a small CSDP police mission has cooperated with NATO in international efforts to secure the country for the West. Good operational cooperation in the field has been facilitated by the establishment of a military-to-military interface at general staff and headquarters levels. There is a permanent EU Cell at NATO's SHAPE and a NATO liaison team in the EUMS.

For issues in which shared strategic interests are less salient, cooperation between the two organizations has suffered. This was the case in Darfur in 2005, when the African Union asked both NATO and the EU to support the deployment of its peacekeeping troops to the area. Washington wanted NATO to coordinate the assistance, while France insisted on a role for the EU (Castle 2005). Both organizations saw the invitation by the African Union as a window of opportunity to showcase themselves and demonstrate their capability and their willingness to be an important part of the global security architecture of the 21st century. Neither organization wasted much time in considering whether it should decline the offer in favor of the other or in coordinating their parallel missions at headquarters level. The result was what one NATO official described as "a political beauty contest between NATO and the EU" (cited in Cascone 2008: 157).

A long-standing challenge for the CSDP-NATO strategic relationship has been a lack of policy coordination. Ambassadorial-level meetings between the EU's PSC and NATO's North Atlantic Council have taken place on a regular basis since the beginning of 2001. Although these meetings should be at the center of policy coordination, they have been bedeviled by political differences among a few states. At their root is a technical issue—information security. According to the Berlin-Plus agreement, only EU states having a bilateral information security arrangement with NATO can participate in strategic discussions between the EU and NATO. The EU state Cyprus—the Greek part of the divided island—does not have such a secure-information agreement with the alliance. Turkey has taken a hard line on Cyprus, whose northern part remains under Turkish control outside the EU, and insisted that Cyprus could not be part of any EU-NATO discussions and decisions on strategic cooperation. Nicosia has disagreed, arguing that the only issues on which it could legitimately be excluded from EU-NATO meetings were those related to EU military operations drawing on NATO capabilities and assets. It has been supported by fellow EU states, notably France and Greece.

As a result of this stalemate, policy coordination on issues of concern to both organizations, such as Afghanistan and Iraq, has been severely curtailed. Insufficient joint political programming and military-strategic and operational planning have prevented the two security providers from taking full advantage of their combined capabilities to develop a comprehensive approach to the stabilization and reconstruction of war-torn countries such as Afghanistan and Kosovo.[15] To alleviate the Turkey/Cyprus problem, informal meetings between the PSC and the North Atlantic Council have been called,[16] in which Greek Cyprus has been allowed to participate. Yet setting up such off-the-record exchanges is subject to political consensus among the members of the two institutions, which makes efforts to call such meetings vulnerable to political posturing (Hofmann and Reynolds 2007). Until the time the Cyprus problem is solved, the EU-NATO coordination problem is unlikely to go away. The best that can be hoped for is amelioration through the creation of informal coordination mechanisms.

Defense planning is another important area in which policy coordination between the EU and NATO is hampered by divergent interests, played out against the backdrop of persistently low defense outlays in most EU states. There are important instances of cooperation on capability development between the EU and NATO, say, on European strategic airlift. Yet such success stories coexist with large-scale instances of wasteful duplication and institutional rivalry. In 1999, NATO agreed to the Defence Capabilities Initiative, intended to create new political momentum for advancing the transformation and upgrade of NATO forces, but the initiative did not deliver. This is not surprising, because the Europeans were busy building up the CSDP. In 2002, NATO took another pledge to strengthen its capabilities. In the Prague Capabilities Commitment, the member states pledged to reinforce the alliance in areas such as intelligence and surveillance, interoperability, and force protection. Because the CSDP capability development process has focused on many of the same areas, to ensure coordination, an EU-NATO Capability Group was established in 2003. However, despite regular meetings, its impact has been limited, and the establishment of EDA in 2004 has further complicated cooperation. The agency's primary task is to promote European solutions to European military capability and technology needs rather than to further transatlantic coordination in this field.

On a US initiative, NATO agreed in 2002 to create the NATO Response Force for military contingencies anywhere on the globe. A standby force that can begin to deploy after five days of a political decision, it was initially intended to comprise up to 25,000 troops, including land, sea, and air components. The force is sustainable in the battlefield for up to thirty days. As Jolyon Howorth (2003) observed, some analysts saw the project as a US ploy to undermine the EU RRF. The NATO Response Force was launched when the EU was getting ready to deploy its first military CSDP operation.[17] Officially, the NATO Response Force has served two main purposes. First, it has given the alliance a sharp tool to tackle the threats and challenges of the new millennium. The force has been trained and certified for a wide range of missions, including humanitarian and rescue tasks, counterterrorism, and high-intensity combat. Second, the NATO Response Force has encouraged European allies to modernize their forces and improve their interoperability. In 2006, the NATO Response Force was declared fully operational. Although it is mainly a European NATO outfit, the United States has pledged crucial "enablers" such as heavy airlift and airborne reconnaissance assets.

Two years after NATO launched its flagship project, the EU agreed to set up its 1,500-strong Battle Groups. As European military policy has been plagued by fiscal constraints and shortages of deployable troops, the EU Battle Groups have inevitably competed with the NATO Response Force for scarce resources. In 2007, the gap between, on the one hand, deployed European forces in Afghanistan, Iraq, the Western Balkans, Lebanon, and elsewhere and, on the other hand, European commitments to the NATO Response Force and the Battle Groups became too large. The NATO Response Force was the weakest link, and NATO was forced to scale down its force as European NATO members reduced their troop pledges. NATO subsequently went back to the drawing board and considerably revised the NATO Response Force.[18]

Toward Closer Transatlantic Security Relations

Assessing EU-NATO relations in 2007, NATO secretary-general Jaap de Hoop Scheffer (2007) described them as being "stuck in the '90s." The bandwidth of cooperation, he complained, remained astoundingly "narrow." Paradoxically, as the situation in Afghanistan worsened, NATO saw its political fortunes rise. The resurgence of the Taliban did not do away with alliance controversies or operational disagreements over Afghanistan (Webber 2009), but it reminded governments of their shared geopolitical interests and of NATO's importance as the military arm of the West. Europeans enhanced their efforts to back the United States in Afghanistan, including through beefed-up troop contributions to the International Security Assistance Force. The reinforcement of NATO's cohesiveness as a community of military action has been accompanied by a new US willingness to embrace CSDP operations as a contribution to allied security.

Washington's support of the CSDP is an acknowledgement that its initial worries that the EU might evolve quickly into a military peer competitor were exaggerated. This reassessment was most clearly expressed by the US National Intelligence Council (2008), which forecast that the EU would not make it into the major league of military powers in the foreseeable future. Another major impetus for US support for the CSDP is the EU's changed place in US strategy. Nicholas Burns (2007), at the time undersecretary of state for political affairs, put it in this way: "The United States' policy toward Europe is no longer about Europe. It's about the rest of the world." What he meant is that Europe is no longer needed as a bulwark against Soviet domination of Eurasia but is needed to provide material support and legitimacy to the US war on terrorism and its interventions in the new strategic hot spots of the greater Middle East. Washington's troubles in Iraq and Afghanistan have played a key role in this reevaluation of the EU's importance. The George W. Bush administration's early optimism about postwar stabilization and reconstruction in these theaters turned out to be misplaced, and it realized that it needed all the help it could get to avoid failure in Iraq and Afghanistan. Hence, it downplayed its earlier predilection for unilateralism and actively sought better relations with its European allies.

An important element of this policy reversal was a new appreciation of the security tasks that are at the center of the CSDP. Unlike its precursor of 2002, the 2006 US National Security Strategy emphasized "conflict interventions . . . to restore peace and stability" and "the hard work of post-conflict stabilization and reconstruction" (White House 2006: 16; see also Brimmer 2007; Dobbins 2006). Acting on this reassessment, the administration reinforced its civilian peace support toolbox. A linchpin in these efforts has been the Office of the Coordinator for Reconstruction and Stabilization, which was created in 2004. Closely related, in its second term, the Bush administration called for or supported new CSDP deployments in Kosovo, Palestine, Afghanistan, and Iraq. After the 2006 war between Israel and Hezbollah, it welcomed the European contributions to the beefed-up UN peacekeeping operation in Lebanon.

In 2008, President Bush expressed the administration's new support for the CSDP in a speech that echoed President Kennedy's famous Atlantic Partnership speech (Kennedy 1962).

> Building a strong NATO Alliance also requires a strong European defense capacity. So at this [NATO] summit, I will encourage our European partners to increase their defense investments to support both NATO and EU operations. America believes if Europeans invest in their own defense, they will also be stronger and more capable when we deploy together. (White House 2008)

The Obama administration has followed the same policy script. Secretary of State Hillary Clinton used words similar to those of President Bush to express her backing of the CSDP. "We do not see the EU as a competitor of NATO, but we see a strong Europe as an essential partner with NATO and with the United States. . . . And we look forward to working together with the EU as it applies its Common Security and Defense Policy to determine how we can best support one another and the United Nations in addressing security challenges" (Clinton 2010). In May 2011, the EU and the United States signed a framework agreement on the participation of civilian US personnel in CSDP operations.[19] NATO's 2010 Strategic Concept expressed the same cooperative spirit (North Atlantic Treaty Organization 2010). This said, US support for the CSDP remains qualified. Its major concern is that the CSDP does not endanger US primacy in transatlantic relations and European security. Hence, further steps in the direction of

EU collective defense, which were initiated by the Lisbon Treaty, would raise serious concerns in Washington, as would the creation of a genuine European army. A more "political" conflict scenario would be the establishment of an EU caucus within NATO, which continues to be a "vision of horror" for US policymakers but a goal of Europeanists (Bitterlich 2007: 19; Larrabee 2009).

As to the Europeans, they have been as willing as the Americans to improve transatlantic relations after the diplomatic woes over Iraq. They have responded positively, some more so than others, to US administration requests for a greater contribution to the stabilization and reconstruction mission in Afghanistan. The return to transatlantic security multilateralism has been facilitated by leadership changes in Germany and France. Those leaders who loudly opposed the US-led invasion of Iraq were replaced by pro-American administrations. President Sarkozy completed France's post–Cold War rapprochement with NATO, and, in 2009, the country rejoined NATO's integrated military structure. Paris wants to shape the development of the alliance and placate fears among some EU states that its support for a stronger CSDP is directed against NATO (d'Aboville 2008; Grand 2009). Furthermore, both Berlin and Paris have come to realize that, as a senior adviser to Chancellor Angela Merkel put it, "the differences between Europe and America are dwarfed by the differences the two of us have with other parts of the world" (cited in McGuire 2007: 28). Part of this new realism in Berlin and Paris is an appreciation of the fact that on most diplomatic-strategic issues of importance the EU is for the time being too weak to accomplish anything without partnering with the United States. In short, as the CSDP entered its teen years, relations with NATO were better than they were throughout most of its first ten years of existence.

Conclusion: A New Transatlantic Division of Labor?

In the wake of the end of the Cold War, the EU and the United States have begun to build a new European security architecture, which has been a conflictual process of trial and error. After September 11, attention among the transatlantic allies has shifted toward global security management. Unaided by an overall grand strategy, a new transatlantic division of labor in security affairs has emerged through policies designed to address practical challenges. During the Cold War, Europeans specialized in the provision of a large number of place-bound troops, while Americans specialized in building, maintaining, and modernizing a large strategic nuclear arsenal as the ultimate deterrent of major war. They also maintained a power projection capability, including the capability to engage in conventional warfare in foreign theaters. Since the 1990s, US armed forces have considerably upgraded their expeditionary warfare capabilities. Taking advantage of the technological revolution in military affairs, they have specialized in both unconventional (Afghanistan) and conventional warfare operations (Iraq) across the globe. More recently, the US has given renewed emphasis to counterinsurgency tasks. Without aiming at it, the EU has acquired the capabilities to deputize for the United States in lower-intensity stabilization and reconstruction assignments. CSDP operations have backfilled for US troops in missions that Washington no longer wants in order to avoid overstretch (for example, peacekeeping in Bosnia). They have been deployed to theaters where the United States cannot go because it is politically too controversial in the concerned country or region. CSDP operations in Georgia, Chad, and the CAR fall into this category. Last but not least, the CSDP has assisted the Americans in cleaning up the mess left over from war fighting, as has been the case in Afghanistan and Iraq. In brief, the CSDP has made the EU more relevant to US security concerns.

In the future, however, the CSDP may well complicate transatlantic relations. In the short to medium term, the danger is that the EU will bite off more than it can chew. Without being prepared for all contingencies, it might get involved in a military operation that goes wrong and from which it needs to be bailed out by the United States (Serfaty 2004). Given its already existing military commitments, such an extra assignment would not be welcome by Washington, though it could hardly say no to its closest allies. Also, an EU operation gone wrong would probably sap the will of EU states to project military power abroad, thus weakening NATO's ability to engage in out-of-area operations. Conversely, if the EU succeeds in the long run in developing the capabilities and political will to forcefully project power abroad in defense of its interests and values, even more serious Euro-US challenges may lie in waiting (see Chapter 14).

Notes

1. The main challenge to the US leadership of the transatlantic community was launched by French president de Gaulle at the end of the 1950s. He proposed that NATO be led by a directorate of Britain, France,

and the United States. When his proposal was rejected by the allies, he gradually removed France from NATO's integrated command structures in protest.

2. The quote is from a joint letter by French president Mitterrand and German chancellor Kohl to the EU in December 1990 (reprinted in Laursen and Vanhoonacker [1992: 313–314]). An important reason for Germany's support for the French initiative was precisely to alleviate fears of German reunification among its neighbors.

3. The notorious highlight of these efforts was the "Bartholomew telegram." Sent to the twelve EU governments in February 1991, it highlighted US red lines in relation to European security cooperation.

4. Capabilities refer to military services, notably planning facilities; and assets refer to tangible objects such as mobile headquarters and AWACS (airborne early warning and control system) airplanes.

5. Incidentally, this was not a case of unrequited love. The WEU Parliamentary Assembly, for instance, refused the overtures of the EU's European Parliament to work together on defense issues.

6. This is how US deputy secretary of state Strobe Talbot put it: Washington does not want to see a European security policy that "comes into being first within NATO but then grows out of NATO and finally grows away from NATO" (cited in Hunter 2002: 58).

7. The European Parliament strongly objected to the agreement (see Chapter 4). The Interim Security Agreement was replaced by a permanent NATO-EU Agreement on the Security of Information in 2003.

8. Also, the EU promised Turkey that if it fulfilled "the Copenhagen political criteria" related to democracy, the market economy, and administrative capacity by the end of 2004, "the European Union [would] open accession negotiations with Turkey without delay." Ankara had first applied for EU membership in 1987.

9. The name Berlin-Plus signifies that the agreement builds on the previously mentioned 1996 agreement between NATO and the WEU, which was made in Berlin. Most of the separate agreements comprising the Berlin-Plus agreement have not been made public.

10. NATO's principal common assets include command, control, and communication systems; an air-defense systems; AWACS airplanes; oil pipelines; bunkers; and airfields.

11. I borrow the term "identity subservience" from Nelson (2002: 60).

12. The "refuseniks" feared that a positive decision would make a military confrontation between the United States and allied nations, on the one side, and Iraq, on the other side, more likely. Within a few days, a compromise was struck, and NATO deployed defensive assets to Turkey.

13. All EU governments had been invited by Belgium to take part in the summit.

14. NATO's new strategic concept, adopted in 2010, has not removed these challenges.

15. Cooperation at the level of general staff and operational headquarters, too, has been affected by the Turkey/Cyprus problem (Duke 2008b).

16. Informal meetings also take place at the level of foreign ministers, the two respective Military Committees, and lower-level bodies.

17. As mentioned previously, all CSDP operations so far have been resourced from the forces declared to the RRF.

18. Agreed in 2009, the new, modular NATO Response Force comprises an immediate response force of about 14,000 troops supplemented by a variable response forces pool that is fed from the general NATO pool of deployable forces.

19. The previous participation of US personnel in CSDP operations was based on ad hoc agreements.

CHAPTER 13

Russia and
European Security Policy

THIS CHAPTER LOOKS AT HOW EU-RUSSIA SECURITY RELATIONS
have evolved since the end of the Cold War. The CSDP has been one,
albeit not a key, element in the relationship. The collapse of the
Soviet Union raised high hopes in the EU that an enfeebled Russia
could be integrated into a European peace order centered on the EU.
In the 1990s relations between Brussels and Moscow improved dra-
matically. Eastern European governments that raised the fear of the
"Russian bear" to expedite their transition from post-Communist
states to EU members were politely but firmly told by the EU that
such Cold War rhetoric was unhelpful. In the new millennium, however, things have changed. Russia has refused to be the EU's junior
partner. Conversely, its offer to be an equal partner in the CSDP has
been rejected by the EU. Russia's resurgence as an assertive regional
power has led to growing tensions over regional and energy security.
In response, the EU has hardened its Russia policy and has started to
challenge Russia in their joint neighborhood. The CSDP has been a
small but not unimportant part of this tougher policy. Yet the EU's
Russia policy remains hampered by disagreements among member
states about whether Russia is a threat to European security, a difficult neighbor, or a strategic partner.

Europe During the Cold War

In the wake of the defeat of Nazi Germany, the Soviet Union established within a few years its control over Central and Eastern Europe,
which it had freed from German occupation. The Communist empire

was periodically shaken by popular uprisings, such as in Hungary in 1956 and Czechoslovakia in 1968. However, its longevity and the threat it posed to the rest of Europe and the capitalist world as a whole were doubted by few Western governments. To stop the expansion of Soviet Communism, they designed a policy of global containment, centered in Europe. The result was a precarious balance of power on the continent between two heavily armed military alliances—NATO and the Communist Warsaw Pact. Even when the Cold War was coldest, peace prevailed but at the cost of little interaction across the Iron Curtain. In the 1970s, relations between Washington and Moscow warmed, which enabled the EU to push through a diplomatic agenda of constructive engagement with the East on a wide range of issues. An East-West dialogue was institutionalized by the 1975 Helsinki Final Act of the CSCE. Whereas the West formally recognized the existing borders in Europe and, hence, Moscow's sphere of influence, the Soviet Union made concessions on human rights and travel restrictions for East Bloc citizens. Both sides agreed to more cultural, economic, and scientific exchanges across the Iron Curtain and military confidence-building measures (Thomas 2002). In the first half of the 1980s, the limited liberalization in the East was threatened by a new cold war and a new wave of repression in Eastern Europe. When Mikhail Gorbachev took over the reins of power in the Kremlin, he gradually introduced policies of glasnost and perestroika at home and a policy of rapprochement with the West. The Cold War drew to a close.

The Rebirth of Sovereign Russia

Toward the end of 1991, Russia, Ukraine, and Belarus announced the creation of the Commonwealth of Independent States.[1] This was the beginning of the end of the Soviet Union, and the multinational empire disintegrated into fifteen independent states. From being at the center of a global military superpower, Moscow was reduced to overseeing the disintegration of its former military prowess (Herspring 2003). Military hardware deployed in the newly independent states was confiscated and used to build up national defense forces. The Soviet military-industrial complex collapsed, as the production chains that linked the territorially dispersed production units were disrupted by sovereign borders. In the process of Western-guided shock therapy and hasty and corrupt privatizations, the Russian economy fell into a virtual free fall. The Russian defense budget was among the first to suffer. As political power seeped away from the central government, the governance capacity of the state weakened precipitously. Economic policymaking became largely captured by oligarchs and Western advisers, while the state's internal sovereignty was undermined by the power grab of regional bosses. Russia became a hollowed-out federation of powerful mini-states (Sakwa 2008a; Nicholson 2003). The country was on the way to losing its place in the major league of geopolitical powers.

Under President Boris Yeltsin, Russia pursued a Western-oriented policy (foreign and domestic), and priority was given to its relationship with the United States. The ideological confrontation of old was replaced by an emphasis on common values such as democracy, human rights, and free markets. Russia's foreign policy rested on two main assumptions. First, the country was and would remain a great power due to its history, size, nuclear capabilities, and permanent seat on the United Nations Security Council. Second, its transformation into a "normal" country would make Russia an equal partner of the United States in the joint management of international affairs. However, Moscow failed to develop a grand strategy based on these assumptions (Herspring and Rutland 2003). The task of elaborating a coherent foreign policy was hampered by rivalry and bureaucratic infighting among the foreign and defense ministries and the presidential administration, new players in the foreign policy field such as oil companies and the Duma, and a lack of resources.

Even as the material foundations of its international influence crumbled in the 1990s, Russia insisted that it remained a great power. It had a right to "occupy a worthy place . . . in the community of civilised peoples of Eurasia and America" (Foreign Minister Andrei Kozyrev, cited in Sakwa 2008b: 366). And indeed, Russia retained sufficient power-projection capabilities to establish its hegemony over post-Soviet space, excluding the Baltic states. Moscow claimed what Yeltsin called a "special responsibility" in this territory. He called on the United Nations and other international actors "to grant Russia special powers as guarantor of peace and stability in this region" (Crow 1993: 28). This is Russia's version of the Monroe Doctrine, which identifies the "near abroad" as its sphere of influence in which it has a right of oversight over local developments. Moscow's robust military response in August 2008 to Georgia's effort to reintegrate the breakaway territory of South Ossetia by force was a manifestation of the doctrine (see Chapter 9). The institutional vehicle by which Russia has sought to pursue its doctrine is the Commonwealth of Independent States. However, both

Russia's weakness and the divergent interests of the member states have limited Moscow's ability to make the organization a powerful institutional platform through which to exercise legitimate regional leadership. For instance, the creation of the Collective Security Treaty in 1992 failed to evolve into an Eastern alternative to NATO.[2] This said, the Commonwealth of Independent States has facilitated and licensed the deployment of Russian troops in post-Soviet space.

Russia's Resurgence as a European Power

There remains a huge gap between the global influence once exercised by the Soviet Union and Russia's ability to shape international events. However, Russia has undoubtedly had a resurgence on the international scene, notably in the Southern Caucasus and in Central Asia (Nygren 2008), dating roughly to the middle of the 2000s. Two key background conditions have contributed to this development. First, in the first half of the 2000s, the Russian petro-economy boomed, fueled by record high prices for hydrocarbons. The windfall profits of the oil and gas industry filled government coffers and enabled the Kremlin to pursue a more robust foreign policy. Although energy prices dropped precipitously in the late 2000s global financial crisis, they have recovered and are expected to remain high in coming decades. Russia's petro-economy will thus continue to underwrite the country's reemergence as a great power. Second, President Vladimir Putin restored the internal conditions for the effective pursuit of Russia's national interest on the international stage. Under his leadership, the governing capacity of the state was rebuilt in the first half of the new millennium. The political power of the oligarchs was curbed, and a similarly robust policy rebalanced federal-regional relations. The prerogatives of the central government were restored by curbing the fiscal and legal competencies of the regions. The downside of the centralization of power has been a limitation of democracy, at least as seen from the West.

Beyond these basic factors, a number of specific policies account for Russia's resurgent capacity to defend its interests abroad. First, Moscow has begun the difficult process of reversing the decline of its military might (Facon 2005; International Institute for Strategic Studies 2008; Isakova 2005).[3] Besides making defense a budget priority, it has moved forward on making the Russian armed forces more professional and capable. Steps have been taken to rebuild and consolidate the military-industrial complex, while emphasis has been put on increasing military exports to finance the process. Second, Moscow has reinvigorated and launched new integration schemes (military and economic) that bind it closer to its near abroad (Malfliet et al. 2007). For instance, the Kremlin took the lead in upgrading the Collective Security Treaty into the Collective Security Treaty Organization. At the heart of the organization, which was agreed to in 2002, is a rapid reaction force designed to combat shared security threats such as terrorism in Central Asia.[4] Third, and most importantly, Moscow has reasserted domestic political control over the strategically important oil and gas industry and entered into a gas alliance with Central Asia. This has given it a powerful tool to engage in economic statecraft vis-à-vis both Eastern Europe and the EU. Russian oil and gas companies have expanded into the EU energy market, buying up assets such as refineries and ports and acquiring part ownership of distribution networks by forming strategic alliances with local partners. Finally, Russian oil and gas companies have struck deals with importers to build new pipelines through which Russian-owned oil and gas will be pumped to EU countries.

The EU's Russia Policy in the 1990s and Early 2000s

Eastern policy (*Ostpolitik*) was pioneered by West Germany in the late 1960s and early 1970s. After World War II, Bonn pursued a policy of isolating Communist East Germany diplomatically and economically. When the policy failed to undermine the rigid regime, West Germany abandoned its hard-line policy. It began to promote good neighborly relations with East Germany and the rest of the East Bloc and to encourage the Communist regimes to adhere to basic human rights and civil liberties. To this end, West Germany offered them economic and other incentives. Through the EPC, German *Ostpolitik* was uploaded to the EU level. The peaceful end of the Cold War confirmed to many in Western Europe that *Ostpolitik* really worked and thus remained the taken-for-granted EU policy toward Russia after the end of the Cold War. The promotion of democracy, the rule of law, human rights, and free markets in Russia was to be achieved through practical engagement with the country and the active diffusion of Western norms and values. Security concerns were an important driver of the EU's Russia policy, because Brussels was worried about uncontrolled migration toward Western Europe, flourishing organized crime, and ethnic warfare. A particular concern was nuclear safety in Russia and the risk of trafficking in radioactive materials.

At the beginning of the 1990s, the EU put in place a new program, Technical Aid to the Commonwealth of Independent States (TACIS), which assisted Russia's transition to democracy and a market economy and financed nuclear safety and cleanup projects. A few years later, Brussels and Moscow signed a Partnership and Cooperation Agreement, which established an institutional framework for close political dialogue. In addition to the Permanent Partnership Council, which meets in different ministerial formats, there are semiannual EU-Russia summits and additional diplomatic- and expert-level talks. The EU's 1996 Action Plan on Russia emphasized cooperation in the fields of democratization and nuclear safety. In the following years, the EU agreed to the Northern Dimension policy, whose main non-EU participant is Russia.[5] Northern Dimension projects with Russia center on regional cross-border cooperation and cover issues such as border control, environmental pollution, and nuclear safety. In 1999, the EU adopted a Common Strategy on Russia aimed at bundling Europe's manifold initiatives on Russia with a view to making them more coherent and more effective in promoting a "stable, open and pluralistic democracy in Russia" (European Council 1999a, Annex II). The strategy was not a success, and when it expired in 2003 it was not renewed. Instead, Brussels and Moscow agreed to reinforce the Partnership and Cooperation Agreement with Four Common Spaces: (1) economy; (2) freedom, security, and justice; (3) external security; and (4) research and education. Yet the Spaces lack specific commitments and have not contributed to a convergence of views and policies between the EU and Russia. Their limited impact is indicative of the failure of the EU's ambitious policy of trying to establish its "normative hegemony" over Russia (Haukkala 2010). Unimpressed by EU exhortations, Moscow has turned toward illiberal policies at home and has displayed a growing assertiveness in the neighborhood it shares with the EU. Russia's resurgence as a regional power was brought home to the EU by disagreements with Moscow over secessionist conflicts and by Moscow's use of its energy weapon (for Russia's view, see Merlingen et al. 2009).

EU-Russia Disagreements over Secessionist Conflicts in Eastern Europe

In the wake of the end of the Cold War, a number of ethnic conflicts flared up in Eastern Europe, and Russia meddled in all of them. Its peacekeepers subsequently played a central role in maintaining a precarious peace among the parties. Especially in Georgia and Moldova, Moscow actively sided with the secessionists. In the new millennium, it has stepped up its efforts to obstruct any resolution of the conflicts that would entail losing the breakaway territories to pro-Western governments. For example, it has supported the secessionists diplomatically by seconding their political demands and opposing Western peace initiatives; militarily, by maintaining its troops in the breakaway territories; economically, by providing free energy to them; and politically, by granting Russian citizenship to the concerned populations. Russia's policy prompted countries such as Germany and France, which have a history of pursuing accommodating policies toward Moscow, to harden their positions.

A consensus emerged within the EU that Moscow instrumentalizes the conflicts in Georgia and Moldova to maintain its strategic influence in the region. To begin with, the EU accuses Russia of using the unresolved conflicts as a pretext for the forward deployment of its troops. The EU was particularly critical of Russia's willingness to resort to war in 2008 to defend its interests in Georgia. Also, it deplores the continuing deployment of Russian forces in the breakaway Georgian territories of South Ossetia and Abkhazia after the war. The EU considers these troops, as well as those stationed in the Moldovan breakaway territory of Transdniestria, as a means through which Moscow exerts political pressure on Tbilisi and Chişinău. Second and closely related, the EU accuses Russia of having undermined the European security order with its policy in the wake of the war with Georgia. Moscow violated international law and its commitment to the principles of the OSCE (the successor to the CSCE) when it recognized the self-declared sovereignty of South Ossetia and Abkhazia. Third, in the eyes of Brussels, the Kremlin treats the disputed territories in Georgia and Moldova as a bargaining chip in its relations with the EU and more broadly the West. Finally, by standing in the way of a peaceful resolution of the secessionist conflicts, Russia limits the spread of democracy, human rights, and prosperity.

The EU regards the secessionist governments of Abkhazia, South Ossetia, and Transdniestria as more or less corrupt political elites at the helm of quasi-state structures. It criticizes especially South Ossetia and Transdniestria for presiding over widespread poverty and human rights abuses while maintaining close links to organized crime networks. Brussels sees the secessionist territories as posing a twofold danger to EU security. First, they are sources of or transit territories for the illicit movement of people, including terrorists, and the smuggling of goods into the EU. Closely related, they negatively affect EU energy security by introducing an additional and significant element of instability into a region that is an important energy corridor linking the EU to Caspian oil and gas. Second, Brussels regards the existence of civilizational black holes in its proximity as a threat to its international standing. It is concerned that failure to translate its vision of a well-governed EU neighborhood into reality may prompt the international community to perceive it as weak—if not in its own backyard, where else in the world can the EU expect to make a difference?

EU Concerns over Russia's Energy Weapon

East-West energy relations have a long history. As early as the late 1960s, the Soviet Union delivered natural gas to Western European markets. By the mid-1980s, the Soviet Union had become the world's largest gas producer and an important supplier for Western Europe. In the wake of the breakup of the Soviet Union, Russian gas exports to Europe stagnated but began to rise again in the second half of the 1990s. The majority state-owned company Gazprom, the successor to the Soviet Ministry of Gas Industry, has played a crucial role in the recovery. Since 2000, the EU and Russia have conducted regular consultations in the framework of the Energy Dialogue, which was initiated in recognition of the importance of their trade in gas and oil. Yet despite cooperation at the level of experts and senior officials, the EU has become increasingly worried about its energy security. These concerns derive from both structural and policy factors. The EU is structurally dependent on energy imports from abroad. On current trends, "in the next 20 to 30 years around 70 percent of the Union's energy requirements, compared to 50 percent today, will be met by imported products" (European Commission 2006: 3). To meet its energy needs, the EU has to import hydrocarbons from Africa, the Middle East, and, especially, Russia. The latter accounts for about 50 percent of the total gas imports of the EU and for over 30 percent of its oil imports.[6] World energy markets are predicted to become tighter in the next decades, which will inevitably increase the power of resource holders. In view of these prospects, European decisionmakers have become increasingly uneasy about their energy relationship with Moscow. These concerns, in turn, have increased the geo-economic salience of the Southern Caucasus, Moldova, and Ukraine as (potential) energy corridors. Also, Europe wants to gain direct access to Central Asia's rich energy resources and bypass Russia.

Moscow's actions in the new millennium have reminded the EU of its dependency on Russia's gas and oil spigot. Moscow has raised the price it charges for energy deliveries to pro-Western Moldova and Georgia and to Ukraine when it has been governed by pro-Western governments. At the same time, it has provided free energy to Abkhazia and South Ossetia (Proedrou 2007). More ominously, it has repeatedly cut oil and gas deliveries to Belarus and Ukraine, when their governments have proved "difficult" in their relations with Moscow. For instance, at the beginning of 2009, a gas row between Moscow and Kiev led to major gas shortages in Eastern EU states, with effects felt in Western Europe. Many EU capitals have interpreted incidents of this sort as a worrisome manifestation of what the former EU ambassador to Moscow called "Gazprom politics" (cited in Edwards 2006: 159). In this view, Russia is not a reliable energy supplier but is ready to violate contractual obligations and to use energy as "a currency of power in the international system" to gain political leverage in target countries (Enno Harks, cited in Triantaphyllou 2007: 290). Moscow's refusal to agree to transparent investment, competition, and transit rules has reinforced the perception that Russia's energy policy poses a threat to the EU.[7] One day, the argument goes, the EU may well find itself the target of economic blackmail by the Kremlin.

Toward a More Assertive EU Policy on Russia

In response to security concerns about Moscow's foreign policy, the EU has forged a new, more assertive Russia policy, in which CFSP instruments figure prominently. Until recently EU efforts have been least impressive on the energy front. Brussels has tried to forge a common external energy policy vis-à-vis Russia that would take account of the "geo-political dimensions of energy-related security issues" (European Commission and High Representative for the CFSP 2006: 3). Initially, such efforts were largely unsuccessful because member states have divergent interests. Some have struck special deals with Russia to secure energy deliveries, while others want to limit their energy dependency on Russia. These cross-national differences have so far prevented agreement on a common line. This prompted the high representative for the CFSP to complain that "too often, we see . . . the defence of narrow, national interests at the expense of broader, European interests" (Solana 2008). In recent years there has been a growing recognition among EU governments that if they make deals with Russia individually, they have considerably less leverage than if they act together. This has led to a new willingness to deepen cooperation in the field of external energy policy, leading to an agreement to adopt a long-term EU energy strategy (see, for example, European Commission 2010).

The EU has had more success in widening and deepening its involvement in post-Soviet Eastern Europe with a view to limiting Russian influence. The main tool with which the EU seeks to bind its eastern neighbors more closely to itself is the European Neighbourhood Policy (ENP), which is designed to replicate the success story of the EU's eastward enlargement by using conditionality, technical assistance, and generous aid to shape the domestic and foreign policies of the states participating in the EU scheme.[8] In 2009, the EU upgraded the ENP by establishing the Eastern Partnership, which provides additional incentives to the eastern neighbors to entice them to come closer into the EU orbit. Also, the EU stepped up its CFSP involvement in the region. It appointed EUSRs for Moldova (in 2005), the Southern Caucasus (in 2003), and the crisis in Georgia (in September 2008); dispatched the CSDP rule-of-law mission EUJUST Themis to Georgia (2004–2005); put in place the follow-up EU Border Support Team (in 2005); and deployed the EUMM to the country (in October 2008) to verify the cease-fire agreement between Russia and Georgia.[9]

Three cases illustrate Brussels's new willingness to challenge Russia's long-standing geopolitical influence in post-Soviet space. First, in 2003, Russia made a proposal—the Kozak Memorandum—to resolve the secessionist conflict in Moldova. Like Finland during the Cold War, Moldova would have become a nonaligned country outside the orbit of the West and of Russia.[10] Although Moscow saw its proposal as a viable compromise, Brussels and Washington were not willing to abandon their goal of incorporating the country into Western political, economic, and military structures. The EU and the United States exerted pressure on the government in Moldova to reject the Russian-sponsored peace plan, and Chişinău did so after it had initially welcomed Moscow's initiative. Second, most EU countries recognized, over vocal opposition by Moscow, Kosovo's unilateral declaration of independence from Serbia in February 2008, while Russia supported Serbia's demand that its territorial integrity not be violated.[11] The EU subsequently sent a large CSDP mission to Kosovo to help build up its judiciary and law enforcement. Also, it appointed an EUSR to provide overall guidance to the state-building project. Third, during and after the 2008 war between Russia and Georgia, the EU gave its full diplomatic and financial backing to Tbilisi. It strongly condemned Russia's military actions; put pressure on it to end its offensive and withdraw to the positions held prior to the war; rejected Russia's recognition of the self-declared independence of South Ossetia and Abkhazia; and warned Moscow that if it continued to behave improperly, relations with the EU would further deteriorate.

The former Communist EU states, especially Poland and the Baltic states, have done much to bring about a more forceful EU policy toward Russia. Moscow's foreign policy toward Georgia, Ukraine, and Moldova and its embrace of illiberal domestic policies have raised alarm bells in eastern EU capitals, which strongly back anchoring the borderland between themselves and Russia to the EU and NATO. They see the integration of the concerned countries into the Euro-Atlantic structures as a means to improve their security by stabilizing and democratizing their environment. More ambitiously, they want to create a bridgehead deep within post-Soviet space from which to Westernize Russia or, if this fails, to contain Russia. Closely related, they advocate a more determined use of the CFSP in post-Soviet space, including more forceful CSDP deployments. They have found strong supporters of their tough line on Russia in some Western European countries, such as Britain and Sweden.

The EU's Russia policy has become less timid and more assertive in the new millennium. But it remains bedeviled by a number of important limitations. The EU has shied away from using its new CSDP capabilities to resolve the secessionist conflicts. The speedy deployment of the EUMM to Georgia in the aftermath of the war with Russia was an impressive display of the CSDP, yet the civilian mission has no executive powers to enforce the EU-Russia peace plan. The EU plays the leading role in the Geneva peace talks convened to address the fallout from the war (Merlingen and Ostrauskaitė 2010). However, it is only an observer in the conflict settlement talks on Transdniestria and has no formal role in the negotiations between Armenia and Azerbaijan over secessionist Nagorno-Karabakh. As to the European Neighbourhood Policy and the Eastern Partnership, they face a formidable challenge. When compared to the previous former Communist accession countries, such as Hungary and the Czech Republic, the EU neighbors in the East start out at a much lower level of development (democracy, economy, rule of law, etc.). This makes the EU's objective of remaking these countries in its own image exceedingly difficult (Kelley 2006). Moreover, the EU has put itself at a disadvantage in its rivalry with Russia by not offering its eastern neighbors the prospect of EU membership, which is the most powerful foreign policy instrument the EU possesses. Last but not least, EU foreign policy in post-Soviet space has been handicapped by persistent disagreements among EU governments. The recent convergence of national views on Russia notwithstanding, the EU has not been able to agree to a common grand strategy toward the country. Member states continue to have fundamentally different views of the nature of Russia and its role in Europe. Some EU states, notably Germany, France, and Italy, regard Russia as a difficult but inevitable partner in managing European security. They are thus wary of stepping too hard on Moscow's toes. Other EU states such as Lithuania regard Russia as a threat to EU security and would like to see much tougher EU policies toward Russia. (On the views of the Eastern European EU states on Russia, see Chapter 7.)

The CSDP in EU-Russia Relations

Russia's view of the CSDP has evolved differently from that of the United States, which responded to the creation of the CSDP with some trepidation, fearing that the CSDP might undermine NATO. It was only later that these fears gave way to a pragmatic embrace of the CSDP. Conversely, Russia warmly welcomed the creation of the CSDP only to be frustrated later on by how it evolved.

When the CSDP was launched, President Putin declared his willingness to work closely with Brussels on security and defense matters. "Europe [could] consolidate its reputation as a powerful and truly independent centre of world politics, firmly and for the long term, if it [could] join its own capabilities with Russia's possibilities" (Putin, cited in Mark Smith 2004: 1; see also Allison et al. 2006; Monaghan 2004). Moscow proposed to begin negotiations on joint peace operations and military-industrial cooperation. One goal was simply to ensure that the CSDP would not negatively affect Russia's interests in Europe. A more far-reaching goal was to cooperate with the EU to reassert what Russia's EU strategy called the "responsibility of European States for the future of the continent" (Russian Ministry of Foreign Affairs 1999). Clearly, Russia expected that the

EU would use the CSDP to emancipate itself from its security dependence on the United States and US-led NATO, which would be in Russia's interest. Moscow has considered NATO a Cold War institution that has outlived its usefulness in post–Cold War Europe.[12] Moscow's misunderstanding of the implications of the creation of the CSDP were clearly revealed in a statement by the Russian envoy to NATO, who declared that the EU's RRF was "a dagger pointed at NATO's heart" (cited in Reid 2004: 179).[13] These expectations could not but lead to Russian frustration with how the CSDP has evolved in the new millennium.

At first, the EU welcomed the Russian overtures and stated that Russia might "be invited to take part in the EU-led operations" (European Council 1999b). Soon thereafter, the EU and Russia adopted a joint declaration "on strengthening dialogue and cooperation on political and security matters in Europe" (EU-Russia Summit 2000). In 2001, monthly meetings on foreign and security policy between the EU's PSC and the Russian ambassador to the EU were agreed to. However, the EU showed no intention of giving Russia a say in the CSDP, nor did it wish to develop an EU-Russia equivalent of the close military cooperation between the EU and NATO or draw on Russian military hardware to plug CSDP capability gaps. Hence, Moscow's goal of close military and intelligence cooperation with the EU, including shared responsibility for the planning and implementation of CSDP operations, remained unfulfilled. This prompted Foreign Minister Igor Ivanov to declare that "some of our European partners [were] not yet psychologically ready for equal collaboration with Russia" (cited by Merlingen et al. 2009: 109).

There are two main reasons for Brussels's lukewarm response to Moscow's advances. First, the EU regards the CSDP as an instrument for implementing a transformational security policy. Its objective is to promote peaceful, law-abiding market democracies. The EU believes that close association of the CSDP with illiberal Russia would undermine this objective. Second, the EU understands that if it were to affiliate Russia tightly with the CSDP, Washington would in all likelihood be alarmed and would interpret the move as an attempt to marginalize its role in European security (Forsberg 2004: 257). Moreover, not even the Europeanist EU governments wish to gang up with Russia against the United States. Hence, there is no demand within the EU for forging close links between the CSDP and Russia. When Moscow realized that the EU intended neither to replace NATO by the CSDP nor to closely associate the CSDP with Russia, it lost much of its interest in the

CSDP. It has reverted back to its traditional view of the EU as a trading power with no muscles and dismisses the CSDP as a "paper project" (Polikanov 2007: 117).[14] This said, Russia cooperates in a limited fashion with the CSDP. It made small contributions to the CSDP police mission in Bosnia and the military mission in Chad and the CAR.

With the deepening of the structural fissures between the EU and Russia in recent years, the prospect of a closer security partnership centered on the CSDP has receded further.[15] Indeed, security relations may even worsen in the future. A vocal group of EU governments make the case for a more forceful use of the CSDP in the Eastern neighborhood to roll back Russian influence, spread European values, and promote European interests. Any such hardening of the CSDP in post-Soviet space would certainly not be welcomed by Moscow and would lead to considerable tensions between the two sides unless the Kremlin was granted a significant voice in designing and implementing the operations. This is what it wanted in the first place when it tried to develop a strategic partnership with the EU based on the CSDP.

The Future of EU-Russia Security Relations

EU-Russia relations have become strained, underpinned by different foreign and security policy role conceptions. Because Russia is a sovereignty-bound state, the lamppost guiding its foreign and security policy is the national interest. The universalistic credo of the Soviet years has been abandoned. As Russian foreign minister Ivanov put it, "Russia has consciously given up the global Messianic ideology that had been intrinsic to the former USSR and at the end of its existence had come into insurmountable contradiction with the national interests of the country" (cited in Sakwa 2008a: 272). In recent years, the idea of sovereign democracy has been crafted into the historical self-image of Russia as a great power. Sovereign democracy implies resistance to interference by outsiders in domestic affairs. The Kremlin expects the EU to accept Russia as a sovereign policymaker rather than a policy-taker, both in domestic and foreign affairs (Light 2009: 84). As to the EU, policymakers think of their collective foreign and security policy as being a postnational, value-based enterprise (Cooper 2003). At its heart is the international diffusion of universal Western norms and values. Thus both the EU and Russia have role conceptions that are incompatible. Indeed, in recent years the perception and value gap between the two sides has increased

(Haukkala 2010). Unless carefully managed, these ideational differences provide a fertile ground for the proliferation of policy conflicts over concrete issues. As former US secretary of state Henry Kissinger observed some time ago, "No power will submit to a settlement, however well-balanced and however 'secure,' which seems totally to deny its vision of itself" (Kissinger 1973: 146).

The different role conceptions of the EU and Russia translate into contrasting foreign and security policy objectives. While Russia wants an alliance with the EU that is founded on shared interests, the EU wants a relationship that is founded on common values. For the time being, these objectives do not have a common denominator. From Moscow's perspective, the EU's Eastern policy is about the pursuit of power and interest. From Brussels's perspective, Russia's refusal to be inducted into an EU-centered Western community of values looks like the affirmation of illegitimate imperial aspirations. The conceptual differences are so profound that they may even become the ideational enablers of a new cold war. However, there are also powerful countervailing forces of a more material nature. The EU and Russia are bound together in a relationship of mutual economic interdependence. As discussed, the EU is dependent on Russian hydrocarbons, while Russia's economic dependence on the EU is similarly pronounced.[16] Moreover, on a number of important strategic issues, the EU and Russia have similar concerns, including the acquisition of nuclear weapons by Iran, China's economic and military rise, order and security in Afghanistan, and Islamic terrorism.

Notes

1. Following this announcement, the organization was formed by twelve of the fifteen successor states of the Soviet Union. The three Baltic states did not join. Turkmenistan downgraded its membership to associate member in 2005. Following its war with Russia in 2008, Georgia withdrew from the organization in August 2009.

2. The signatories of the alliance treaty were Armenia, Belarus, Kazakhstan, Kyrgyzstan, Russia, and Tajikistan.

3. This said, much remains to be done to streamline and modernize the armed forces. For an analysis of the limitations of defense reforms, and the causes thereof, see Barany (2007).

4. The founding members of the organization are Armenia, Belarus, Kazakhstan, Kyrgyzstan, Russia, and Tajikistan. Uzbekistan formally joined the organization in 2008, when it ratified the accession treaty.

5. The other two non-EU participants in the Northern Dimension framework are Iceland and Norway.

6. By 2020, the numbers are expected to rise to 70 percent and 50 percent, respectively. Cf. Proedrou (2007: 334).

7. Moscow signed but never ratified the 1994 Energy Charter Treaty and its Transit Protocol. In 2009, it withdrew from the treaty.

8. The majority of the states participating in the ENP are Mediterranean countries. In Eastern Europe, Armenia, Azerbaijan, Belarus, Georgia, Moldova, and Ukraine participate in the EU scheme. In response to the "Arab Spring," the ENP was relaunched in May 2011 with more funds to increase the EU's leverage over the reform processes of the southern and eastern EU neighbors.

9. The mandates of the EUSRs for the Southern Caucasus and Moldova were allowed to expire at the end of February 2011 without a decision to appoint new officeholders. At the time of writing, there are discussions in Brussels to appoint a new EUSR for the Southern Caucasus and to merge the portfolio of the officeholder with that of the EUSR for the crisis in Georgia.

10. The 2003 memorandum would have federalized Moldova by placing the two state entities, Moldova and Transdniestria, on an equal constitutional footing. Transdniestria would have had the right to leave the federation.

11. The dispute followed the 1999 controversy over NATO's military intervention in the province aimed at stopping interethnic fighting. Most EU countries fully backed the use of force, even though it was strongly opposed by Russia and occurred in the absence of UN authorization.

12. In the early 1990s, Russia believed that NATO would either wither away or be turned into a new pan-European security organization in which Russia would have its rightful place (Baranovsky 2003). Neither scenario unfolded. After a period of calm, when Moscow seemed to have reconciled itself to the fact that NATO was here to stay and enlarging its geographical reach to the East, the alliance moved back to the top of Moscow's security concerns in 2008. Foreign Minister Sergei Lavrov (2008) stated that his country would consider it "a substantial negative geopolitical shift" if Georgia and Ukraine were to join the alliance. Since then, the prospect of (early) NATO membership for Georgia and Ukraine has faded. Russia, in turn, has stopped fussing about NATO.

13. The same comment was apparently made by John Bolton prior to becoming undersecretary of state in the George W. Bush administration (cited in Layne 2007: 114).

14. This is the dominant "pragmatic nationalist" view. Fundamentalist nationalists remain concerned about the CSDP, either because they see it as an appendage of a hostile NATO or because they fear the geopolitical consequences for Russia of a militarily powerful and independent EU (Allison et al. 2006: 77).

15. These fissures remain even when the political atmosphere between EU states and Russia improves. For instance, in the wake of the crash in Russia of the Polish plane carrying the Polish president and high-ranking Polish officials, bilateral relations superficially improved because Russia's leadership appeared to share the grief of the shocked Polish nation. Such sentiments,

however, do not get rid of the deep-seated differences in values and interests between the EU and Russia, which have been analyzed in this chapter.

16. Russia ships about 88 percent of its total oil exports and about 70 percent of its gas exports to the EU, with few if any short- to medium-term alternatives. The EU represents about 50 percent of overall Russian imports, whereas Russia accounts for about 6.5 percent of EU exports and about 10.5 percent of EU imports (European Commission 2011a, 2011b).

PART 4

Conclusion

CHAPTER 14

The EU: A Superpower in the Making?

WHEN THE CSDP WAS LAUNCHED, THE EU HAD NO INDEPEN-dent military option. Previous chapters have shown that since then the EU has put in place the capabilities and the institutional and ideational infrastructure that make for a weighty military power. They have also documented that important shortfalls remain. These problems notwithstanding, today's EU has the expeditionary forces, decisionmaking institutions, command and control capabilities, doctrines, and strategy required for performing the full spectrum of military tasks short of large-scale warfare. And yet, the CSDP deployment record is that of a small power. The concluding chapter looks beyond the current record to ask what the future might hold for the military CSDP and international order. Is the EU destined to remain a small power in international military affairs or will it transform itself into a major military player, perhaps even a rival to the United States?

Two Future Scenarios

Drawing on the discussion of international relations theories in Chapter 2, the chapter sketches two future scenarios. In the realist scenario, the EU balances the United States. In the liberal-constructivist scenario, the EU and the United States cooperate in managing the liberal international order.[1] The chapter evaluates the plausibility of these scenarios by looking at the preliminary evidence that can be garnered to support them or to cast doubt on them.

The Realist Scenario

This scenario is premised on the argument that states balance against the concentration of power in the international system. This makes the United States, which enjoys unprecedented military preponderance, a prime target for balancing behavior. The EU is currently one of the few international actors with the necessary material resources to check US power. With the creation of the CSDP, the EU has started doing precisely this and has begun to build up its military power. It wants to balance against the United States because there is no guarantee that unchecked US power will not one day negatively affect, either deliberately or unintentionally, important European interests (Art 2006; Jones 2007; Layne 2007; Posen 2006). What future for the CSDP and international order does this scenario predict? The anarchical structure of the international system pushes the EU to become a major military player. Only if the EU acts on this pressure will it be able to defend and promote its values and interests in an increasingly competitive multipolar world. However, to turn itself into a military power the EU has to implement a "radical change" in how it runs the CSDP (Waltz 2000: 32). Two alternative institutional routes to great powerdom are available to the EU. First, the CSDP is federalized and run by Brussels, as opposed to EU states. Second, a hegemon (most likely Germany) or a small group of powerful EU states impose their leadership on the CSDP. However it emerges, military power in Europe will stake out its claim to strategic leadership in particular geographic regions such as Eastern Europe and Central Asia. It will seek to limit US geopolitical preeminence in others, such as the Middle East, which is vital to Europe's security. Between an aspiring regional leader and a waning global leader, conflict is likely. NATO will be the first victim of the growing transatlantic rivalry as the EU rebels against an organization that is "mainly . . . a means of maintaining and lengthening America's grip on the foreign and military policies of European states" (Waltz 2000: 20).

What preliminary evidence can be marshaled for and against this scenario? Support comes from CSDP capability development. The Europeans have for the first time embarked on a process of building up considerable military power outside NATO and hence independently of US supervision. Importantly, this process has involved significant duplication of existing US and NATO capabilities and assets.

Such duplication has, for instance, occurred in the area of space-based assets, battlefield reconnaissance systems, and autonomous headquarters options. Closely related, the capability development work of EDA has prioritized high-tech assets, which are at the core of network-enabled warfare. The EU thus emulates US policy and acquires assets required for full-spectrum war fighting. However, these assets do not help it become the world's leading peace support operator. The latter role would be more in line with the EU's self-description as a different kind of international actor: less violent and more cooperative. A final piece of circumstantial evidence supporting the balance-of-power scenario is that out of seven military CSDP operations only two have drawn on NATO capabilities and assets. What is more, in both cases EU troops took over from NATO troops. Hence, it was natural for the EU to borrow alliance capabilities and assets already in place. The reluctance of the EU to make use of the Berlin-Plus agreement in other theaters of operation suggests that it does not want to lock the CSDP into an unequal relationship with US-dominated NATO or depend on the alliance for the military strategic planning, command, and control of CSDP operations.

Evidence against the balance-of-power scenario includes the strong support for the United States by the Atlanticist EU states.[2] Indeed, not even the leader of the Europeanist camp, France, wishes to see the United States reduce its commitment to NATO and European security. Also, the close cooperation on the ground between US and CSDP operations in places such as Kosovo, Palestine, and Afghanistan is at odds with the theory's predictions. So is the fact that EU civilian missions largely outnumber military operations. If the CSDP is primarily about aggregating European capabilities to balance the United States, why does the EU busy itself with deploying so many civilian CSDP missions? Furthermore, some critics argue that the realist balancing scenario overlooks that international intergovernmental institutions such as the EU are structurally incapable of balancing behavior. The consensus-based CSDP decisionmaking process condemns the EU to pursue the foreign and security policy of a small power (Howorth and Menon 2009; Toje 2010). It is structurally incapable of pushing back against US military dominance. The uses to which the EU has put the CSDP so far lend some support to this conclusion.

The Liberal-Constructivist Scenario

This scenario is premised on the priority of international institutions, rules, and norms over the balance of power (Ikenberry 2001). It argues that the transatlantic order is a peace system (Deutsch 1957; Wæver 1998), and there is no security dilemma dividing Europe from the United States. The transatlantic order is held together by shared values; a common culture and a collective identity, particularly dense relations of economic interdependence; and strong international institutions (Moravcsik 1993b; Risse 2002). The EU has no incentives to disrupt this order, nor does it wish to end the US-led global extension of liberal order, because it benefits materially from liberal internationalism and identifies with its constitutive values and norms. Hence, the CSDP cannot be understood as an instrument for checking US power (Risse 2002). Rather, it is an outgrowth of European political integration and a tool to support the United States in managing liberal world order. The CSDP contributes to a transatlantic division of labor in international security. Joint security management is founded on mutual interests, shared values, and complementary tasks based on the relative strengths of each side. While the US military focuses on high-tech warfare operations (conventional and unconventional), complemented by counterinsurgency, the CSDP focuses on humanitarian interventions, peacekeeping, and nation-building (Moravcsik 2003).

What future for the military CSDP and international order does the liberal-constructivist scenario predict? As the allies seek to stay on top of rising global security interdependence, the transatlantic division of labor will be consolidated and deepened. The EU will further upgrade its ability to fit the military CSDP into its comprehensive foreign and security policy toolbox. It will become better at implementing what Stephan Keukeleire calls structural foreign policy—policy aimed at shaping the political, legal, economic, and security contexts in foreign countries (Keukeleire and MacNaughtan 2008). More to the point, the EU will continue to strengthen its military capabilities, procuring technologically more sophisticated intervention capabilities, though on a much lower scale than that of the United States. High-tech military power enables the EU to act more effectively as the US junior partner in joint security operations. Also, it enables it to do more demanding stabilization and reconstruction operations on its own. Finally, the liberal-constructivist scenario assumes that in the long run a posthegemonic order will likely emerge (Ikenberry 2009). The most powerful states will cooperate as equals to maintain global liberal order and to keep the benefits that flow from it.

What arguments can be marshaled for and against the liberal-constructivist scenario? Beginning with supporting evidence, the public pronouncements of European policymakers make it clear that the

EU strongly backs the current liberal world order. This has been expressed most eloquently by former British prime minister Blair. In a speech in 2000, he spoke of "an EU whose vision of peace is matched by its vision of prosperity; a civilised continent united in defeating brutality and violence; a continent joined in its belief in social justice: A superpower, but not a superstate" (Blair 2000). In 2007, British foreign secretary David Miliband (2007: 3) talked about the EU as a model power, "a role model that others follow." EU citizens seem instinctively to support the idea that European foreign and security policy ought to defend liberal decency in the international realm. Polls show that a large majority wants the EU to deal with international problems and threats by spending money on development assistance, using trade to influence other countries, and committing troops to peacekeeping missions. Moreover, a majority wants the EU to address international security problems in partnership with the United States (German Marshall Fund of the United States 2007: 8, 23–26). Both elite and public attitudes suggest that the future of the CSDP lies in peacemaking and peace-building, not in balancing US power.

Second, any European policymaker keen to balance US power would be hard-pressed to answer the why-bother question. The EU and the United States share the same world order vision—a world safe for democracy, human rights, and capitalism. Further, the economies of the EU and the United States are tightly integrated, in terms of both trade and financial flows. Transatlantic cooperation is crucial to maintain the rules of an open world economy, of which the United States and the EU are among the principal beneficiaries. Both emphasize similar threats—terrorism, nuclear proliferation, and state failure. Cooperation on these issues is good, including through NATO, albeit not without friction. In many theaters, CSDP and US personnel have worked closely together. Common interests and values, shared threat perceptions, and operational cooperation lend credence to the liberal-constructivist argument that the EU has no reason to and does not fear US superior military power.

What are the arguments against the liberal-constructivist scenario? To start, since the 1970s the Europeans have diligently sought to enhance their collective role and influence in world politics. This was a driving force behind the creation of the CSDP. It seems unlikely that the EU will suddenly cease this quest and be content with the role of an extra on the world stage. Moreover, the better the EU is equipped to backfill and deputize for US forces, the better its position to challenge US leadership. Last but not least, the recent global financial crisis has tightened fiscal constraints in Europe, which has reinforced the pressure on EU states to deepen and widen their military cooperation. If they were to agree to joint armament production and procurement and to merge their separate armed forces, they could realize considerable savings. What is more, such a development would enhance EU capabilities and in all likelihood firm up EU attitudes on the use of force. An EU that can draw on a well-equipped supranational Euro-army is likely to be an EU that musters the political will to move beyond a small-power role of conflict preventer and postconflict stabilizer. Paradoxically, fiscal retrenchment may be the midwife of the EU's birth as a great military power.

Conclusion

The EU launched the CSDP at a time when the United States was the world's lone superpower, and the US still remains without a military peer competitor. After September 11, US military outlays increased considerably, reinforcing a trend that had been under way since the mid-1990s. No such growth spurt occurred in the EU. But US global military supremacy is unlikely to be sustainable. US overstretch and uneven economic growth favoring emerging powers will enable countries such as China and India to narrow the gap in hard military power between themselves and the leader. The EU, too, is likely to improve its military position relative to the United States in the long run. It is determined to build up its military capabilities, rationalize its military decision processes, construct a robust strategic culture, and deepen EU military cooperation. What remains to be seen is how the shift in the international balance of power over the next two decades or so will shape how the EU employs the CSDP and how the CSDP affects US-EU relations and more generally international order. Both the realist scenario and the liberal-constructivist scenario can point to supporting evidence. For the time being, the jury is still out on what the EU will make of the CSDP and thus of itself. What can be predicted with some confidence is that, as they build up the CSDP, EU decisionmakers will be faced with a persistent question. It is a question that Albright, then US ambassador to the United Nations, asked of the chairman of the US Joint Chiefs of Staff, General Colin Powell, when he opposed military intervention in Bosnia in the 1990s to stop the ethnic fighting. "What's the point of having this superb military you're always talking about if we can't use it?" Indeed, the question has already begun to be asked of the CSDP (Burgess 2008). Ignoring it will become politically increasingly difficult for the EU in the future.

Notes

1. This scenario is based on combining insights from both liberalism and constructivism. Such eclecticism is in line with calls by a number of scholars to join arguments from the two theories that have been aptly described as birds of a feather (Sterling-Folker 2000; also Fearon and Wendt 2002; Finnemore and Sikkink 1998). The liberal-constructivist scenario is broadly compatible with a governance scenario. However, a fully fledged governance theory scenario would put more emphasis on the erosion of sovereignty and on the role of nonstate actors in global security affairs.

2. Most Central and Eastern EU governments are concerned not about the concentration of military power in US hands but about the growth of power of Germany and Russia. They want a strong US in Europe to contain Germany and protect them against a resurgent Russia. Incidentally, there is a realist explanation for this. "Accepting the leadership of [the US] prevents a balance of power from emerging in Europe, and better the hegemonic power should be at a distance than next door" (Waltz 2000: 26). The fact that realism can be used to predict EU opposition to US influence over Europe and continued EU support for this state of affairs supports the claim of critics that contemporary realism is worryingly elastic because it can "support diametrically opposed arguments" about the CSDP (Rynning 2011: 28).

Acronyms

AMM	Aceh Monitoring Mission
AMM-IMP	AMM–Initial Monitoring Presence
ASEAN	Association of Southeast Asian Nations
C^4	command, control, communications, computers
CAR	Central African Republic
CFSP	Common Foreign and Security Policy, of which CSDP is an integral part
CIVCOM	Committee for Civilian Aspects of Crisis Management
CMC	Crisis Management Concept
CMPD	Crisis Management and Planning Directorate
CONOPS	Concept of Operations
COREPER	Committee of Permanent Representatives
CPCC	Civilian Planning and Conduct Capability
CSCE	Conference on Security and Cooperation in Europe
CSDP	Common Security and Defence Policy
DRC	Democratic Republic of Congo
EC	European Community (pre-Maastricht)
EDA	European Defence Agency
EDC	European Defence Community
ENP	European Neighbourhood Policy
EPC	European Political Cooperation
ESDP	European Security and Defence Policy, pre-Lisbon
ESS	European Security Strategy

EU	European Union
EU COPPS	EU Co-ordination Office for Palestinian Police Support
EUFOR	EU Force
EUMC	EU Military Committee
EUMM	EU Monitoring Mission
EUMS	EU Military Staff
EU NAVCO	EU Naval Coordination Cell
EUPM	CSDP police mission in Bosnia
EUPOL	EU Police Mission
EUSRs	EU special representatives
EUTM	Somalia EU Training Mission Somalia
GAM	Free Aceh Movement
ISTAR	intelligence, surveillance, target acquisition, and reconnaissance
MAP	Military Assessment and Planning
MINURCAT	UN Mission in the Central African Republic and Chad
MONUC	UN Organization Mission in the Democratic Republic of Congo
MSO	Military-Strategic Option
NATO	North Atlantic Treaty Organization
NTM-A	NATO Training Mission–Afghanistan
OSCE	Orgainsation for Security an Cooperation in Europe
OHQ	operational headquarters
OPLAN	Operation Plan
PMG	Politico-Military Working Group
PSC	Political and Security Committee
R2P	Responsibility to Protect
RELEX	Foreign Relations Councillors
RRF	(EU) Rapid Reaction Force
SHAPE	NATO's Supreme Headquarters Allied Powers Europe
SitCen	Joint Situation Centre
SSR	security sector reform
TACIS	Technical Aid to the Commonwealth of Independent States
WEU	Western European Union, 1954

Bibliography

Abrahams, Fred (1998) *Police Violence in Macedonia: Official Thumbs Up*, Human Rights Watch Report no. 10, New York.

Adler, Emanuel (1997) "Seizing the Middle Ground: Constructivism in World Politics," *European Journal of International Relations* vol. 3, no. 3, pp. 319–363.

Adler, Emanuel, and Michael Barnett (1998) "A Framework for the Study of Security Communities," in Emanuel Adler and Michael Barnett (eds.) *Security Communities* (Cambridge, UK: Cambridge University Press), pp. 29–65.

Aggestam, Lisbeth (ed.) (2008) "Special Issue: The EU as an Ethical Power," *International Affairs* vol. 84, no. 1.

Allen, David (1998) "'Who Speaks for Europe?' The Search for an Effective and Coherent External Policy," in John Peterson and Helene Sjursen (eds.) *A Common Foreign Policy for Europe? Competing Visions of the CFSP* (London: Routledge), pp. 41–58.

Allison, Roy, Margot Light, and Stephen White (2006) *Putin's Russia and the Enlarged Europe* (Oxford, UK: Blackwell).

Amnesty International (2009) "Open Letter to the Security Council," London.

Anderson, Stephanie B. (2008) *Crafting EU Security Policy: In Pursuit of a European Identity* (Boulder, CO: Lynne Rienner).

Andréani, Gilles, Christoph Bertram, and Charles Grant (2001) *Europe's Military Revolution* (London: Centre for European Reform).

Archer, Clive (ed.) (2008) *New Security Issues in Northern Europe: The Nordic and Baltic States and the ESDP* (London: Routledge).

Art, Robert J. (2004) "Europe Hedges Its Security Bets," in T.V. Paul and James J. Wirtz (eds.) *Balance of Power Revisited: Theory and Practice in the 21st Century* (Palo Alto, CA: Stanford University Press), pp. 179–213.

——— (2006) "Striking the Balance," *International Security* vol. 30, no. 3, pp. 177–185.

——— (2007) "The Four Functions of Force," in Robert J. Art and Robert Jervis (eds.) *International Politics: Enduring Concepts and Contemporary Issues* (New York: Pearson), pp. 141–148.

Asmus, Ronald D. (2006) "The European Security Strategy: An American View," in Roland Dannreuther and John Peterson (eds.) *Security Strategy and Transatlantic Relations* (London: Routledge), pp. 17–29.

Bagayoko, Niagalé (2004) "L'Opération Artémis, un tournant pour la politique européenne de sécurité et de défense?," *Afrique contemporaine*, no. 209, pp. 101–116.

Bailes, Alyson J. K. (2004) "EU and US Strategic Concepts: A Mirror for Partnership and Difference?," *The International Spectator* vol. 39, no. 1, pp. 19–33.

Balzacq, Thierry (ed.) (2009) *The External Dimension of EU Justice and Home Affairs: Governance, Neighbours, Security* (Basingstoke, UK: Palgrave Macmillan).

Baranovsky, Vladimir (2003) "Russian Views on NATO and the EU," in Anatol Lieven and Dmitri Trenin (eds.) *Ambivalent Neighbors: The EU, NATO and the Price of Membership* (Washington, DC: Carnegie Endowment for International Peace), pp. 269–294.

Barany, Zoltan (2007) *Democratic Breakdown and the Decline of the Russian Military* (Princeton, NJ: Princeton University Press).

BBC News (2010) "US Names Bissau 'Drug Kingpins,'" 9 April.

Bentégeat, Henri (2008) "1998–2008: 10 Years of ESDP," *Impetus: Bulletin of the EU Military Staff*, no. 6, pp. 6–7.

Bertin, Thomas (2008) "The EU Military Operation in Bosnia," in Michael Merlingen and Rasa Ostrauskaitė (eds.) *European Security and Defence Policy: An Implementation Perspective* (London: Routledge), pp. 61–77.

Bickerton, Chris J. (2011) "Towards a Social Theory of EU Foreign and Security Policy," *Journal of Common Market Studies* vol. 49, no. 1, pp. 171–190.

Bickerton, Christopher J., Bastien Irondelle, and Anand Menon (2011) "Security Co-operation Beyond the Nation-State: The EU's Common Security and Defence Policy," *Journal of Common Market Studies* vol. 49, no. 1, pp. 1–21.

Bildt, Carl (2008) "Strengthening the ESDP: The EU's Approach to International Security," speech given in Helsinki on 19 September.

Biscop, Sven (2005) *The European Security Strategy: A Global Agenda for Positive Power* (Aldershot, UK: Ashgate).

——— (2007) *A "European Army" for the EU and NATO?*, paper presented at the 48th International Studies Association (ISA) Annual Convention, Chicago, 28 February–3 March.

——— (2008) "Permanent Structured Cooperation and the Future of ESDP," Egmont Paper no. 20 (Brussels: Royal Institute for International Relations [EGMONT]).

Biscop, Sven, and Jo Coelmont (2011) *Europe, Strategy, and Armed Forces* (London: Routledge).

Bitterlich, Joachim (2007) "How to Get Europe's Common Foreign Policy out of the Doldrums," *Europe's World*, no. 6, pp. 15–19.

Blair, Tony (2000) "Address by Tony Blair to the Polish Stock Exchange," Warsaw, 6 October.

Blitz, James, and Frederick Studemann (2010) "NATO End Date 'Plays into Hands' of Taliban," *Financial Times*, 29 June.

Bono, Giovanna (2005) "National Parliaments and EU External Military Operations: Is There Any Parliamentary Control?," *European Security* vol. 14, no. 3, pp. 203–229.

——— (2006) "Challenges of Democratic Oversight of EU Security Policies," *European Security* vol. 15, no. 4, pp. 431–449.

Bono, Gosalbo (2006) "Some Reflections on the CFSP Legal Order," *Common Market Law Review* vol. 43, no. 2, pp. 337–394.

Bozo, Frédéric (2001) "Continuity or Change? The View from Europe," in S. Victor Papacosma, Sean Kay, and Mark R. Rubin (eds.) *NATO After Fifty Years* (Wilmington, DE: Scholarly Resources Inc.), pp. 53–72.

Braud, Pierre-Antoine, and Giovanni Grevi (2005) *The EU Mission in Aceh: Implementing Peace*, Occasional Paper no. 61 (Paris: EU Institute for Security Studies).

Brauss, Heinrich (2007) "The European Security and Defence Policy (ESDP)—Current State and Prospect," *European Security and Defence*, no. 2, pp. 5–7.

Brenner, Michael (1998) *Terms of Engagement: The United States and the European Security Identity* (Westport, CT: Praeger).

——— (2003) "The CFSP Factor: A Comparison of United States and French Strategies," *Cooperation and Conflict* vol. 38, no. 3, pp. 187–209.

Breuer, Fabian (forthcoming) "Sociological Institutionalism, Socialisation and the Brusselisation of CSDP," in Xymena Kurowska and Fabian Breuer (eds.) *Explaining EU's Common Security and Defence Policy: Theory in Action* (Basingstoke, UK: Palgrave Macmillan).

Brimmer, Esther (2007) *Seeing Blue: American Vision of the EU*, Chaillot Paper no. 105 (Paris: EU Institute for Security Studies).

Brok, Elmar, and Norbert Gresch (2004) "Untitled contribution," in Nicole Gnesotto (ed.) *EU Security and Defence Policy: The First Five Years (1999–2004)* (Paris: EU Institute for Security Studies), pp. 179–188.

Brooks, Stephen G., and William C. Wohlforth (2008) *World Out of Balance: International Relations and the Challenge of American Primacy* (Princeton, NJ: Princeton University Press).

Brown, Keith S. (2000) "In the Realm of the Double-Headed Eagle: Parapolitics in Macedonia, 1994–9," in Jane K. Cowan (ed.) *Macedonia: The Politics of Identity and Difference* (London: Pluto Press), pp. 122–139.

Brummer, Klaus (2007) "Superficial, Not Substantial: The Ambiguity of Public Support for Europe's Security and Defence Policy," *European Security* vol. 16, no. 2, pp. 183–201.

Building on Success: The London Conference on Afghanistan (2006) "The Afghanistan Compact," London, 31 January–1 February.

Bulmer, Simon, and Wolfgang Wessels (1987) *The European Council: Decision-Making in European Politics* (Basingstoke, UK: Palgrave Macmillan).

Bulut, Esra (2009) "EUPOL COPPS (Palestinian Territories)," in Giovanni Grevi, Damien Helly, and Daniel Keohane (eds.) *European Security and Defence Policy: The First 10 Years (1999–2009)* (Paris: EU Institute for Security Studies), pp. 287–298.

Burgess, Mark (2008) "Saving Congo: Whither the EU?" (Washington, DC: Foreign Policy in Focus), 4 December.

Burns, R. Nicholas (2007) "Remarks to the Atlantic Council," Washington DC, 21 February.

Cascone, Gabriele (2008) "ESDP Operations and NATO: Co-operation, Rivalry or Muddling-Through?," in Michael Merlingen and Rasa Ostrauskaitė (eds.) *European Security and Defence Policy: An Implementation Perspective* (London: Routledge), pp. 143–158.

Castle, Stephen (2005) "NATO Turf War on Airlift Delays Help for Darfur," *The Independent*, 10 June.

Christiansen, Thomas, and Torbjörn Larsson (eds.) (2007) *The Role of Committees in the Policy-Process of the European Union: Legislation, Implementation and Deliberation* (Cheltenham, UK: Edward Elgar).

Christiansen, Thomas, and Sophie Vanhoonacker (2008) "At a Critical Juncture? Change and Continuity in the Institutional Development of the Council Secretariat," *West European Politics* vol. 31, no. 4, pp. 751–770.

Clément, Caty (2009) "EUSEC RD Congo," in Giovanni Grevi, Damien Helly, and Daniel Keohane (eds.) *European Security and Defence Policy: The First 10 Years (1999–2009)* (Paris: EU Institute for Security Studies), pp. 243–254.

Clinton, Hillary (2010) "Speech given to the Atlantic Council in Washington, DC," 22 February.

Cogan, Charles G. (2001) *The Third Option: The Emancipation of European Defense, 1989–2000* (Westport, CT: Praeger).

Cohen, William S. (2000) "Press conference, NATO Informal Ministerial Meeting, Washington, DC," 10 October.

Cooper, Robert (2003) *The Breaking of Nations: Order and Chaos in the 21st Century* (London: Atlantic Books).

Cornell, Svante E., and S. Frederick Starr (eds.) (2009) *The Guns of August 2008: Russia's War in Georgia* (Armonk, NY: M. E. Sharpe).

Cornish, Paul, and Geoffrey Edwards (2005) "The Strategic Culture of the European Union: A Progress Report," *International Affairs* vol. 81, no. 4, pp. 801–820.

Council of the European Union (2004) "Conceptual Framework on the ESDP Dimension of the Fight Against Terrorism," Brussels, 18 November.

——— (2005) "Council Joint Action of 9 September on the European Union Monitoring Mission in Aceh (Indonesia) (Aceh Monitoring Mission [AMM])," 2005/643/CFSP, Brussels.

——— (2008a) "Declaration by the Presidency on Behalf of the European Union on the Deployment of EULEX," Brussels, 28 November.

—— (2008b) "Draft Declaration on Strengthening Capabilities," Brussels, 5 December.

—— (2008c) "Factsheet: EU Support to the African Union Mission in Darfur—AMIS," Brussels.

Crow, Suzanne (1993) *Russia Seeks Leadership in Regional Peacekeeping*, Research Report no. 15 (Prague, Czech Republic: Radio Free Europe/Radio Liberty [RFL/RL]).

Crowe, Brian (2005) *Foreign Minister of Europe* (London: Foreign Policy Centre).

d'Aboville, Benoît (2008) "The Thinking Behind France's NATO Rapprochement," *Europe's World*, no. 10, pp. 69–73.

Darnis, Jean-Pierre, Giovanni Gasparini, Christoph Grams, Daniel Keohane, Fabio Liberti, Jean-Pierre Maulny, and May-Britt Stumbaum (2007) *Lessons Learned from European Defence Equipment Programmes*, Occasional Paper no. 69 (Paris: EU Institute for Security Studies).

Davis, Laura (2009) *Justice-Sensitive Security System Reform in the Democratic Republic of Congo* (Brussels: Initiative for Peace-Building).

Delpech, Thérèsè (2002) *International Terrorism in Europe*, Chaillot Paper no. 56 (Paris: EU Institute for Security Studies).

Dempsey, Judy (2009) "Training of Afghan Police by Europe Is Found Lacking," *New York Times*, 18 November.

Deutsch, Karl Wolfgang (1957) *Political Community and the North Atlantic Area: International Organization in the Light of Historical Experience* (Princeton, NJ: Princeton University Press).

Dietrich, Sascha (2006) *Europäische Sicherheits- und Verteidigungspolitik (ESVP)* (Baden-Baden, Germany: Nomos).

Dijkstra, Hylke (2008) "The Council Secretariat's Role in the Common Foreign and Security Policy," *European Foreign Affairs Review* vol. 13, no. 2, pp. 149–166.

—— (2010) "Explaining Variation in the Role of the EU Council Secretariat in First and Second Pillar Policy-Making," *Journal of European Public Policy* vol. 17, no. 4, pp. 527–544.

Dobbins, James (2006) "Friends Again?," in Marcin Zaborowski (ed.) *Friends Again? EU-US Relations After the Crisis* (Paris: EU Institute for Security Studies), pp. 21–28.

Dobbins, James, Seth G. Jones, Keith Crane, Christopher S. Chivvis, Andrew Radin, F. Stephen Larrabee, Nora Bensahel, Brooke K. Stearns, and Benjamin W. Goldsmith (2008) *Europe's Role in Nation-Building: From the Balkans to the Congo* (Santa Monica, CA: Rand).

Dover, Robert (2007) *Europeanization of British Defence Policy* (Aldershot, UK: Ashgate).

Duchêne, François (1973) "The European Community and the Uncertainties of Interdependence," in Max Kohnstamm and Wolfgang Hager (eds.) *A Nation Writ Large? Foreign Policy Problems Before the European Community* (London: Macmillan), pp. 1–21.

Duke, Simon (2000) *The Elusive Quest for European Security: From EDC to CFSP* (Basingstoke, UK: Palgrave Macmillan).

—— (2007) "The Role of Committees and Working Groups in the CFSP Area," in Thomas Christiansen and Torbjörn Larsson (eds.) *The Role of*

Committees in the Policy-Process of the European Union: Legislation, Implementation and Deliberation (Cheltenham: Edward Elgar), pp. 120–151.

—— (2008a) "Consensus Building in ESDP: Lessons of Operation Artemis," UCD Dublin European Institute Working Paper 08-7, Dublin.

—— (2008b) "The Future of EU-NATO Relations: A Case of Mutual Irrelevance Through Competition?," *Journal of European Integration* vol. 30, no. 1, pp. 27–43.

Duke, Simon, and Sophie Vanhoonacker (2006) "Administrative Governance in the CFSP: Development and Practice," *European Foreign Affairs Review* vol. 11, no. 2, pp. 163–182.

The Economist (2005) "Europe's Cassandra Complex," 27 October.

Edwards, Geoffrey (2006) "The New Member States and the Making of EU Foreign Policy," *European Foreign Affairs Review* vol. 11, no. 2, pp. 143–162.

Ehrhart, Hans-Georg (2008) *Assessing EUFOR Chad/CAR*, European Security Review, no. 42 (Brussels: International Security Information Service [ISIS]), pp. 20–22.

Eliasson, Johan (2004) "Traditions, Identity and Security: The Legacy of Neutrality in Finnish and Swedish Policies in Light of European Integration," *European Integration online Papers (EIoP)* vol. 8, no. 6.

EU Military Staff (2007) "Impetus: Bulletin of the EU Military Staff," no. 4, Brussels.

—— (2008) "EU Concept for Military Planning at the Political and Strategic Level," Council Document 10687/08, Brussels.

European Commission (2003) "Reference: Conclusions of the Seville European Council," Bulletin of the European Union, no. 6-2003.

—— (2006) "Green Paper: A European Strategy for Sustainable, Competitive and Secure Energy," COM (2006) 105 final, Brussels.

—— (2008a) "Kosovo (Under UNSCR 1244/99) 2008 Progress Report," Brussels, 5 November.

—— (2008b) "Progress Report on the Occupied Palestinian Territory: Communication from the Commission to the Council and the European Parliament on the Implementation of the European Neighbourhood Policy in 2007," Brussels.

—— (2009) "Kosovo Under UNSCR 1244/99 2009 Progress Report," Brussels, 14 October.

—— (2010) "Energy 2020: A Strategy for Competitive, Sustainable and Secure Energy," communication from the Commission to the European Parliament, the Council, the European Economic and Social Committee, and the Committee of the Regions, COM (2010) 639 final, Brussels, 10 November.

European Commission (2011a) "Datasheets on Trade Between the EU and Its Main Trading Partners—Russia," Brussels.

—— (2011b) "EU-Russia Energy Dialogue: The First Ten Years: 2000–2010," Brussels.

European Commission and High Representative for the CFSP (2006) "An External Policy to Serve Europe's Energy Interests: Paper from Commission/SG/HR for the European Council," Brussels.

European Council (1999a) "Presidency Conclusions of the European Council," Cologne, 3–4 June.

—— (1999b) "Presidency Conclusions of the European Council," Helsinki, 10–11 December.

—— (2000) "Presidency Conclusions of the European Council," Nice, 7–9 December.

—— (2002) "Presidency Conclusions of the European Council," Brussels, 24–25 October.

—— (2003) "A Secure Europe in a Better World—European Security Strategy," Brussels, 12 December.

—— (2008) "Presidency Conclusions of the European Council," Brussels, 11–12 December.

European Defence Agency (2010a) "Defence Data 2009," Brussels.

—— (2010b) "European—United States Defence Expenditure in 2009," Brussels.

EU-Russia Summit (2000) "Joint Declaration on Strengthening Dialogue and Cooperation on Political and Security Matters in Europe," Paris, 30 October.

European Security and Defence Assembly of Western European Union (2010) "European Cooperation on Military Helicopters," report submitted on behalf of the Defence Committee by Claire Curtis-Thomas, Rapporteur (United Kingdom, Socialist Group), Document A/2075, Paris.

European Security Review (2010) *Feature—Somalia*, no. 49 (Brussels: International Security Information Service [ISIS]), p. 13.

European Union Naval Force, Public Affairs Office (2010) "EU NAVFOR Operation Atalanta," Northwood, UK.

Facon, Isabelle (2005) "Putin, the Army and Military Reform," in Jakob Hedenskog, Vilhelm Konnander, Bertil Nygren, Ingmar Oldberg, and Christer Pursiainen (eds.) *Russia as a Great Power: Dimensions of Security Under Putin* (London: Routledge), pp. 203–226.

Faria, Fernanda (2004) *Crisis Management in Sub-Saharan Africa: The Role of the European Union*, Occasional Paper no. 51 (Paris: EU Institute for Security Studies).

Fearon, James, and Alexander Wendt (2002) "Rationalism v. Constructivism: A Skeptical View," in Walter Carlsnaes, Thomas Risse, and Beth A. Simmons (eds.) *Handbook of International Relations* (London: Sage), pp. 52–72.

Ferreira-Pereira, Laura C. (2006) "Inside the Fence but Outside the Walls," *Cooperation and Conflict* vol. 41, no. 1, pp. 99–122.

Filippini, Carlo (2007) "Beyond the Triadic World Order: The Role and Patterns of Trade and Economics in EU-Asia Relations," in Peter Anderson and Georg Wiessala (eds.) *The European Union and Asia: Reflections and Re-orientations* (Amsterdam: Rodopi), pp. 147–171.

Finnemore, Martha, and Kathryn Sikkink (1998) "International Norm Dynamics and Political Change," *International Organization* vol. 52, no. 4, pp. 887–917.

Flessenkemper, Tobias (2008) "EUPOL Proxima in Macedonia, 2003–05," in Michael Merlingen and Rasa Ostrauskaitė (eds.) *European Security and Defence Policy: An Implementation Perspective* (London: Routledge), pp. 78–96.

Forsberg, Tuoams (2004) "The EU-Russia Security Partnership: Why the Opportunity Was Missed," *European Foreign Affairs Review* vol. 9, no. 2, pp. 247–267.

Forster, Anthony (2006) *Armed Forces and Society in Europe* (Basingstoke, UK: Palgrave Macmillan).

Fouilleux, Eve, Jacques de Maillard, and Andy Smith (2007) "Council Working Groups: Spaces for Sectorized European Policy Deliberations," in Thomas Christiansen and Torbjörn Larsson (eds.) *The Role of Committees in the Policy-Process of the European Union: Legislation, Implementation and Deliberation* (Cheltenham, UK: Edward Elgar), pp. 96–119.

Franco-British Summit (1998) "Joint Declaration on European Defence," Saint-Malo, France, 4 December.

Fursdon, Edward (1980) *The European Defence Community: A History* (London: Macmillan).

Gallis, Paul (2003) *NATO's Decision-Making Procedure*, Congressional Research Service Report for Congress, RS21510, Washington, DC.

Gegout, Catherine (2005) "Causes and Consequences of the EU's Military Intervention in the Democratic Republic of Congo: A Realist Explanation," *European Foreign Affairs Review* vol. 10, no. 3, pp. 427–443.

—— (2007) "The EU and Security in the Democratic Republic of Congo in 2006: Unfinished Business," *CFSP Forum* vol. 4, no. 6, pp. 5–9.

—— (2009) "The West, Realism and Intervention in the Democratic Republic of Congo (1996–2006)," *International Peacekeeping* vol. 16, no. 2, pp. 231–244.

General Secretariat of the Council of the EU (2007a) "EUSR Factsheet," Brussels.

—— (2007b) "Factsheet: Financing of ESDP Operations," Brussels.

—— (2009) "Factsheet: EUFOR Chad/Central African Republic," Brussels.

—— (2010) "Factsheet: EU Engagement in Afghanistan," Brussels.

German Marshall Fund of the United States (2007) "Transatlantic Trends: Key Findings 2007," Washington, DC.

Giegerich, Bastian (2006) *European Security and Strategic Culture: National Responses to the EU's Security and Defence Policy* (Baden-Baden, Germany: Nomos).

—— (2008) *European Military Crisis Management: Connecting Ambition and Reality*, Adelphi Paper no. 397 (London: International Institute for Strategic Studies).

Giegerich, Bastian, and Eva Gross (2006) "Squaring the Circle? Leadership and Legitimacy in European Security and Defence Cooperation," *International Politics* vol. 43, no. 4, pp. 500–509.

Giegerich, Bastian, and Alexander Nicoll (eds.) (2008) *European Military Capabilities: Building Armed Forces for Modern Operations* (London: International Institute for Strategic Studies).

Ginsberg, Roy H. (2001) *The European Union in International Politics: Baptism by Fire* (Lanham, MD: Rowman & Littlefield).

Glarbo, Kenneth (1999) "Wide-Awake Diplomacy: Reconstructing the Common Foreign and Security Policy of the European Union," *Journal of European Public Policy* vol. 6, no. 4, pp. 634–651.

Glasius, Marlies, and Mary Kaldor (eds.) (2006) *A Human Security Doctrine for Europe: Project, Principles, Practicalities* (London: Routledge).

Gnesotto, Nicole (1997) "Common European Defence and Transatlantic Relations," in Philip H. Gordon (ed.) *NATO's Transformation: The Changing Shape of the Atlantic Alliance* (Lanham, MD: Rowman & Littlefield), pp. 39–51.

—— (2004) "Introduction—ESDP: Results and Prospects," in Nicole Gnesotto (ed.) *EU Security and Defence Policy: The First Five Years (1999–2004)* (Paris: EU Institute for Security Studies), pp. 11–31.

—— (2009) "The Need for a More Strategic EU," in Álvaro de Vasconcelos (ed.) *What Ambitions for European Defence in 2020?* (Paris: EU Institute for Security Studies), pp. 29–38.

Gordon, Philip H. (1993) *A Certain Idea of France: French Security Policy and the Gaullist Legacy* (Princeton, NJ: Princeton University Press).

—— (1997) "The Western European Union and NATO's 'Europeanisation,'" in Philip H. Gordon (ed.) *NATO's Transformation: The Changing Shape of the Atlantic Alliance* (Lanham, MD: Rowman & Littlefield), pp. 257–270.

—— (2002) "Reforging the Atlantic Alliance," *The National Interest*, no. 69, pp. 91–97.

Grand, Camille (2009) "Sarkozy's Three-Way NATO Bet," *Europe's World*, no. 13, pp. 36–41.

Grant, Robert P. (1997) "France's New Relationship with NATO," in Philip H. Gordon (ed.) *NATO's Transformation: The Changing Shape of the Atlantic Alliance* (Lanham, MD: Rowman & Littlefield), pp. 53–76.

Grevi, Giovanni (2007) *Pioneering Foreign Policy: The EU Special Representatives*, Chaillot Paper no. 106 (Paris: EU Institute for Security Studies).

Grieco, Joseph M. (1996) "State Interests and Institutional Rule Trajectories: A Neorealist Interpretation of the Maastricht Treaty and European Economic and Monetary Union," *Security Studies* vol. 5, no. 3, pp. 261–306.

Gross, Eva (2009a) *The Europeanization of National Foreign Policy: Continuity and Change in European Crisis Management* (Basingstoke, UK: Palgrave Macmillan).

—— (2009b) "Security Sector Reform in Afghanistan: The EU's Contribution," Occasional Paper no. 78 (Paris: EU Institute for Security Studies).

Haine, Jean-Yves (2003) *From Laeken to Copenhagen—European Defence: Core Documents*, Chaillot Paper no. 57 (Paris: EU Institute for Security Studies).

Haine, Jean-Yves, and Bastian Giegerich (2006) "In Congo, a Cosmetic EU Operation," *International Herald Tribune*, 12 July.

Hall, Peter A., and Rosemary C. R. Taylor (1996) "Political Science and the Three New Institutionalisms," *Political Studies* vol. 44, no. 5, pp. 936–957.

Haukkala, Hiski (2010) *The EU-Russia Strategic Partnership: The Limits of Post-Sovereignty in International Relations* (London: Routledge).

Hayes-Renshaw, Fiona, and Helen Wallace (2006) *The Council of Ministers* (Basingstoke, UK: Palgrave Macmillan).

Helly, Damien (2006) "EUJUST Themis in Georgia: An Ambitious Bet on Rule of Law," in Agnieszka Nowak (ed.) *Civilian Crisis Management: The EU Way*, Chaillot Paper no. 90 (Paris: EU Institute for Security Studies), pp. 87–102.

——— (2009) "EU NAVFOR Somalia: The EU Military Operation Atalanta," in Giovanni Grevi, Damien Helly, and Daniel Keohane (eds.) *European Security and Defence Policy: The First 10 Years (1999–2009)* (Paris: EU Institute for Security Studies), pp. 391–402.

Her Majesty's Government (2010) "Securing Britain in an Age of Uncertainty: The Strategic Defence and Security Review," Norwich, UK.

Herspring, Dale R. (2003) "Putin and the Armed Forces," in Dale R. Herspring (ed.) *Putin's Russia: Past Imperfect, Future Uncertain* (Lanham, MD: Rowman and Littlefield), pp. 155–175.

Herspring, Dale R., and Peter Rutland (2003) "Putin and Russian Foreign Policy," in Dale R. Herspring (ed.) *Putin's Russia: Past Imperfect, Future Uncertain* (Lanham, MD: Rowman and Littlefield), pp. 225–255.

Hill, Christopher J. (1993) "The Capability-Expectations Gap, or Conceptualizing Europe's International Role," *Journal of Common Market Studies* vol. 31, no. 3, pp. 305–328.

Hoffmann, Stanley (1995) *The European Sisyphus: Essays on Europe, 1964–94* (Boulder, CO: Westview Press).

Hofmann, Stephanie C. (2009) "Overlapping Institutions in the Realm of International Security: The Case of NATO and ESDP," *Perspectives on Politics* vol. 7, no. 1, pp. 45–52.

——— (2011) "Why Institutional Overlap Matters: CSDP in the European Security Architecture," *Journal of Common Market Studies* vol. 49, no. 1, pp. 101–120.

Hofmann, Stephanie C., and Christopher Reynolds (2007) *Die EU-NATO-Beziehungen: Zeit für Tauwetter*, SWP-Aktuell, no. 37 (Berlin: Stiftung Wissenschaft und Politik—Deutsches Institut für Internationale Politik und Sicherheit).

Howorth, Jolyon (2000) *European Integration and Defence: The Ultimate Challenge?*, Chaillot Paper no. 43 (Paris: EU Institute for Security Studies).

——— (2003) "ESDP and NATO: Wedlock or Deadlock?," *Cooperation and Conflict* vol. 38, no. 3, pp. 235–254.

——— (2004) "Discourse, Ideas, and Epistemic Communities in European Security and Defence Policy," *West European Politics*, vol. 27, no. 2, pp. 211–234.

——— (2009) "The Case for an EU Grand Strategy," in Sven Biscop, Jolyon Howorth, and Bastian Giegerich (eds.) *Europe: A Time for Strategy*, Egmont Paper no. 27 (Brussels: Royal Institute for International Relations [EGMONT]), pp. 15–23.

——— (2010) "The Political and Security Committee: A Case Study in 'Supranational Inter-Governmentalism,'" *Les Cahiers Européens*, no. 1.

Howorth, Jolyon, and Anand Menon (2009) "Still Not Pushing Back," *Journal of Conflict Resolution* vol. 53, no. 5, pp. 727–744.

Human Rights Watch (2007) "*World Report 2007*," New York.

——— (2009) "*World Report 2009*," New York.

Hunter, Robert (2002) *The European Security and Defense Policy: NATO's Companion—or Competitor?* (Santa Monica, CA: Rand).

Hyde-Price, Adrian (2006) "'Normative' Power Europe: A Realist Critique," *Journal of European Public Policy* vol. 13, no. 2, pp. 217–234.

Ifestos, Panayiotis (1987) *European Political Cooperation: Towards a Framework of Supranational Diplomacy?* (Aldershot, UK: Avebury).

Ikenberry, G. John (2001) *After Victory: Institutions, Strategic Restraint, and the Rebuilding of Order After Major Wars* (Princeton, NJ: Princeton University Press).

—— (2007) *Grand Strategy as Liberal Order Building*, paper given at the conference After the Bush Doctrine: National Security Strategy for a New Administration, University of Virginia, Charlottesville, 7–8 June.

—— (2009) "Liberal Internationalism 3.0: America and the Dilemmas of Liberal World Order," *Perspectives on Politics* vol. 7, no. 1, pp. 71–87.

International Crisis Group (2003) *Congo Crisis: Military Intervention in Ituri*, Africa Report no. 64, Nairobi/New York/Brussels.

—— (2006) *Security Sector Reform in the Congo*, Africa Report no. 104, Nairobi/Brussels.

—— (2007) *Reforming Afghanistan's Police*, Asia Report no. 138, Kabul/Brussels.

—— (2010) *The Rule of Law in Independent Kosovo*, Europe Report no. 204, Pristina/Istanbul/Brussels.

International Institute for Strategic Studies (2008) "The Military Balance 2008," pp. 205–224, London.

Ioannides, Isabelle (2007) "Police Mission in Macedonia," in Michael Emerson and Eva Gross (eds.) *Evaluating the EU's Crisis Missions in the Balkans* (Brussels: Centre for European Policy Studies), pp. 81–125.

Irondelle, Bastien (2003) "Europeanization Without the European Union? French Military Reforms 1991–96," *Journal of European Public Policy* vol. 10, no. 2, pp. 208–226.

Isakova, Irina (2005) *Russian Governance in the Twenty-First Century: Geostrategy, Geopolitics and Governance* (London: Frank Cass).

Jacoby, Wade, and Christopher Jones (2008) "The EU Battle Groups in Sweden and the Czech Republic: What National Defense Reforms Tell Us About European Rapid Reaction Capabilities," *European Security* vol. 17, no. 2, pp. 315–338.

Jakobsen, Peter Viggo (2006) "The ESDP and Civilian Rapid Reaction: Adding Value Is Harder Than Expected," *European Security* vol. 15, no. 3, pp. 299–321.

Järvinen, Taina (2007) *Aceh Monitoring Mission and the EU's Role in the Aceh Peace Process*, paper presented at the 48th International Studies Association (ISA) Annual Convention, Chicago, 28 February–3 March.

Jokela, Juha (2011) *Europeanization and Foreign Policy: State Identity in Finland and Britain* (London: Routledge).

Jones, Seth G. (2007) *The Rise of European Security Cooperation* (Cambridge, UK: Cambridge University Press).

Jørgensen, Knud Erik (1997) "PoCo: The Diplomatic Republic of Europe," in Knud Erik Jørgensen (ed.) *Reflective Approaches to European Governance* (Basingstoke, UK: Palgrave Macmillan), pp. 167–180.

Juncos, Ana E. (2007) "Police Mission in Bosnia and Herzegovina," in Michael Emerson and Eva Gross (eds.) *Evaluating the EU's Crisis Missions in the Balkans* (Brussels: Centre for European Policy Studies), pp. 46–80.

——— (2011) "The Other Side of EU Crisis Management: A Sociological Institutionalist Analysis," in Eva Gross and Ana E. Juncos (eds.) *EU Conflict Prevention and Crisis Management: Roles, Institutions and Policies* (London: Routledge), pp. 84–99.

Juncos, Ana E., and Karolina Pomorska (2006) "Playing the Brussels Game: Strategic Socialisation in the CFSP Council Working Groups," *European Integration online Papers (EIoP)*, vol. 10.

Juncos, Ana E., and Christopher Reynolds (2007) "The Political and Security Committee: Governing in the Shadow," *European Foreign Affairs Review* vol. 12, no. 2, pp. 127–147.

Kelleher, Catherine (2008) "The European Security Strategy and the United States: The Past as Prologue," in Sven Biscop and Jan Joel Andersson (eds.) *The EU and the European Security Strategy: Forging a Global Europe* (London: Routledge), pp. 139–165.

Kelley, Judith (2006) "New Wine in Old Wineskins: Promoting Political Reforms Through the New European Neighbourhood Policy," *Journal of Common Market Studies* vol. 44, no. 1, pp. 29–55.

Kennedy, John F. (1962) "Address at Independence Hall," Philadelphia, PA, 4 July.

Keohane, Daniel (2008) "The Absent Friend: EU Foreign Policy and Counter-Terrorism," *Journal of Common Market Studies* vol. 46, no. 1, pp. 125–146.

Keohane, Robert O. (1984) *After Hegemony: Cooperation and Discord in the World Political Economy* (Princeton, NJ: Princeton University Press).

Keukeleire, Stephan (2001) "Directorates in the CFSP/CESDP of the European Union: A Plea for 'Restricted Crisis Management Groups,'" *European Foreign Affairs Review* vol. 6, no. 1, pp. 75–101.

Keukeleire, Stephan, and Jennifer MacNaughtan (2008) *The Foreign Policy of the European Union* (Basingstoke, UK: Palgrave Macmillan).

Khaliq, Urfan (2008) *Ethical Dimensions of the Foreign Policy of the European Union: A Legal Appraisal* (Cambridge, UK: Cambridge University Press).

Kirchner, Emil, and James Sperling (2007) *EU Security Governance* (Manchester, UK: Manchester University Press).

Kirchner, Emil, and James Sperling (eds.) (2010) *National Security Cultures* (London: Routledge).

Kirshner, Jonathan (ed.) (2006) *Globalization and National Security* (London: Routledge).

Kirwan, Paul (2008) "From European to Global Security Actor: The Aceh Monitoring Mission in Indonesia," in Michael Merlingen and Rasa Ostrauskaitė (eds.) *European Security and Defence Policy: An Implementation Perspective* (London: Routledge), pp. 128–142.

Kissinger, Henry (1973) *A World Restored: Castlereagh, Metternich and the Restoration of Peace, 1812–1822* (Boston, MA: Houghton Mifflin Company).

Klein, Nadia (2011) "Conceptualizing the EU as a Civilian-Military Crisis Manager: Institutional Actors and Their Principals," in Eva Gross and Ana E. Juncos (eds.) *EU Conflict Prevention and Crisis Management: Roles, Institutions and Policies* (London: Routledge), pp. 66–83.

Koeth, Wolfgang (2010) "State Building Without a State: The EU's Dilemma in Defining Its Relations with Kosovo," *European Foreign Affairs Review* vol. 15, no. 2, pp. 227–247.

Korski, Daniel (2008) *Time for a European Civilian Reserve* (London: Institute for Public Policy Research).

Korski, Daniel, and Richard Gowan (2009) *Can the EU Rebuild Failing States? A Review of Europe's Civilian Capacities* (London: European Council on Foreign Relations).

Krahmann, Elke (2003) *Multilevel Networks in European Foreign Policy* (Aldershot, UK: Ashgate).

——— (2005) "Security Governance and Networks: New Theoretical Perspectives in Transatlantic Security," *Cambridge Review of International Affairs* vol. 18, no. 1, pp. 15–30.

Kupchan, Charles A. (2004–2005) "The Travails of Union: The American Experience and Its Implications for Europe," *Survival* vol. 46, no. 4, pp. 103–120.

Kurowska, Xymena (2008) "More Than a Balkan Crisis Manager: The EUJUST Themis in Georgia," in Michael Merlingen and Rasa Ostrauskaitė (eds.) *European Security and Defence Policy: An Implementation Perspective* (London: Routledge), pp. 97–110.

Kurowska, Xymena, and Fabian Breuer (eds.) (forthcoming) *Explaining European Security and Defence Policy: Theory in Action* (Basingstoke, UK: Palgrave Macmillan).

Ladrech, Robert (2010) *Europeanization and National Politics* (Basingstoke, UK: Palgrave Macmillan).

Larrabee, F. Stephen (2009) "The United States and the Evolution of ESDP," in Álvaro de Vasconcelos (ed.) *What Ambitions for European Defence in 2020?* (Paris: EU Institute for Security Studies), pp. 51–60.

Larsen, Henrik (2005) *Analysing the Foreign Policy of Small States in the EU: The Case of Denmark* (Basingstoke, UK: Palgrave Macmillan).

Laurent, Pierre-Henri (2001) "NATO and the European Union: The Quest for a Security/Defense Identity, 1948–1999," in S. Victor Papacosma, Sean Kay, and Mark R. Rubin (eds.) *NATO After Fifty Years* (Wilmington, DE: Scholarly Resources), pp. 141–161.

Laursen, Finn, and Sophie Vanhoonacker (eds.) (1992) *The Intergovernmental Conference on Political Union: Institutional Reform, New Policies and International Identity of the European Community* (Dordrecht, Netherlands: Martinus Nijhoff).

Lavenex, Sandra, and Frank Schimmelfennig (2009) "EU Rules Beyond EU Borders: Theorizing External Governance in European Politics," *Journal of European Public Policy* vol. 16, no. 6, pp. 791–812.

Lavenex, Sandra, and Frank Schimmelfennig (eds.) (2010) *EU External Governance: Projecting EU Rules Beyond Membership* (London: Routledge).

Lavrov, Sergei (2008) "We Are Trying to De-ideologize our Politics," *Russia Beyond the Headlines* (Moscow: Rossiyskaya Gazeta).

Layne, Christopher (2007) *The Peace of Illusions: American Grand Strategy from 1940 to the Present* (Ithaca, NY: Cornell University Press).

Leonard, Mark, and Richard Gowan (2004) *Global Europe: Implementing the European Security Strategy* (Brussels: Foreign Policy Centre and British Council).

Leonard, Mark, and Nicu Popescu (2007) *A Power Audit of EU-Russia Relations* (London: European Council on Foreign Relations).

Lewis, Jeffrey (2000) "The Methods of Community in EU Decision-Making and Administrative Rivalry in the Council's Infrastructure," *Journal of European Public Policy* vol. 7, no. 2, pp. 261–289.

Light, Margot (2009) "Russia and Europe and the Process of EU Enlargement," in Elana Wilson Rowe and Stina Torjesen (eds.) *The Multilateral Dimension in Russian Foreign Policy* (London: Routledge), pp. 83–96.

Lindstrom, Gustav (2007) *Enter the EU Battlegroups*, Chaillot Paper no. 97 (Paris: EU Institute for Security Studies).

Longhurst, Kerry, and Marcin Zaborowski (2006) "The European Union as a Security Actor: The View from Poland," in Gisela Müller-Brandeck-Bocquet (ed.) *The Future of the European Foreign, Security and Defence Policy After Enlargement* (Baden-Baden, Germany: Nomos), pp. 55–66.

Loriaux, Michael (1999) "Realism and Reconciliation: France, Germany and the European Union," in Ethan B. Kapstein and Michael Mastanduno (eds.) *Unipolar Politics: Realism and State Strategies After the Cold War* (New York: Columbia University Press), pp. 354–384.

Lucarelli, Sonia, and Ian Manners (eds.) (2008) *Values and Principles in European Union Foreign Policy* (London: Routledge).

Lutterbeck, Derek (2005) "Blurring the Dividing Line: The Convergence of Internal and External Security in Western Europe," *European Security* vol. 14, no. 2, pp. 231–253.

Mace, Catriona (2003) "Operation Concordia: Developing a 'European' Approach to Crisis Management?," *International Peacekeeping* vol. 11, no. 3, pp. 474–490.

Major, Claudia (2005) "Europeanisation and Foreign and Security Policy—Undermining or Rescuing the Nation State?," *Politics* vol. 25, no. 3, pp. 175–190.

——— (2009) "EUFOR RD Congo," in Giovanni Grevi, Damien Helly, and Daniel Keohane (eds.) *European Security and Defence Policy: The First 10 Years (1999–2009)* (Paris: EU Institute for Security Studies), pp. 311–323.

Malfliet, Katlijn, Lien Verpoest, and Evgeny Vinokurov (eds.) (2007) *The CIS, the EU and Russia: The Challenges of Integration* (Basingstoke, UK: Palgrave Macmillan).

Manners, Ian (2002) "Normative Power Europe: A Contradiction in Terms?," *Journal of Common Market Studies* vol. 40, no. 2, pp. 235–258.

March, James G., and Johan P. Olsen (1989) *Rediscovering Institutions: The Organizational Basis of Politics* (New York: The Free Press).

—— (2009) "The Logic of Appropriateness," Arena Working Papers 04/9 (Oslo: Centre for European Studies at the University of Oslo).

Martinelli, Marta (2008) "Implementing the ESDP in Africa: The Case of the Democratic Republic of Congo," in Michael Merlingen and Rasa Ostrauskaitė (eds.) *European Security and Defence Policy: An Implementation Perspective* (London: Routledge), pp. 111–127.

Matlary, Janne Haaland (2009) *European Union Security Dynamics: In the New National Interest* (Basingstoke, UK: Palgrave Macmillan).

Mayer, Hartmut, and Henri Vogt (eds.) (2006) *A Responsible Europe? Ethical Foundations of EU External Affairs* (Basingstoke, UK: Palgrave Macmillan).

McGuire, Stryker (2007) "Europe's Iron Lady," *Newsweek*, pp. 27–28.

Mearsheimer, John J. (1990) "Back to the Future: Instability in Europe After the Cold War," *International Security* vol. 15, no. 4, pp. 5–56.

—— (2010) "Why Is Europe Peaceful Today?," *European Political Science* vol. 9, no. 3, pp. 387–397.

Menon, Anand (2009) "Empowering Paradise? The ESDP at Ten," *International Affairs* vol. 85, no. 2, pp. 227–246.

—— (2011) "Power, Institutions and the CSDP: The Promise of Institutionalist Theory," *Journal of Common Market Studies* vol. 49, no. 1, pp. 83–100.

Mérand, Frédéric (2008) *European Defence Policy: Beyond the Nation State* (Oxford, UK: Oxford University Press).

—— (2010) "Pierre Bourdieu and the Birth of European Defense," *Security Studies* vol. 19, no. 2, pp. 342–374.

Mérand, Frédéric, Stéphanie C. Hofmann, and Bastien Irondelle (2011) "Governance and State Power: A Network Analysis of European Security," *Journal of Common Market Studies* vol. 49, no. 1, pp. 121–147.

Merlingen, Michael (2007) "Everything Is Dangerous: A Critique of 'Normative Power Europe,'" *Security Dialogue* vol. 38, no. 4, pp. 435–453.

—— (2009) "The EU Police Mission in Bosnia and Herzegovina (EUPM)," in Giovanni Grevi, Damien Helly, and Daniel Keohane (eds.) *European Security and Defence Policy: The First 10 Years (1999–2009)* (Paris: EU Institute for Security Studies), pp. 161–171.

—— (2011) "From Governance to Governmentality in CSDP: Towards a Foucauldian Research Agenda," *Journal of Common Market Studies* vol. 49, no. 1, pp. 149–169.

—— (forthcoming-a) "Applying Foucault's Toolkit to CSDP," in Xymena Kurowska and Fabian Breuer (eds.) *Explaining EU's Common Security and Defence Policy: Theory in Action* (Basingstoke, UK: Palgrave Macmillan).

—— (forthcoming-b) "The CSDP in the Western Balkans: From Experimental Pilot to Security Governance," in Sven Biscop and Richard Whitman (eds.) *Routledge Handbook of European Security* (London: Routledge).

Merlingen, Michael, Manuel Mireanu, and Elena B. Stavrevska (2009) "The Current State of European Security," in Institute for Peace Research and Security Policy at the University of Hamburg (ed.) *OSCE-Yearbook 2008: Yearbook on the Organization for Security and Co-operation in Europe (OSCE)* (Baden-Baden, Germany: Nomos), pp. 91–117.

Merlingen, Michael, and Rasa Ostrauskaitė (2005a) "A Dense Policy Space? The Police Aid of the OSCE and the EU," in Institute for Peace Research and Security Policy at the University of Hamburg (ed.) *OSCE-Yearbook 2004: Yearbook on the Organization for Security and Co-operation in Europe (OSCE)* (Baden-Baden, Germany: Nomos), pp. 341–357.

————— (2005b) "Power/Knowledge in International Peacebuilding: The Case of the EU Police Mission in Bosnia," *Alternatives: Global, Local, Political* vol. 30, no. 3, pp. 297–323.

————— (2010) "EU Peacebuilding in Georgia: Limits and Achievements," in Stephen Blockmans, Jan Wouters, and Tom Ruys (eds.) *The European Union and Peacebuilding: Policy and Legal Aspects* (The Hague, Netherlands: T.M.C. Asser Press), pp. 269–293.

Merlingen, Michael, with Rasa Ostrauskaitė (2006) *European Union Peacebuilding and Policing: Governance and the European Security and Defence Policy* (London: Routledge).

Meyer, Christoph O. (2006) *The Quest for a European Strategic Culture: Changing Norms and Defence in the European Union* (Basingstoke, UK: Palgrave Macmillan).

Meyer, Christoph O., and Eva Strickmann (2011) "Solidifying Constructivism: How Material and Ideational Factors Interact in European Defence," *Journal of Common Market Studies* vol. 49, no. 1, pp. 61–81.

Middle East Quartet (2003) "A Performance-Based Road Map to a Permanent Two-State Solution to the Israeli-Palestinian Conflict," joint statement by the United States, the European Union, the Russian Federation, and the United Nations (New York, NY: United Nations).

Middleton, Roger (2008) *Piracy in Somalia: Threatening Global Trade, Feeding Local Wars* (London: Chatham House).

Miliband, David (2007) "Europe 2030: Model Power Not Superpower," speech given to the College of Europe, Bruges, Belgium, 15 November.

Miskimmon, Alister (2007) *Germany and the Common Foreign and Security Policy of the European Union: Between Europeanisation and National Adaptation* (Basingstoke, UK: Palgrave Macmillan).

Missiroli, Antonio (2002) "Turkey and EU-NATO Cooperation in Crisis Management: No Turkish Delight for ESDP," *Security Dialogue* vol. 33, no. 1, pp. 9–26.

————— (2004/5) "Central Europe: Between the EU and NATO," *Survival* vol. 46, no. 4, pp. 121–136.

Möckli, Daniel (2008) *European Foreign Policy During the Cold War: Heath, Brandt, Pompidou and the Dream of Political Unity* (London: I. B. Tauris).

Monaghan, Andrew (2004) "Does Europe Exist as an Entity for Military Cooperation? Evolving Russian Perspectives, 1991–2004," *Connections: The Quarterly Journal* vol. 3, no. 2, pp. 47–62.

Moravcsik, Andrew (1991) "Arms and Autarky in Modern European History," *Daedalus* vol. 120, no. 4, pp. 23–45.

—— (1993a) "Armaments Among Allies: European Weapons Collaboration, 1975–1985," in Peter B. Evans, Harold K. Jacobson, and Robert D. Putnam (eds.) *Double-Edged Diplomacy: International Bargaining and Domestic Politics* (Berkeley, CA: University of California Press), pp. 128–167.

—— (1993b) "Preferences and Power in the European Community: A Liberal Intergovernmentalist Approach," *Journal of Common Market Studies* vol. 31, no. 4, pp. 473–524.

—— (1994) *Why the European Community Strengthens the State: Domestic Politics and International Institutions*, Working Paper Series no. 52 (Cambridge, MA: Centre for European Studies).

—— (1998) *The Choice for Europe: Social Purpose and State Power from Messina to Maastricht* (Ithaca, NY: Cornell University Press).

—— (2003) "Striking a New Transatlantic Bargain," *Foreign Affairs* vol. 82, no. 4, pp. 74–89.

—— (2009) "Europe: The Quiet Superpower," *French Politics* vol. 7, no. 3/4, pp. 403–422.

—— (2010) "Europe: Quietly Rising Superpower in a Bipolar World," in Alan Alexandroff and Andrew Cooper (eds.) *Rising States, Rising Institutions: Challenges for Global Governance* (Washington, DC: Brookings Institution Press), pp. 151–174.

Mühlmann, Thomas (2008) "The Police Mission EUPM in Bosnia, 2003–05," in Michael Merlingen and Rasa Ostrauskaitè (eds.) *European Security and Defence Policy: An Implementation Perspective* (London: Routledge), pp. 43–60.

Müller-Brandeck-Bocquet, Gisela (ed.) (2006) *The Future of the European Foreign, Security and Defence Policy After Enlargement* (Baden-Baden, Germany: Nomos).

Nash, Pat (2008) "Chad—Facing Challenges: Questions to Lt. General Pat Nash," *Impetus: Bulletin of the EU Military Staff*, no. 5, pp. 18–19.

National Intelligence Council (2008) *Global Trends 2025: A Transformed World*, Washington, DC.

Nelson, Daniel N. (2002) "Transatlantic Transmutations," *Washington Quarterly* vol. 25, no. 4, pp. 51–66.

Nicholson, Martin (2003) "Characterising Centre-Periphery Relations in the Yeltsin Era," in Graeme P. Herd and Anne Aldis (eds.) *Russian Regions and Regionalism: Strength Through Weakness* (London: Routledge), pp. 3–18.

North Atlantic Council (1991) "The Alliance's New Strategic Concept," agreed on by the Heads of State and Government participating in the Meeting of the North Atlantic Council, 7–8 November, Rome.

—— (1994) "Declaration of Heads of State and Government," Ministerial Meeting of the North Atlantic Council/North Atlantic Cooperation Council, Ministerial Communiqué, Brussels, 10–11 January.

North Atlantic Treaty Organization (2010) "Strategic Concept," adopted by Heads of State and Government in Lisbon, 19 November.

Nuttall, Simon J. (1992) *European Political Co-operation* (Oxford, UK: Clarendon Press).
––––– (2000) *European Foreign Policy* (Oxford, UK: Oxford University Press).
Nye, Joseph S. (2002) *The Paradox of American Power: Why the World's Only Superpower Can't Go It Alone* (Oxford, UK: Oxford University Press).
Nygren, Bertil (2008) *The Rebuilding of Greater Russia: Putin's Foreign Policy Towards the CIS Countries* (London: Routledge).
O'Donnell, Clara Marina (2009) *The EU Finally Opens Up the European Defence Market*, Policy Brief (London: Centre for European Reform).
O'Sullivan, David (2011) "Setting Up the EEAS," speech given to the Institute of International and European Affairs (IIEA), Dublin, 14 January.
Oakes, Mark (2001) *European Security and Defence Policy: Nice and Beyond* (London: The Stationery Office).
Observatoire de l'Afrique (2008) *Security Sector Reform in Guinea-Bissau*, Africa Briefing Report, Brussels.
Official Journal of the European Community (1992) "Treaty on European Union (Masstricht Treaty)" (Luxembourg: Publications Office of the European Community).
Official Journal of the European Union (2006) "Consolidated Versions of the Treaty on European Union and of the Treaty Establishing the European Community (Nice Treaty)" (Luxembourg: Publications Office of the EU).
––––– (2010) "Consolidated Versions of the Treaty on European Union and the Treaty on the Functioning of the European Union (Lisbon Treaty)" (Luxembourg: Publications Office of the EU).
Oikonomou, Iraklis (forthcoming) "A Historical Materialist Approach to CSDP," in Xymena Kurowska and Fabian Breuer (eds.) *Explaining European Security and Defence Policy: Theory in Action* (Basingstoke, UK: Palgrave Macmillan).
Ojanen, Hanna (2006) "The EU and NATO: Two Competing Models for a Common Defence Policy'," *Journal of Common Market Studies* vol. 44, no. 1, pp. 57–76.
Olsen, Gorm Rye (2002) "The EU and Conflict Management in African Emergencies," *International Peacekeeping* vol. 9, no. 3, pp. 87–102.
––––– (2009) "The EU and Military Conflict Management in Africa: For the Good of Africa or Europe?," *International Peacekeeping* vol. 16, no. 2, pp. 245–260.
Organisation for Security and Cooperation in Europe (2008) "Background Report—Human Rights, Ethnic Relations and Democracy in Kosovo (Summer 2007—Summer 2008)," Pristina, 5 September.
Osica, Olaf (2004) "A Secure Poland in a Better Union? The ESS as Seen from Warsaw's Perspective," *German Foreign Policy in Dialogue* vol. 5, no. 14.
Oxfam (2009) *Oxfam and the Chad Crisis—March 2009*, Oxford, UK.
Pape, Robert A. (2005) "Soft Balancing Against the United States," *International Security* vol. 30, no. 1, pp. 7–45.
Patten, Chris (2000) "The EU's Evolving Foreign Policy Dimension: The Common European Security and Defense Policy After Helsinki," speech given at a joint meeting of the European Parliament's Foreign Affairs

Committee with members of the NATO Parliamentary Assembly, 22 February, Brussels.

———— (2005) *Not Quite the Diplomat: Home Truths About World Affairs* (London: Allen Lane).

Pedersen, Thomas (2002) "Cooperative Hegemony: Power, Ideas and Institutions in Regional Integration," *Review of International Studies* vol. 28, no. 4, pp. 677–696.

Peral, Luis (2009) "EUPOL Afghanistan," in Giovanni Grevi, Damien Helly, and Daniel Keohane (eds.) *European Security and Defence Policy: The First 10 Years (1999–2009)* (Paris: EU Institute for Security Studies), pp. 325–337.

Perlo-Freeman, Sam, Olawale Ismail, Noel Kelly, and Carina Solmirano (2010) "Military Expenditure Data, 2000–2009," *SIPRI Yearbook 2010: Armaments, Disarmament and International Security* (Oxford, UK: Oxford University Press), pp. 201–242.

Petrov, Petar (2011) "Introducing Governance Arrangements for EU Conflict Prevention and Crisis Management Operations," in Eva Gross and Ana E. Juncos (eds.) *EU Conflict Prevention and Crisis Management: Roles, Institutions and Policies* (London: Routledge), pp. 49–65.

Polikanov, Dmitry (2007) "Russia-EU Relations: Opportunities for a Security Dialogue," in David Brown and Alistair J. K. Shepherd (eds.) *The Security Dimensions of EU Enlargement: Wider Europe, Weaker Europe?* (Manchester, UK: Manchester University Press), pp. 115–128.

Pollack, Mark A. (2009) "The New Institutionalisms and European Integration," in Antje Wiener and Thomas Diez (eds.) *European Integration Theory*, 2nd ed. (Oxford, UK: Oxford University Press), pp. 125–143.

Pond, Elizabeth (1999) "Kosovo: Catalyst for Europe," *The Washington Quarterly* vol. 22, no. 4, pp. 77–92.

Pop, Valentina (2008) "EU Begins Anti-Piracy Mission off Somali Coast," Euobserver.com, 8 December.

———— (2010) "Nato to Unveil New Goals for Austerity-Hobbled Alliance," EUobserver.com, 19 November.

Posen, Barry (2006) "European Union Security and Defence Policy: Response to Unipolarity?," *Security Studies* vol. 15, no. 2, pp. 149–186.

Proedrou, Filippos (2007) "The EU-Russia Energy Approach Under the Prism of Interdependence," *European Security* vol. 16, nos. 3–4, pp. 329–355.

Quille, Gerrard (2003) "'Battle Groups' to Strengthen EU Military Crisis Management?," *European Security Review*, no. 22 (Brussels: International Security Information Service [ISIS]), pp. 1–2.

Radaelli, Claudio M. (2000) "Whither Europeanization? Concept Stretching and Substantive Change," *European Integration online Papers (EIoP)* vol. 4, no. 8.

Rathbun, Brian (2008) "A Rose by Any Other Name: Neoclassical Realism as the Logical and Necessary Extension of Structural Realism," *Security Studies* vol. 17, no. 2, pp. 294–321.

Rayment, Sean (2009) "Overstretch Pushes British Troops to the Brink," *The (UK) Telegraph*, 10 January.

Reichard, Martin (2006) *The EU-NATO Relationship: A Legal and Political Perspective* (Aldershot, UK: Ashgate).

Reid, T. R. (2004) *The United States of Europe: The Superpower Nobody Talks About—From the Euro to Eurovision* (London: Penguin).

Rettman, Andrew (2010) "Berlin, Paris and Warsaw Keen to Beef Up EU Military Muscle," EUobserver.com, 13 December.

Riding, Alan (1991) "Conflict in Yugoslavia: Europeans Send High-Level Team," *New York Times*, 29 June, available at http://www.nytimes.com.

Rieker, Pernille (2006) *Europeanization of National Security Identity: The EU and the Changing Security Identities of the Nordic States* (London: Routledge).

Risse, Thomas (2002) "US Power in a Liberal Security Community," in John G. Ikenberry (ed.) *America Unrivaled: The Future of the Balance of Power* (Ithaca, NY: Cornell University Press), pp. 260–283.

Ross, Andrew L. (2009) "Global Governance, Security Governance, and an Imperious United States," in Charlotte Wagnsson, James A. Sperling, and Jan Hallenberg (eds.) *European Security Governance: The European Union in a Westphalian World* (London: Routledge), pp. 79–93.

Russian Ministry of Foreign Affairs (1999) "Medium-Term Strategy for the Development of Relations Between the Russian Federation and the European Union (2000–2010)," Moscow.

Rynning, Sten (2005) "Return of the Jedi: Realism and the Study of the European Union," *Politique Européenne*, no. 17, pp. 11–33.

——— (2011) "Realism and the Common Security and Defence Policy," *Journal of Common Market Studies* vol. 49, no. 1, pp. 23–42.

Sabiote, Maria A. (2008) "EUPOL COPPS In the Palestinian Territories: A Neutral Force or a Protagonist in the Shadow?," *CFSP Forum* vol. 6, no. 3, pp. 5–7.

Sakwa, Richard (2008a) *Putin: Russia's Choice* (London: Routledge).

——— (2008b) *Russian Politics and Society*, 4th ed. (London: Routledge).

Schake, Kori (2006) "An American Eulogy for European Defence," in Anne Deighton with Victor Mauer (ed.) *Securing Europe? Implementing the European Security Strategy*, Zürcher Beiträge zur Sicherheitspolitik, no. 77 (Zürich: Center for Security Studies), pp. 101–107.

Scheffer, Jaap de Hoop (2007) Keynote speech, "NATO and the EU: Time for a New Chapter," Berlin, 29 January.

Schimmelfennig, Frank, and Ulrich Sedelmeier (2004) "Governance by Conditionality: EU Rule Transfer to the Candidate Countries of Central and Eastern Europe," *Journal of European Public Policy* vol. 11, no. 4, pp. 661–679.

Schmitter, Philippe C. (1970) "A Revised Theory of Regional Integration," *International Organization* vol. 24, no. 4, pp. 836–868.

——— (2004) "Neo-Neofunctionalism," in Antje Wiener and Thomas Diez (eds.) *European Integration Theory* (Oxford, UK: Oxford University Press), pp. 45–74.

Selden, Zachary (2010) "Power Is Always in Fashion: State-Centric Realism and the European Security and Defence Policy," *Journal of Common Market Studies* vol. 48, no. 2, pp. 397–416.

Serfaty, Simon (2004) "Thinking About and Beyond NATO," in Hall Gardner (ed.) *NATO and the European Union: New World, New Europe, New Threats* (Aldershot, UK: Ashgate), pp. 79–90.

Shaw, Martin (2000) *Theory of the Global State: Globality as an Unfinished Revolution* (Cambridge, UK: Cambridge University Press).

Shepherd, Alistair J. K. (2006) "Irrelevant or Indispensable? ESDP, the 'War on Terror' and the Fallout from Iraq," *International Politics* vol. 43, no. 1, pp. 71–92.

Silber, Laura, and Allan Little (1997) *Yugoslavia: Death of a Nation* (New York: Penguin Books).

Simon, Luis (2010) *Command and Control? Planning for EU Military Operations*, Occasional Paper no. 81 (Paris: EU Institute for Security Studies).

Sjöstedt, Gunnar (1977) *The External Role of the European Community* (Westmead, UK: Saxon House).

Slaughter, Anne-Marie (2004) *A New World Order* (Princeton, NJ: Princeton University Press).

Sloan, Stanley (2000) *The United States and European Defence*, Chaillot Paper no. 39 (Paris: EU Institute for Security Studies).

—— (2005) *NATO, the European Union and the Atlantic Community: The Transatlantic Bargain Challenged* (Lanham, MD: Rowman & Littlefield).

Smith, Mark A. (2004) *Russia and the EU Under Putin*, Russian Series no. 04/20 (Swindon, UK: Conflict Studies Research Centre, Defence Academy of the United Kingdom).

Smith, Michael E. (2004a) *Europe's Foreign and Security Policy: The Institutionalization of Cooperation* (Cambridge, UK: Cambridge University Press).

—— (2004b) "Toward a Theory of EU Foreign Policy-Making: Multi-Level Governance, Domestic Politics, and National Adaptation to Europe's Common Foreign and Security Policy," *Journal of European Public Policy* vol. 11, no. 4, pp. 740–758.

Soder, Kirsten (2010) "EU Crisis Management: An Assessment of Member States: Contributions and Positions," unpublished manuscript.

Solana, Javier (2004a) "Intelligent War on Terror," *The Korea Herald*, 8 November.

—— (2004b) "Preface," in Nicole Gnesotto (ed.) *EU Security and Defence Policy: The First Five Years (1999–2004)* (Paris: EU Institute for Security Studies), pp. 5–10.

—— (2007) "Presentation to the United Nations Security Council by the EU High Representative for the CFSP on the Democratic Republic of Congo / EUFOR," New York, 9 January.

—— (2008) "The External Energy Policy of the European Union," speech at the Annual Conference of the French Institute of International Relations," Paris, 1 February.

Sommer, Theo (2004) "Untitled contribution," in Nicole Gnesotto (ed.) *EU Security and Defence Policy: The First Five Years (1999–2004)* (Paris: EU Institute for Security Studies).

Sperling, James A. (2009) "Introduction: Security Governance in a Westphalian World," in Charlotte Wagnsson, James A. Sperling, and Jan Hallenberg (eds.) *European Security Governance: The European Union in a Westphalian World* (London: Routledge), pp. 1–15.

Statewatch Bulletin (2005) *EU: SITCEN's Emerging Role*, 15/1.

Steinmann, Thomas, and Gerhard Hegmann (2010) "Airbus verzweifelt am A400M," *Financial Times Deutschland*, 11 November.

Sterling-Folker, Jennifer (2000) "Competing Paradigms or Birds of a Feather? Constructivism and Neoliberal Institutionalism Compared," *International Studies Quarterly* vol. 44, no. 1, pp. 97–119.

Stockholm International Peace Research Institute (ed.) (2006) *SIPRI Yearbook 2006: Armaments, Disarmament and International Security* (Oxford, UK: Oxford University Press).

——— (ed.) (2007) *SIPRI Yearbook 2007: Armaments, Disarmament and International Security* (Oxford, UK: Oxford University Press).

——— (ed.) (2008) *SIPRI Yearbook 2008: Armaments, Disarmament and International Security* (Oxford, UK: Oxford University Press).

Taliaferro, Jeffrey W. (2006) "State Building for Future Wars: Neoclassical Realism and the Resource-Extractive State," *Security Studies* vol. 15, no. 3, pp. 464–495.

Tallberg, Jonas (2006) *Leadership and Negotiation in the European Union* (Cambridge, UK: Cambridge University Press).

Thomas, Daniel C. (2002) *The Helsinki Effect: International Norms, Human Rights, and the Demise of Communism* (Princeton, NJ: Princeton University Press).

Toje, Asle (2005) "The 2003 European Union Security Strategy: A Critical Appraisal," *European Foreign Affairs Review* vol. 10, no. 1, pp. 117–133.

——— (2008) "The Consensus-Expectations Gap: Explaining Europe's Ineffective Foreign Policy," *Security Dialogue* vol. 39, no. 1, pp. 121–141.

——— (2010) *The European Union as a Small Power: After the Post–Cold War* (Basingstoke, UK: Palgrave Macmillan).

Tonra, Ben (1997) "The Impact of Political Cooperation," in Knud Erik Jørgensen (ed.) *Reflective Approaches to European Governance* (Basingstoke, UK: Palgrave Macmillan), pp. 181–198.

——— (2001) *The Europeanisation of National Foreign Policy: Dutch, Danish and Irish Foreign Policy in the European Union* (Aldershot, UK: Ashgate).

——— (2003) "Constructing the Common Foreign and Security Policy: The Utility of a Cognitive Approach," *Journal of Common Market Studies* vol. 41, no. 4, pp. 731–756.

Tonra, Ben, and Thomas Christiansen (eds.) (2004) *Rethinking European Union Foreign Policy* (Manchester, UK: Manchester University Press).

Treacher, Adrian (2004) "From Civilian Power to Military Actor: The EU's Resistable Transformation," *European Foreign Affairs Review* vol. 9, no. 1, pp. 49–66.

Triantaphyllou, Dimitrios (2007) "Energy Security and Common Foreign and Security Policy (CFSP): The Wider Black Sea Area Context," *Southeast European and Black Sea Studies* vol. 7, no. 2, pp. 289–302.

Ulriksen, Ståle, Catriona Gourlay, and Catriona Mace (2004) "Operation Artemis: The Shape of Things to Come?," *International Peacekeeping* vol. 11, no. 3, pp. 508–525.

United Nations (2008) "Special Inquiry into the Bas Congo Events of February and March 2008" (Kinshasa: UN Mission in the Democratic Republic of Congo).

United Nations Office on Drugs and Crime (2007) "UNODC Warns of Cocaine Trafficking Threat in West Africa," press release, New York.

United Nations Security Council (2006) "Letter from the Secretary-General Addressed to the President of the Security Council," 12 April 2006, New York.

—— (2008) "Report of the Secretary-General on the United Nations Interim Administration Mission in Kosovo," New York, June.

United States Department of Defense (2002) "Allied Contributions to the Common Defense," Washington, DC.

Valášek, Tomáš (2005) "New EU Members in Europe's Security Policy," *Cambridge Review of International Affairs* vol. 18, no. 2, pp. 217–228.

Van Staden, Alfred (2005) "Close to Power?," in Hans Mouritzen and Anders Wivel (eds.) *The Geopolitics of Euro-Atlantic Integration* (London: Routledge), pp. 64–81.

Vinocur, John (2007) "A Dilemma of Distance in German Approach," *International Herald Tribune*, 3 July.

Wæver, Ole (1998) "Insecurity, Security and Asecurity in the West European Non-War Community," in Emanuel Adler and Michael Barnett (eds.) *Security Communities* (Cambridge, UK: Cambridge University Press), pp. 69–118.

Wagner, Wolfgang (2006a) "The Democratic Control of Military Power Europe," *Journal of European Public Policy* vol. 13, no. 2, pp. 200–216.

—— (2006b) "Missing in Action? Germany's Bumpy Road from Institution-Building to Substance in European Security and Defence Policy," in Gunther Hellmann (ed.) *Germany's EU Policy on Asylum and Defence: De-Europeanization by Default?* (Basingstoke, UK: Palgrave Macmillan), pp. 91–155.

Wagnsson, Charlotte, James A. Sperling, and Jan Hallenberg (eds.) (2009) *European Security Governance: The European Union in a Westphalian World* (London: Routledge).

Wallace, William, and David Allen (1977) "Political Cooperation: Procedure as Substitute for Policy," in Helen Wallace, William Wallace, and Carole Webb (eds.) *Policy-Making in the European Communities* (London: John Wiley & Sons), pp. 227–247.

Walt, Stephen M. (1987) *Origins of Alliances* (Ithaca, NY: Cornell University Press).

Waltz, Kenneth N. (1979) *Theory of International Politics* (Reading, MA: Addison-Wesley).

—— (2000) "Structural Realism After the Cold War," *International Security* vol. 25, no. 1, pp. 5–41.

Watanabe, Lisa (2010) *Securing Europe: European Security in an American Epoch* (Basingstoke, UK: Palgrave Macmillan).

Webber, Mark (2009) "NATO: The United States, Transformation and the War in Afghanistan," *The British Journal of Politics and International Relations* vol. 11, no. 1, pp. 46–63.

Webber, Mark, Stuart Croft, Jolyon Howorth, Terry Terriff, and Elke Krahmann (2004) "The Governance of European Security," *Review of International Studies* vol. 30, no. 1, pp. 3–26.

Weber, Katja, Michael E. Smith, and Michael Baun (2007) *Governing Europe's Neighbourhood: Partners or Periphery?* (Manchester, UK: Manchester University Press).

Wessel, Ramses A. (2001) "The EU as Black Widow: Devouring the WEU to Give Birth to a European Security and Defence Policy," in V. Kronenberger (ed.) *The European Union and the International Legal Order: Discord or Harmony?* (The Hague, Netherlands: T.M.C. Asser Press), pp. 405–434.

Western European Union (1984) "Rome Declaration," Rome, 27 October.

―― (1987) "The Platform on European Security Interests," The Hague, Netherlands, 27 October.

―― (1992) "Petersberg Declaration," Bonn, 19 June.

―― (1999) "Luxembourg Declaration," Luxembourg, 22–23 November.

Westlake, Martin (1999) *The Council of the European Union* (London: Catermill).

Westlake, Martin, and David Galloway (eds.) (2006) *The Council of the European Union* (London: John Harper Publishing).

White House (2006) "The National Security Strategy of the United States of America," Washington, DC.

―― (2008) "President Bush Visits Bucharest, Romania, Discusses NATO" (Bucharest: Office of the Press Secretary), 2 April.

Whitman, Richard G. (1999) *Amsterdam's Unfinished Business? The Blair Government's Initiative and the Future of the Western European Union*, Occasional Paper no. 7 (Paris: EU Institute for Security Studies).

Whitman, Richard G. (ed.) (2010) *Normative Power Europe: Empirical and Theoretical Perspectives* (Basingstoke, UK: Palgrave Macmillan).

Whitney, Craig R. (1991) "War in the Gulf: Europe: Gulf Fighting Shatters Europeans' Fragile Unity," *New York Times*, 25 January, available at http://www.nytimes.com.

Wiessala, Georg (2002) *The European Union and Asian Countries* (Sheffield, UK: Sheffield Academic Press).

Witney, Nick (2008) *Re-energising Europe's Security and Defence Policy* (London: European Council on Foreign Relations).

Wong, Reuben Y. (2006) *The Europeanization of French Foreign Policy: France and the EU in East Asia* (Basingstoke, UK: Palgrave Macmillan).

Woodward, Susan L. (1995) *Balkan Tragedy: Chaos and Dissolution After the Cold War* (Washington, DC: Brookings Institution Press).

Zaborowski, Marcin (2004) *From America's Protegé to Constructive European: Polish Security Policy in the Twenty-first Century*, Occasional Paper no. 56 (Paris: EU Institute for Security Studies).

Index

About the Book

WHAT IS THE EUROPEAN UNION'S SECURITY AND DEFENCE policy (CSDP)? How does it work? Does it make a difference in international security affairs? How do other global actors react to Europe's new assertiveness? And how do theories of international relations account for the trajectory of EU integration in the high politics of national security? In this comprehensive survey and analysis, Michael Merlingen brings together the key issues, themes, and debates related to the CSDP.

Merlingen explores the construction and inner workings of EU security policy, as well as its impact both regionally and globally. He also looks carefully at relationships between the EU and other world powers. Taking stock of the CSDP—its successes and failures, accomplishments and limitations—he highlights the challenges and opportunities that await the EU as it continues to reinforce its position as an important security actor on the world stage.

MICHAEL MERLINGEN is associate professor of international relations and European studies at the Central European University. His publications include *European Union Peacebuilding and Policing: Governance and the European Security and Defence Policy* and *The European Security and Defence Policy: An Implementation Perspective.*